S0-ESC-132

The Complete Book of Product Publicity

The Complete Book of Product Publicity

James D. Barhydt

amacom
American Management Association

*This book is available at a special
discount when ordered in bulk quantities.
For information, contact Special Sales Department,
AMACOM, a division of American Management Association,
135 West 50th Street, New York, NY 10020.*

Library of Congress Cataloging-in-Publication Data

Barhydt, James D.
    The complete book of product publicity.

    Includes index.
    1. Public relations. 2. Marketing—Management.
I. Title.
HD59.B35   1987   659.2   86-47592
ISBN 0-8144-5668-5

© 1987 AMACOM, a division of
American Management Association, New York.
All rights reserved.
Printed in the United States of America.

This publication may not be reproduced,
stored in a retrieval system,
or transmitted in whole or in part,
in any form or by any means, electronic,
mechanical, photocopying, recording, or otherwise,
without the prior written permission of AMACOM,
a division of American Management Association,
135 West 50th Street, New York, NY 10020.

Printing number

10 9 8 7 6 5 4 3 2 1

Acknowledgments

This book would never have been written without the encouragement and support of Bob Nightengale, a director of communications in Du Pont's External Affairs Department. I also owe much to several of my colleagues, for whom I have the highest admiration as creative and skilled publicity professionals. Many of the approaches I suggest are what they do so well every day in support of marketing.

Thanks also to AMACOM Acquisitions Editor Phil Henry for his counsel as this was being written, and to Managing Editor Barbara Horowitz for pulling it all together. Copy editor Marty Stuckey has my highest regard. She showed me how very valuable a copy editor can be.

There is one other person to whom I owe the greatest thanks: my wife, Frances. She was behind the project all the way—throughout the many evenings, weekends, and vacations it took to write this book over the past two years.

Preface

For all but a few years of my public relations career, I have focused on product publicity. And from my first day with the Du Pont Company on July 22, 1962, I have worked with my advertising counterparts in promoting a wide range of products and services. It wasn't until 1980, however, that this relationship was formalized: about 35 public relations professionals joined with our advertising colleagues to become part of a new and aptly named Marketing Communications Department.

As we learned to work together more effectively, we began to really appreciate what each one of us did. And marketing benefited a lot. Editors often refer to a "church and state" separation between the advertising side of media and the editorial function. But it soon became clear to me that it did *not* have to be this way in communications.

As the months went by in our new department, public relations people took on advertising responsibilities, and ad people began supervising product publicity. But it became apparent that our advertising colleagues needed a better understanding of product publicity to help them take on the responsibilities of directing a communications program that included publicity (it must also be said that many public relations professionals have little knowledge of advertising).

So when I became press officer for marketing communications in July, 1983, I developed a two-day seminar on product publicity, primarily to give advertising professionals a quick but intensive overview that would help them plan and manage product publicity. We have since expanded the seminar to include marketing and management people.

On the basis of my experience with the seminar and the very positive reception it got from its more than 100 participants, I thought it made sense to expand the scope of the subject into a book. I want to emphasize that this is not a "here's-how-we-do-publicity-at-my-company" book. Rather, these are my own views on product publicity, reflecting what I've learned in 30 years of educational, agency, and corporate public relations and what I've absorbed from working with so many talented people and with media of every description.

My objective is to cover product publicity in such a way that any company or organization can use the book to help it develop a program that will suit its own needs and markets. Thus, I will define the role of publicity in communications—and the valuable contribution it makes in reaching your important audiences. I will take you through an ideal publicity plan. And I will delve into such topics as selecting the right public relations agency, developing good relations with the press, writing and selling publicity stories, taking attention-getting photographs, using media effectively, conducting press conferences, and measuring the effectiveness of all these efforts.

To make sure I was not just relying on what worked best for me but was on solid ground in giving advice, I spoke to a great many people in management, marketing, public relations, and product publicity. I interviewed more than 30 editors from the print and broadcast media (a product publicity program goes nowhere unless it meets the needs of these editors). I exchanged views with my colleagues and successful public relations practitioners from other companies and agencies. And from talking to and working with product and marketing managers, sales representatives, and technical and research people, I have a pretty good idea of what can help them get the most from product publicity—and what they need to know to help them understand it, and use it, better.

Another reason for my writing this book is the apparent lack of literature that covers in detail all the important aspects of product publicity. It is true that many of these topics have been written about previously—and some, quite extensively. But so far they have not been incorporated in one volume with an emphasis on a well-planned, strategic approach.

After all, the key to any effective communications program is planning—and planning well. In today's results-oriented business environment, we can no longer afford to show management executives a scrapbook-full of clippings and expect them to assume we're doing a good job. And *they* can no longer take on mere faith what we public relations people can do for them. Once they gain an appreciation of what a well-planned and well-executed product publicity program can do for them, they become enthusiastic supporters, better able to determine whether they're getting what they're paying for.

I am also a firm believer in working closely with *everyone* involved in communications. We tend to be parochial, thinking that our respective disciplines best serve our clients in marketing and management. This is unfortunate, because the truth is that we serve our clients best when we cooperate and use all the techniques and tactics available in a strategic and well-planned program.

The most talented people I know on the corporate and agency sides of our business are those who put their creative skills (be they in marketing, advertising, publicity, technical, or sales) together to make product publicity as important as any other element of a communications program. Each time this takes place, the synergy is remarkable. The program's reach is greater. More key audiences are

Preface

moved to respond and take action. And most importantly, the return on investment is far bigger than when the focus was on one area alone.

In the final analysis, after all, this is what the book aims to do. When we begin to think of what we do as a business instead of a profession, this book, in helping us develop better product publicity programs, can help us get better *business* results for our clients. And for us.

Contents

1	The Power of Publicity	1
2	Preparing a Publicity Plan That Works	13
3	The Role and Responsibilities of the Publicity Manager	37
4	Selecting and Working with Public Relations Agencies	47
5	Developing Good Relations with the Press	69
6	Getting into Print	95
7	Getting It on Paper	128
8	Attracting Attention with the Right Photos	150
9	Strategies for Using Broadcast Media	171
10	Successful Press Conferences	192
11	Support Services and How They Fit	232
12	Measuring Publicity Effectiveness	251
13	Reporting and Merchandising	268
	Appendix **A**: Trivial Pursuit® — A Case Study of a Publicity Campaign at Its Best	276
	Appendix **B**: Tip Sheet	279
	Appendix **C**: Media Briefing Manual	282
	Appendix **D**: PR Data Reports for Snow Skis, Inc.	286
	Index	301

1
The Power of Publicity

Publicity professionals have not always been completely successful at explaining their work to others. Even business colleagues tend to say things like, "Publicity? That's just free advertising, right?"

Not exactly—although their objectives and targets are the same.

Publicity can teach, just like advertising, but often in more depth.

Publicity can say more, provide more detail.

And publicity carries with it the credibility of having been endorsed by a neutral third party: the editor, the authority. A publication will, within the limits of editorial policy and good taste, include in its pages any advertisement for which payment is received. But that same publication will include among its editorial material (editorial meaning all the articles, photos, announcements: everything but the advertisements) only those items of publicity that the editor has decided are valuable to the readers.

Or sometimes publicists hear questions like, "Publicity? You mean like press releases?"

Well, yes, publicity means press releases. It also means backgrounders, feature stories, press conferences, media tours, special events, roundup stories, special promotions, television clips, mat and syndication releases, and lots more.

All these individual pieces are the *tools* of publicity. We might also call them tactics. But publicity is not just tactics—no matter how skillfully executed—but the integrated strategy behind them. And planning is what makes the publicity strategy fit smoothly with the advertising strategy and the sales promotion strategy. Together, they constitute the communications strategy.

When publicity is planned as an integral part of a total marketing communications program, with advertising and promotion the other two partners, what you have is a wonderful synergy, with all the parts reinforcing and enhancing one another.

One other clarification: "Publicity" is used here to mean something distinct from "public relations." In this book I hope to present all the strategic and tactical elements of public relations that can be used to support marketing an organization's products or services. The best way to describe the support of marketing by public relations is to call it product publicity.

A product publicist nearly always works with marketing, while the public relations practitioner's efforts are directed primarily to corporate issues. Many, of course, do both. But the publicist measures success on the contribution to sales and earnings, the public relations person on the performance of the stock and the way the company is regarded by its many publics, investors, regulatory agencies—in short, the corporate image.

Product publicity can play a role at every stage of a product's life cycle. Whether it is a leading role, a supporting role, or a walk-on depends to a large extent on the maturity of the product (see Chapter 2). It is the main element of any new product introduction, a vital element in any new market exploration, and, with creative planning, a means of maintaining market interest.

The results of these efforts can have a significant but indirect effect on a company's sales and earnings. The effect can be measured in ways far more appropriate, far more useful, than the traditional scrapbook full of clippings.

Those who would undertake the practice of product publicity need to understand where it fits in a total communications plan. In addition, certain skills are needed to get "publicity" from the typewriter or word processor to the media. The pages to follow will help point the way.

Marketing Communications . . .

The term "marketing communications" has come into our business language only in recent years. As a definition, we can say it is a planned, strategic, persuasive, and coordinated approach to communicating to key markets and buying influences the benefits, advantages, and properties of a company's or organization's products or services through a well-planned, creative program. The program uses the disciplines of advertising, product publicity, and promotion as integral elements, creatively and with a full understanding of and appreciation for what each can contribute to the whole.

Other elements include sales literature, trade shows, exhibits, audiovisual presentations, direct mail, telephone and direct-response marketing—all to support a company's marketing objectives. Marketing communications is a sophisticated but straightforward way to move information from one place to another.

The audiences with which a company wishes to communicate get their information in any number of ways: product literature, television, radio, print media,

The Power of Publicity

trade shows and conventions, by letters, phone calls, direct mail, salespeople, the competition, and word of mouth.

Selecting the proper media, setting priorities, budgeting, staffing, and executing, all to get communications moving and keep them moving—these are key elements in a marketing communications program. And it should be scheduled so they all work together, like the proverbial clockworks.

Communicators must work together to bring to their clients the most effective and measurable programs possible. When ad people and publicity people in a corporation go their separate ways, it is a waste of both resources.

. . . and Where Product Publicity Fits

Product publicity is a highly effective means of communicating the benefits and properties of products and services to virtually any target audience through the editorial pages of magazines and newspapers and over broadcast outlets.

The outlets for publicity are many and varied. There are nearly 8,000 magazines, on every subject under the sun. There are some 1,700 daily newspapers and more than 8,000 weekly newspapers. There are more than 10,000 radio stations, some 1,400 television stations, and nearly 7,000 cable system outlets.

Publicity in any or all of these media can contribute greatly to a communications program, helping to reach such program objectives as

- Create and build a market presence.
- Position a product or service, either short-term or long-term.
- Scout and prospect new markets.
- Introduce a product.
- Position a company as an authority on a certain industry or subject.

But to reach those media in the first place, publicity must be so presented that its thrust coincides with the media interest. Print editors and television and radio news directors or producers are the final arbiters on whether the publicist is successful.

The company or agency that plans publicity and uses proven marketing principles has the best chance of success. This means understanding the media and matching the messages or "news" to the needs of the audiences to which the media are directed. Media can't be force fed with stories that do not meet the editors' own marketing objectives. Stories that work are those that provide readers with information that can help them solve problems or tell them something they didn't know before.

Publicity and Advertising

Advertising and publicity may be — and usually are — directed to the same markets, and with the same objectives. But there are important differences between the two. Advertising can be run any time. The message does not have to be delivered in an "editorial" writing style, the points conveyed do not have to be fully supported by facts and, as long as they are in good taste, they can be repeated and no one at the publication will change them or decide not to run the advertisement.

There are differences in the way advertising and publicity professionals approach their work:

- Advertising professionals make judgments on advertising tactics, on when, how, and where (after answering why). They buy time, space, direct mail materials, promotional literature; and, indirectly through agencies, they buy the talents of copywriters, photographers, media experts, market researchers, art directors, and a host of others.

- Publicity professionals need to make editorial judgments; they must think like editors and relate their work to readers, listeners, and viewers. They sell ideas to media that they hope will be developed into feature stories mentioning their company and its products. They present "news." They find "angles" to make the dull interesting and the non-news, news. They write, they create. They do all these tasks so that they can more effectively market news about a company's product, its services, and sometimes its people.

- Long-range planning is easier for advertising. It can be timed to the exact print issue or the precise minute of radio or television time. Many publicity activities have a timing element as an objective; for example, a publicist needs to plan for special features or press conferences, which have set timings. Of course, there is no guarantee the timed objective will be achieved with the targeted media.

- The publicist, and in turn the editor, must make decisions about audience perception of the media. What do people *think* of this publication, or why do *some* people watch *this* news show? In contrast, an ad person looks at such items as demographics, psychographics, cost per thousand, and number of insertions. Although they may view the media differently, publicists and advertisers often do direct their efforts toward the same publications, since audience targets are frequently alike.

- The primary contact between the publication and the ad person is often a space salesperson. The advertising person is a buyer and must be convinced the right decision is made. The person who manages a publicity program seldom sees a sales rep; conversely, ad people seldom have a need to talk to the editor (although they could learn a great deal about the vehicle for their advertising if they took the opportunity).

There are also differences in the characteristics of the work they produce:

- Editorial copy must impart "news" in a straightforward, pithy manner; it can't oversell. Ad copy is designed to sell.
- Ad copy can use virtually any superlative. Unsupported superlatives in editorial copy (and even a lot of supported superlatives) raise editors' eyebrows.
- Brand-name mentions in editorial copy must be kept to a minimum. There is no limit in advertising copy—it's often the more the merrier, to please the client.
- Editorial copy contains complete sentences, and is written using good grammar. Ad copy can break the rules, and often does. Ad copy sent when news is required will result in the material not being used, and the sender will be regarded as unprofessional. (So if the product manager rewrites your copy because "it doesn't get the name out there enough," tactfully explain to him the difference between advertising and publicity.)

While the two disciplines need to be fully understood, there is no reason one person cannot directly supervise a marketing communications program that includes both advertising and publicity. Hats must be changed from time to time, however, so that editors do not feel any pressures, real or imagined, when contacted by this communications professional. The most important requisites for effective management are that both disciplines be studied, learned, and practiced.

What Publicity Can Do

- A good publicity campaign can help establish your company as an authority in its field, which can have a positive effect on how your customers and potential customers see you. As a result, communication between your company and the media becomes two-way. You will be more likely to get calls from editors planning a story that relates to your industry once you have established that you are an authority, have access to other authorities and experts, and are a good source of ideas and reliable information. This in turn will give your company and its products even more exposure.
- Product publicity also can extend the reach of advertising. With a limited budget, advertising may have to be concentrated in one or two publications. Publicity can carry your message to the other media reaching your target markets.
- Product publicity can provide a third-party endorsement for your products and services because the "authority" becomes the medium in which a story appears. The assumption is that the more respected the publication (or television show), the more believable or valid the story. Taking this one step further, if another party is involved—a happy customer, a technical expert, or a recognized authority—this endorsement carries even more weight.

- Product publicity can reach more people. The readership of editorial material is generally higher than that for ads. In business-to-business or trade publications the ad message is often directed to just a segment of the readers, but the editors select articles and news items of interest to a majority. For example, not everyone reading *Chemical Week* is interested in *buying* sulfuric acid, so many might overlook an ad for it. But because it is a highly useful and essential chemical in many industries, readers may be very interested in an article on how the market is performing, industry capacity, shipping rates, and so on. Similarly, most readers look at the editorials in *Chemical Week*, since what's written there applies to their businesses and to the industry. In general, editorial material will appeal to a high proportion of readers of any given consumer publication.

There may be tradeoffs here. Editorial matter may have higher readership, but it appears only once, whereas ads are often repeated (six ads in a given trade publication usually is the limit) because there is some justification to the belief that readership is gained each time.

- Product publicity also is a way to announce new developments and products and to educate specific targeted audiences about them. Publicity will take the product message to the markets in detail — background it, describe it, comment on it, support it.
- Product publicity can help promote products and services at all stages of growth, through introduction to obsolescence, although publicity's effectiveness diminishes along with the product's newness.
- Product publicity can help a company develop a "presence" in the media, and thus in the marketplace.
- Publicity, just as advertising, will pay off in qualified inquiries for followup by salespeople.

What Publicity Cannot Do

- Publicity cannot promote a product that has been widely covered by media or whose uses or name has become well known. There is no "news" for the media to offer its readers or viewers.
- Publicity cannot deliver a message that is loaded with superlatives or delivered as brief copy points about a product's benefits or properties. In its brochure "How to Get Your News in a Business Publication," Maclean Hunter Publishers advises publicists against exaggerating a product's performance or benefits.
- Publicity cannot compete with advertising. Once a product has been advertised as new, publicity cannot deliver the identical message. Timing is critical. Publicity leads; advertising follows. Editors read competitive publications, including the advertising. They are not easily fooled.

- Publicity cannot deliver a message word for word as it is submitted. It is always subject to rewrite. The message may be interpreted by an editor, or the editor may solicit and include opinions on the same subject from others, even competitors.
- Publicity cannot make promises. No matter how well a publicist knows an editor, there is no assurance any submitted material will be used.
- Publicity cannot work miracles; it cannot create a story where there genuinely is none. For many products it may not be productive to use publicity, simply because there is absolutely no editorial interest. If it is necessary to "keep the name out there," a modest advertising program should be considered instead. Advertising can be a far better and more successful way of keeping customers aware of the product and its benefits, and letting the market know the company still makes the product.

As an example, several years ago I was given a publicity assignment for a number of industrial products. One was used to reduce odors in municipal sewage treatment plants—hardly an exciting product, but one that did make money for the company. My predecessor had developed two case histories on cities that had success with our product. The publicity problem was that virtually every treatment plant in the country used either our product or a very similar one from the competition. There was no *news*.

In such situations, publicists must learn to resist pressure from others in the company: "You're the expert, get me a story." Trying to force, cajole, or otherwise convince editors that there is a story, when none exists, will get you immediate bad marks, and will reduce your chances of success when you really have a story to tell.

The Basic Ingredients of Publicity

A good publicity program, as we have said before, is part of an integrated communications plan. This plan—and each of its individual components (publicity, advertising, and promotion)—is *strategic:* Objectives can be defined clearly and goals can be measured. Here it may be helpful to note the basic tasks that make up most strategic publicity programs; all are discussed in detail in subsequent chapters.

The basic elements of publicity, for both print and broadcast media, are:

Print News Release

A news release is usually sent to more than one publication in a specific marketing area, because there usually are several that may be interested in the news or information it conveys. A release should provide "news" to a given market, news that educates, solves problems, or otherwise provides information the media audience is unaware of. Most print releases for product publicity run only two to three pages; most are accompanied by photographs and captions.

A news release is used to announce new products, new equipment, new plant or office capacity, a new application of a product, the publication of product literature or technical data, new distributors, personnel changes, and information condensed from speeches or position statements that may have an effect on a market.

The news release is by far the most common tool used in product publicity. The odds of it being used by a publication—assuming it has something to say and is sent to the proper media—can be increased if it is well written and meets an editor's criteria for news. The release approach also is very much overused, when other techniques, such as exclusives, might be more productive. A news release is an inexpensive way to reach a market, but it is money wasted if it doesn't provide information of value.

Broadcast News Release

Releases sent to television are frequently called news clips or video news releases (VNRs). They are produced on broadcast-quality videotape and sent to stations by overnight air or first class mail, depending upon the urgency or timeliness of the message. They can also be transmitted directly to the stations via satellite. The printed matter enclosed with the tape or sent in advance of a satellite transmission describes briefly what is being sent. Television news clips should be

---

Tasks of Publicity Professionals

Plan and give direction to programs	Counsel external contacts
Manage outside services	Manage inquiry handling
Administer budgets	Conduct press events
Merchandise efforts	Prepare press kits
Advocate programs	Manage media tours
Maintain editorial contacts	Manage exhibit publicity
Identify story opportunities	Conduct interviews
Research stories	Prepare electronic news material
Write copy	Manage movie and videotape production
Edit copy	Write speeches
Travel	Write newsletters
Counsel internal contacts	Edit technical papers

used sparingly. They are quite expensive to produce—often twice as much as the cost of a press event. In 1986, I paid about $10,000, including distribution.

Unlike print releases, VNRs often have to be presold. They are regarded with some suspicion by television news directors, who are highly sensitive to anything that smacks of commercialism. There also are a growing number of agencies and independent producers making and distributing them, which suggests that some, at least, will be distributed that do not meet the criteria of news value and high visual interest. TV clips are becoming the bane of the broadcast news director, just as the written release is of the print news editor.

There are two basic types: (1) those used in connection with a newsworthy event such as the announcement of a new product development (released at the same time it is announced to the print media), and (2) "evergreen" stories, those that do not have an immediate or "hard" news angle.

Radio News Release

These are not "releases" in the sense that a print release is. Print releases are never sent to a radio station; they are far too long and detailed, and the photos that go with them are meaningless to a radio news director. What is useful is a brief statement of why the product is newsworthy, and how it relates to the station's audiences by demographic or high local interest.

Radio releases can be sent over a telephone line if the station expresses interest. A radio release should have the name of a person who can be contacted for further information, plus the offer of a source for an expert's interview (also over the phone). The expert can be a company spokesperson, an outside authority, or both. Radio releases should be sent to arrive at the station in advance of a print release; once the story has appeared in the local newspaper, it is of no value to a radio station.

Feature Stories

Features are not written like news releases; they run much longer, depending upon the needs and style of a given publication. It's just not what you say, but how you say it and the amount of detail and supporting data you offer that will determine whether a given feature will be used.

Features are most often exclusives—they are developed with and sent to just *one* publication. However, it is quite proper to rewrite a feature for later placement in a noncompetitive publication, or recast it as a short news release for other media in the market area—but only *after* it has appeared in the first publication.

Exclusives may be written by a company publicist, an agency writer, a free-lance writer retained by the agency or company, an editor at the publication, or someone assigned by the publication. There is no hard and fast rule on who does them, even with highly technical pieces.

Seven Basic Types of Features

1. The *case history* is an account of someone's experience with a product. Most often this is a customer, although the story may also be written from the point of view of a person who has researched or tested a given product. It provides a third-party endorsement of a product or application.

2. *Roundups* report on the latest developments of a number of products in a particular business or consumer interest area. They are developed and written by a publication, based on information requested by or contributed to it. They are often scheduled well in advance, and many are listed on media calendars prepared by the publications or in media directories.

3. Closely related to the roundup is the *trend story*, which describes and explains a trend taking place within a given industry. The line between roundups and trends is often blurred; both types of stories usually involve a number of different products from a number of different companies.

4. *Technical articles* also are exclusive and can be either initiated by editors or suggested by publicists. They usually discuss a narrow research or development area. It's most important that the publicist thoroughly understand the editorial thrust of a publication before approaching it on a technical article.

5. Another type of exclusive is an *application story*, describing how a product is used. The line between this and other types of exclusives can be fuzzy. Case histories, roundups, and trend stories, or stories that combine all three, can involve an application.

6. *New product stories* can sometimes be offered as exclusives. Doing so may well motivate an editor to cover the development extensively, but the publicist risks offending other publications covering the same potential markets. This type of exclusive should be done only for industries that are covered by just a very few publications, as a rule, only with *the* leading publication reaching the industry.

7. *Roundtables* are another way to develop exclusives. They work this way: Experts on a given discipline—technical, research, marketing, management—are brought together with *one* editor who has responded favorably to a publicist by showing interest in developing an in-depth feature on a development or a new product and its significance in a market. The experts are not necessarily always from the company. Bringing in one or more outside experts may help validate some of the points made by company people.

Press Events

Another fundamental element of any publicity program. They take several forms, from the structured press conference to the more informal "event" with a party atmosphere. But all have a serious purpose: to bring together media to announce at one time a development that has a high news (and often visual) value.

Photography

This is a basic and vital part of any publicity program. It is important in *all* print media, with the exception of newsletters and some technical journals, and it is a vital element of any program through the entire life cycle of a product.

Editorial Relations

Perhaps the single most important basic element of publicity is editorial relations. It is far easier to carry out all the separate tasks if the editorial relationship is cordial, professional, and founded on trust. The publicist who will be successful in working with all these elements is the one who takes the time to develop a thorough understanding of the needs of the media and the audiences they reach.

Tying It All Together

The publicity plan often starts to take shape several months before it is actually scheduled to go into effect. Such a plan should respond to and reflect marketing objectives. These objectives are directed to such areas as:

- Educating the marketplace of the value of a product or service.
- Positioning a product against its competition or, if there is no in-kind competition, as a new or unique entity.
- Building awareness of the product's properties among its potential markets.
- Exploring new market areas where the product might be successful.

All these call for *strategic* programming over a given period of time.

Too often, however, publicity actions are tactical, and respond only to a call for a news release or a customer support feature. These tactics are used to support a selling effort *now,* and to hope for a response *now.* There is nothing wrong with tactical actions at times; publicity is sometimes opportunistic and must be responsive in this way. And any publicity program is composed of a sequence of specific tasks — tactics, if you will. But publicity can be most effective when it is planned, and when it is an integral part of a strategic marketing communications program.

Linda Pezzano, president of Pezzano+Company of New York, defines marketing public relations "as either the primary means of marketing communication or as an important adjunct to advertising and promotion efforts. But in all cases, a successful public relations program must be consistent with the client's overall marketing objectives. For every organization, from small businesses and corporations to hospitals and colleges, survival depends on continued sales—either of a product, service, or idea. We exist to produce sales inquiries. We strive to create a favorable selling environment by increasing positive awareness."

Andrew W. Ballentine, distinguished lecturer in marketing in the College of Business Administration at the University of South Carolina, says:

> Product publicity can be a valuable medium when it addresses specific marketing objectives and when it is orchestrated with other segments of the communications plan. Unfortunately, this seldom happens in many companies.
>
> There are several reasons for this. First, the business unit managers do not view publicity, advertising, and other communications vehicles as strategic resources. Rather, they are considered tactically and often are used sporadically. They are viewed as selling expenses rather than resources in the strategic marketing process.
>
> It is imperative that communications professionals and managers understand the role and effectiveness of publicity in the communications mix. Then take appropriate actions to ensure that business management understands the role of communications in the marketing mix.
>
> When this happens and when product publicity is used strategically, it will become understood and its role will be appreciated as a contributor to the health of the enterprise.

2
Preparing a Publicity Plan That Works

The best product publicity plans are those prepared with the same attention to detail as is given to advertising and promotion. Because publicity should be an integral part of the marketing communications plan, the plans should be developed at the same time as the other communications sectors, and as a joint effort by marketing communications professionals.

Cooperative planning by all segments of a communications program—jointly defining objectives and setting up a system to measure results—is extremely important. By insisting that measurable objectives be spelled out, that realistic forecasts be established, and that target markets be identified, marketing management is far better able to budget and allocate resources and measure results against the communications objectives set. The final publicity plan, then, becomes part of the total marketing communications plan; advertising, sales promotion, and publicity all work together to support marketing objectives.

Some public relations people have difficulty approaching publicity planning this way; to them it seems cold and analytical. But the measure of success can no longer be scrapbooks filled with clippings, broadcast reports, or a list of editors who have been contacted for future stories. This would be like the salesperson listing the customers called upon, but with no report on whether an order was written. Success in publicity means only one thing: that the targeted media actually carried the agreed-upon messages; that they were indeed delivered to the target audiences through media reaching those audiences. This takes careful and detailed planning.

In this chapter we will look at three major aspects of the planning process: the strategic and tactical elements of the plan, its budget, and its timing vis-à-vis the life cycle of the product. For another perspective on what's involved in good strategies, tactics, and plans, see the case study of a well-designed and implemented publicity campaign in Appendix A.

Effective Planning

Organizing the Plan

Behind every plan are four questions that must be answered:

1. Who are you talking to? Be very specific. This cannot be expressed in vague generalities. Think individual decision makers, not groups or things.
2. What do you want them to learn?
3. How are you going to convey the message in the most direct and forceful manner?
4. What actions do you want them to take as a result of your activity? With editorial material, you are speaking to an audience through an editor. While you may want your audiences to take some specific actions, you must first structure and deliver your message in such a way that it will be of interest to an editor as "news."

The target media selected for publicity will often be in the same general categories as for advertising. But the publicity plan will probably differ from the advertising plan in concentration. Advertising may be scheduled for only one or two publications reaching a given market, or on one television or radio station. Publicity targets may be a number of media reaching a given audience, or media in which no advertising is planned.

A way to look at the path by which "customers" receive communications from publicity is illustrated in Figure 2-1. The message is created and delivered in the *external world*. If the receiver has an interest in the message or messages, they then enter the receiver's head, or the *internal world*, where a number of steps occur.

The *message* path on the left involves only one message or a single action, transmitted via one vehicle or medium. Examples of such messages include a news release or an exclusive. (An idea spread through word-of-mouth is also a type of message, but I will discuss here only those messages set into motion by a publicist.) Although the message is developed by a publicist, neither he nor marketing control it. It is subject to rewrite by an editor, who also decides whether or not to use it.

Let's assume in this case that the message is left relatively intact and is

Preparing a Publicity Plan That Works

Figure 2-1. Communications path to customers.

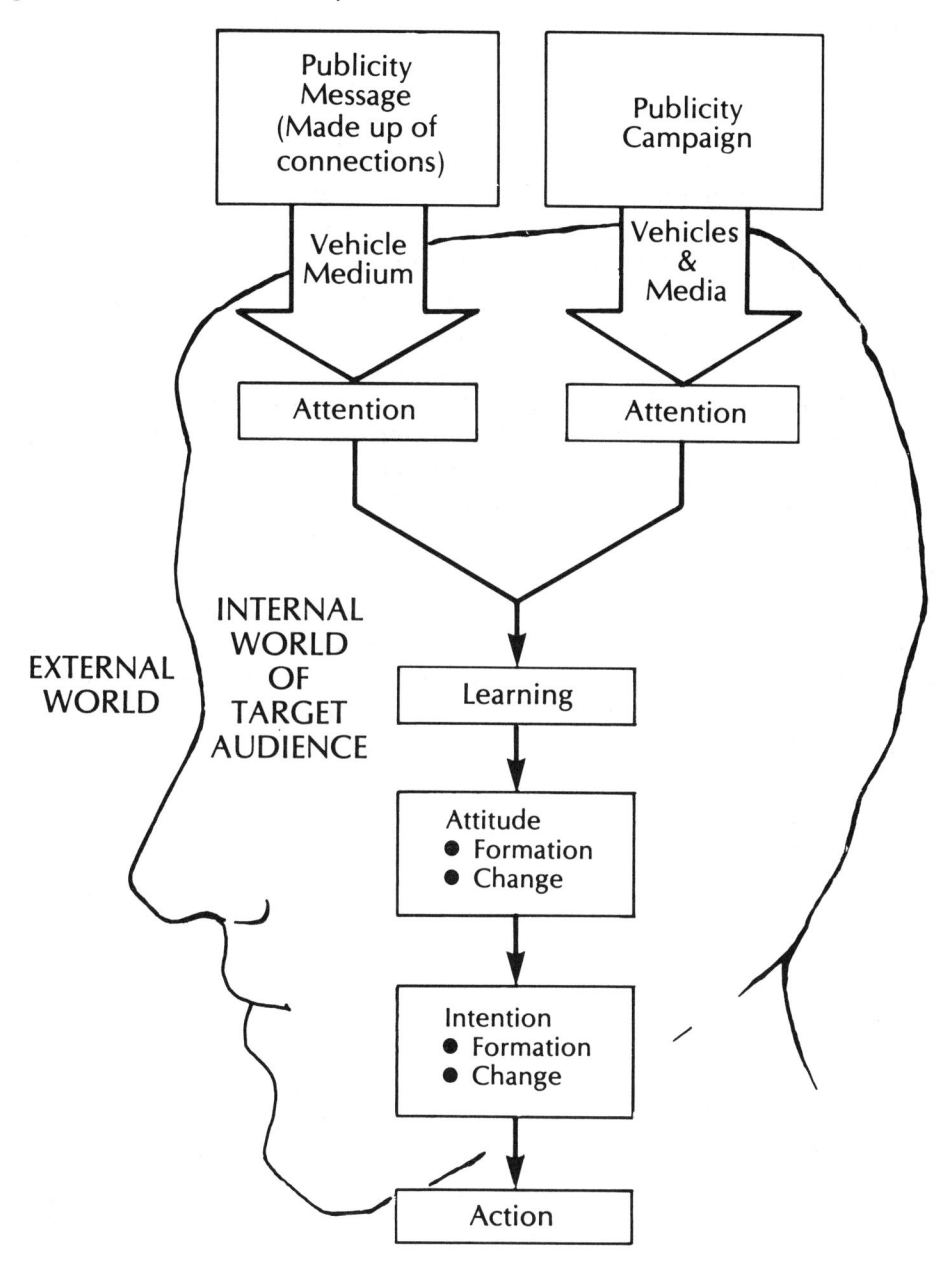

```
Publicity Message          Publicity
(Made up of                Campaign
connections)
    |                          |
Vehicle                    Vehicles &
Medium                      Media
    ↓                          ↓
Attention                  Attention
         \                /
          ↓              ↓
            Learning
               ↓
            Attitude
            • Formation
            • Change
               ↓
            Intention
            • Formation
            • Change
               ↓
             Action
```

EXTERNAL WORLD

INTERNAL WORLD OF TARGET AUDIENCE

Courtesy of Dr. Arthur Beard, Market Research Manager at Du Pont.

delivered to the recipient. Note the *attention* box included inside the head (that is, inside the internal world of the target audience). Before any other responses can take place, the message recipient must *pay attention* to the message. If a message is delivered via the wrong medium and fails to reach the intended audience or is ignored, there is no attention.

The *campaign* path on the right involves just that, a publicity campaign made up of several messages that may be addressed to different types of media. A compaign is a collection of coordinated messages, with lots of activities. Let's assume in this case that they attract the attention we are seeking.

Note that the left and right paths of the figure converge at *learning,* which is the next essential response. If the receiver fails to *learn* anything, no *attitudes* can be formed. The message or messages delivered may also precipitate a change of attitude, which could be either positive or negative.

If the attitude change is positive, then the recipient must form an *intention* to act in order for the publicity to be considered successful.

Finally, if all these steps have occurred, and all reactions have been positive, the result is *action,* which is external. Action can take several forms — for example, writing an inquiry about a product, circling a reader service number on a bingo card, or calling a company or sales office.

The concept of a communications path can also be applied to advertising. The only difference is that advertising is not subject to editing or to an editor's decision to run. The message created will be delivered to the audience in precisely the same way it is written. However, *attention* and all the other internal activities must still take place before advertising can be considered successful.

As you can see, broad exposure or a pile of clippings do not provide a measure of success. The members of a target audience must experience positive thought processes and take some resultant action.

Another tool that is helpful in organizing your thinking about planning is the "five W's and How." (See Chapter 6 for a description of how news writers use this tool.) The "five W's plus" can be modified and applied to planning as follows:

- *Who?* Who is the source for the message? Who is speaking for it?
- *Says what?* What is this company or person saying? What is the content of the message? How do the points relate to the source and to one another?
- *To whom?* Who are the people you want to receive the message?
- *Via which channels?* How are you going to deliver it in the most effective way?
- *How?* In what style or by what means is the contact being made?
- *When?* When do you hope the message will appear? Set a target date (or a hoped-for date) for publicity as well as advertising.
- *Where?* Where do you expect the message to appear? In the new-product section, technical, picture page, special columns?
- *Why?* Assuming you have succeeded, now what do you want your audience

to do? Write a letter, circle a reader service number, telephone you, ask for literature, feel better about your company, respect you?
- *With what effect?* Simply, did they do any of the things you wanted them to do?

There may be markets that can be reached through publicity even though they are too costly for advertising. Equally important, there may be areas where publicity just won't be effective, as seen in Quirk's curve later in this chapter. Publicity won't support a poor product for very long; if a product is not all it is claimed to be, all the editorial contacts, good photos, and excellent writing will not achieve results. Advertising won't help, either, other than by bringing the product to an even quicker demise.

Publicity cannot "sell" a product, and it can't always be used as a substitute for advertising. Thus, the program must be approached with realistic expectations in mind. Even so, reasonable and measurable objectives should be set. Reasonable, because the publicity objectives are targeted to the proper media and have a reasonable chance of success; and measurable, because the people handling publicity must be held accountable for their actions.

Writing the Plan: The Basic Ingredients

The basic elements of a publicity plan are:

1. Market summary
2. Communications analysis
3. Identification of target audiences
4. Statement of role of communications
5. Statement of communications objectives
6. Strategies
7. Tactics
8. Media objectives
9. Budgets

Market Summary

Before any program is written, the advertising and publicity people together should prepare a market or business summary that they can all use. This is seldom written by an agency, because it can best be done by those in the company with access to market and business intelligence and information from several different company sources. It's like a snapshot of "where we are now, and where we want to be, in our business," against which a workable and effective marketing communications program can be written. Once it is done, all parties involved in providing information for the report should agree that it is a true and realistic review and appraisal. It will become a working document, a "state of the business," and a valuable source of information for communications professionals.

Briefly, it covers:

1. The product(s), their properties, advantages, disadvantages, functions, uses, and applications *by markets.*
2. Information on where each product is in its life cycle.
3. Description of how the product features benefit the customers.
4. Complete description of the markets.
5. Complete assessment of the competition.
6. Description of distribution methods.
7. Description of customer attitudes toward each product in each market.
8. Financial information.

These are some of the details that will be needed:

1. Product descriptions. This must be very detailed, for a number of reasons. First, this forces the person preparing the plan and marketing management to make a realistic assessment of the product. It also provides staff and agency with information they need to promote the product and position it against others.

The description must include the apparent advantages of the product as well as its disadvantages. Few products are perfect, and it is far easier to plan a communications program when the negative information is available. As an example, a positive story may be developed on a product's use, but an editor may raise a question about either a real or rumored disadvantage. This type of question can be answered only if the information is available (and it is not proprietary, of course). There may also be recognized disadvantages that become less significant because of the inherent product advantages. These disadvantages can be real in the marketplace, however, and used against the company by competitors.

The summary also must describe how the product functions, either as a single element or as part of another. If the product is industrial, describe the environment in which it works. If it's a consumer product—a food item, a vehicle, or sports equipment—describe its function in relation to its value. For example, there are many manufacturers of skis, but each has built properties into its products that make them different from the competition.

2. Life Cycle. Information on where the product is in its life cycle is important in planning because it will determine what actions are taken to promote it. Is it new, are markets just being developed, is it a mature product, or is it in a declining market? This information is essential to determine the extent and kind of communications support—in money and personnel time—budgeted for the program. Having this information may suggest placing more emphasis on advertising and less on publicity, or vice versa, depending upon its life-cycle position. We will discuss the issue of life cycle and timing at length later in this chapter.

3. *Customer benefits.* Delineate and detail how the product benefits a customer. Does it fill a need for one market group, or cut across several? Is it targeted to fill a need in a particular industry, or an identifiable demographic group? Try to look at the product from a customer's point of view. Are there needs the product is *not* meeting? Is the competition also fulfilling these needs and perhaps doing a more effective job of it? Does this information suggest that marketing or communications plans that may have worked well in the past now need refocusing?

4. *Markets.* Describing the markets can help guide selection of media to reach them. The description should be detailed and closely focused on precisely who purchases the product or service or who makes the purchasing decision. (It should always be a person, not a thing; the gourmet foods manager, not a supermarket.) Be specific. The primary buyer is not, for example, a "purchaser of men's clothing." The buyer is the person, by title, for each target market (chain or individual store unit) who decides whether and where the men's clothing will be sold. It may be more than one person: It may be the buyer *and* the buyer's superior, who approves the decision. Try to describe this person.

What factors influence a purchase decision? If it is an industrial product, the purchase decision may be made because a product meets certain specifications or is offered at the lowest cost. If a market is the military, there are a number of set procedures that must be observed. Or the product may be recommended by a designer, approved by a chief designer, and ordered by a purchasing director.

Market share should be identified as a part of the total potential market. The potential market is not the entire market — unless there is no competition, which is rare. Share is the percentage a company currently holds, and potential share is a reasonable projected portion of the market, a realistic goal over a given period of time, say one to five years. (It is *not* like the potential share statement in a plan I reviewed, which indicated that there were one billion units in use and this offered a "remarkable opportunity for market penetration.")

The report also offers a brief summary of how marketing hopes to achieve this penetration.

5. *The competition.* Who are they, where are they, and what are they selling? Is their product better, as good as, or worse than ours? Is it more expensive or less expensive than ours? What advantages does our product have? Better service? Faster delivery? Longer shelf life? More attractive packaging? More convenient packaging? High quality? Good service?

Knowing how a product measures up against the competition may motivate the communicator to recommend positioning the product and attempting to carve out a particular portion of the market where the competition is vulnerable.

Be realistic. If there is competition, it must be doing something right or there would be little need to position the advantages of your own product.

If your product is higher priced than the competitor's, there have to be some compelling reasons for someone to buy it. It may have to be positioned as having what some of my colleagues call "value in use," which can mean that it will perform better, last longer, is of better quality, will reduce labor costs, and so on, even though it costs more.

A product also may perform better than its competitors because of a combination of properties. By the way, beware of the common phrase "unique combination of properties"; this is poor English and also stretches a point by stating that it is possible to have a unique combination of anything. Instead, try to find out what the properties are.

Sales assistance and technical support also may help gain the sale.

6. *Distribution.* Collect all the data you can. Knowing who distributes and sells the product—company salespeople, distributors, dealers, retailers, jobbers, or combinations thereof—can help you plan the best program to support these activities. The people outside the company helping to market and sell the product are often just as important as the internal marketing staff. You may consider a separate program to support the outside group. Knowing they have support and are important to your company will motivate them to work harder for you.

7. *Customer attitudes.* There is one important question that can't always be answered satisfactorily: What do those people think of us? Our customers, our potential customers, and those other buying influences may hold an opinion of our company, but we are unable to pin it down. Or we just don't know.

Marketing research can frequently find the answers to some of these questions. (Marketing research as it relates directly to measuring publicity activities is covered in Chapter 12.) Marketing research also can determine who makes the important purchase decisions and identify what they consider the most important features of your product. All this information can be gathered for a cost of a few thousand dollars.

8. *Financial information.* Use charts and graphs to clarify data on earnings, return on investment, and sales forecasts. Data should be developed for each product and each market.

If marketing can forecast for a five-year period—or at least two years—this can help define the areas that need attention and marketing communications support. If a pattern is developing that shows a product will be in a declining market in a year or two, for example, there may be no reason to support it with extensive publicity or advertising. Other patterns may forecast a greater market share, or a need for a greater market share in order to become profitable. Marketing communications plans can be developed to meet these goals.

Communications Analysis

This involves summarizing and analyzing the communications programs now being used, both by you and by your competition.

Preparing a Publicity Plan That Works

Studying how the prime competition is communicating can greatly benefit a marketing communications program. This can be done inexpensively by instructing your clipping services to clip stories and advertisements of your competitors. This needs to be detailed with specific media groups defined so that you can track the messages the competition uses to promote its products and the media it uses to deliver them. You should be able to get an estimate of competitive activity, and may wish to add this to your budget. Knowing where your company stands in relation to the competition can be beneficial in developing your programs and may even help when a budget increase must be defended.

Your plan also should include a review of what your company has done in the past year. This is vital to budgeting as well as planning.

Determine if you have been successful and reached your communications objectives. Perhaps no objectives were set to measure against. Ask: Were we (or they) just guessing, based on scrapbooks and attractive advertising and sales literature? It's sometimes difficult to determine just what parts of a publicity program are working, but it's a fact that programs *are measurable* with relatively inexpensive tracking methods such as media reporting services, marketing research, and telemarketing. (See Chapter 12 for more on this.)

Target Audiences

A number of questions should be asked to help you pinpoint your audience, to determine who should be educated or receive useful information.

- Just who are these people we are trying to reach?
- How much do we really know about them?
- Who out of this conglomeration of customers really makes the purchasing decisions?
- What media should be employed to help influence the purchasing decisions?
- How can we exert influence on these decisions?
- Are our marketing communications directed to the right audiences, through the right media?

I heard a very bright young marketing executive say that his advertising and publicity people had directed his promotional program to "industrial designers." He then asked a reasonable question: "Who are these people? I never met one at a trade show, have no idea what they think, how they regard their jobs, or whether they are really specifiers for our products." If he didn't know, his communications staff and agency probably didn't know either. If they could not provide detailed information on this group, they were probably just guessing that these people were influenced by the communications program. Perhaps they were—and perhaps not.

One way to get this information is to check the demographics of the publications to which publicity is directed and in which advertising is scheduled. Another is to develop a market research project to determine who these elusive "designers" are. This could be a carefully structured telephone survey or focus group interviews.

Some of the information you need to get a better fix on the marketing audiences can be obtained from your company's business plans and forecasts, as well as from what was done in marketing communications in the past. But there are other methods of gathering intelligence:

Talk to the old-timers in the company; not necessarily the ones nearing retirement, but people who have been with the company for a number of years. They have experienced the ups and downs of the market swing, have been calling on customers for many years, and are often good sources for market information and customer attitudes. (They are also good sources for story leads.)

Make sales calls with a sales representative or a distributor, to plants, supermarkets, retail stores, offices—wherever your products are sold. See the business from the field side, the competitive arena. Hear directly about what your customers think about your company, including their complaints.

Talk to the people in research and development. Or, if you have a technical support group, talk to them. Many technical people are troubleshooters and can tell you if there are any problems with a product, and will share their views about how customers regard the service the company provides.

Speak to a *friendly* editor. If you know the editor well enough, you often can gather some valuable market information during the course of a meeting or over the phone. But don't call an editor just to pick his brain. Your questions about the business should be an outgrowth of a conversation, not the reason for initiating it.

Don't send an editor a questionnaire and ask him to fill it out. A number of editors I interviewed told me they frequently receive questionnaires or find them included with news releases. They resent them, totally ignore them, and consider this approach quite unprofessional. (Marketing research can be directed to editors, however, and has been done successfully.) In doing a number of interviews, both long and short, for this book, I found all the editors I spoke with extremely cooperative. But they *don't* want questionnaires included in news releases.

Finally, and most important, when you are developing a plan for the future, be sure to research the past. If the plan produced results and met the objectives set a year ago, it may only need to be continued. But with publicity, the longer the product or service has been around, the more difficult it is to create "news" about it. The plan may need extensive refining or new direction based on present realities.

Role of Communications

The role of communications—advertising, promotion, and publicity—should be detailed and related to the market summary. The role should be identi-

Preparing a Publicity Plan That Works

fied for each product and service. (A role of publicity is not to "sell." Rarely does even advertising sell, and publicity *never* does. Sales may result somewhere down the line, but they do so because communications taught something, the receiver of the message took some action, the company delivering the message took some further action, and a sale resulted.) Ask the question: What do you expect communications to achieve?

Communications Objectives

Communications objectives should not be confused with marketing objectives. Marketing and sales personnel may wish to increase market share or increase earnings; these are marketing objectives. Communications objectives are set to help create a climate in which marketing objectives are easier to accomplish. Communications objectives relate to teaching a specified audience something, generating inquiries, helping position a product or service, and increasing awareness if there is an awareness base to begin with. Communications objectives can be measured.

Here are *some* of the tasks publicity can undertake that can be related as communications objectives. (Many could also be undertaken by advertising, of course.)

1. Differentiate or position your product or service against others. (This may entail defining audiences by demographics and psychographics.)
2. Improve or heighten benefits awareness.
3. Improve awareness of "perceived value": properties of your product compared with the competition. (Awareness can be measured, but that created or increased by a publicity program may not be easy to measure, because other communications activities are at work.)
4. Show technical competence.
5. Clear up any misconceptions about the product.
6. Assert leadership role in industry by becoming an authority on a particular subject or in a particular area. (Good editorial relations are important to achieve this.)
7. Teach specific product benefits and advantages. (A way to measure learning as a result of communications activities should be defined.)
8. Introduce the product to new market area, and generate a given number of inquiries.
9. Encourage trial use.
10. Assist distributors and sales agents.

Strategies

Once the communications objectives are set for each market segment, the type of media and the media audiences that the messages will be directed to, as well as the specific media that will be used to reach these audiences, must be identified.

These are called *strategies and tactics.*

There is a great deal of confusion about the difference between strategies and tactics. Perhaps a military analogy will help.

General Eisenhower, as chief of the European Allied forces in World War II, had the objective of winning the war. One of his *strategies* was to invade Europe. Part of the strategy involved selecting the army divisions, air squadrons, and naval armadas that would carry out the objective. Timing was another part of the strategy. His *tactics* included choosing specific regiments (by name) to be deployed and the specific air and naval units for the attack. We can assume he knew the strength of the enemy (the competition) and the terrain (the marketplace).

Here's another example: Your objective is to reach upscale carpet buyers. A strategy is space advertising in home-interest publications. A tactic might be to run a four-color spread in *Architectural Record* every month from March through October. Another strategy might be to develop a publicity program aimed at high-income families to influence them to purchase a particular brand of carpet. A tactic could be developing a story for *Town & Country* about a wealthy family that totally redecorated its home in Brookville, Long Island. The objective is to have the new carpets featured along with the other furnishings, including an antique collection.

When selecting a tactic, try to have a back-up—be flexible whenever you can. Although there is a good chance that if you have set objectives and developed strategies, your tactic will work, there are no guarantees. In the case of your tactic to place stories related to carpets in *Architectural Record* and *Town & Country,* have another publication to fall back on, since it's extremely difficult to get publicity into either of these two. Bear in mind, however, that if your audience can be reached only through these magazines, you must put together a strategy that is sure to work.

Strategies involve ways to reach identified audiences and the primary media areas in which the message is to be delivered. Another example of a strategy: "Reach fashion-conscious women through fashion or lifestyle publications." As part of the strategy, key copy points to be delivered should be listed. What messages are to be conveyed and in what order of importance?

Timing is most important. While the editor makes the decision as to when (and if) a story will run, timing can be set as an *objective* (even if you don't make it) and coordinated with advertising and other promotional efforts.

A new-product launch requires a strategic program. It might include a press event to announce a new product, a combination press/customer event at a trade show or exhibition, a media tour, and exclusive feature stories. It will have an editorial justification and be directed at reaching the objectives set in the publicity plan.

Tactics

Tactics are specific actions directed to specific media. They are the tools used to carry out the strategies to reach the communications objectives. Tactics are directed to specific media: Who will be invited to the press event? Which publications should receive the publicity releases on a certain story? Which television programs have a segment that could take advantage of the visual aspect?

For example, in order to reach the world of high fashion, your tactic might be to send releases to *Women's Wear Daily, Vogue, Harper's Bazaar,* and *Elle,* as well as to fashion columns in newspapers you've decided would be appropriate. If you were able to get a story published in *Women's Wear Daily, Vogue* might then be influenced to use it, too. A specific angle or approach should be identified for each of the target media. Tactics, then, are the specifics of how the strategy is to be accomplished.

To take the fashion example a step further, if you truly have the beginnings of a fashion trend, there's a strong possibility of television interest. The tactic would be to place the story in a highly visual way on selected television channels.

The "tools" listed in Figure 2-5 later in this chapter are tactics. The key to strategic programming is selecting the right tactic, at the right time, and coordinating all the publicity elements with advertising and promotional programs.

Media Objectives

There are a number of ways to measure success. One part of the plan is to set measurable objectives by identifying the primary media for each product group, and directing most of your efforts to those media only. (Distribution lists should then be set up according to primary and secondary media.) A rule of thumb is that if your publicity appears in at least 80 percent of prime media, you have been successful. This makes the most sense when you have targeted at least several outlets. Obviously if your objective had been to develop publicity for two publications, and success was achieved, you would have 100 percent success; but the guideline would have been more meaningful if a number of print or broadcast media were involved.

Another way is to determine if the important copy points for your products were picked up and used. To measure this, set up for each product four or five key messages you want to take to the media.

Were your stories *well* used? Were you able to get relatively good position in the publication? Was the brand name mentioned in the headline or the first paragraph? Was the photo used? If these and other goals you set for yourself averaged out well, you had a successful program.

These media objectives are just as important as all the others. Unless the messages are delivered in media reaching your primary markets, you have not had a successful program. But you should not ignore media identified as secondary. If an editor who is not too important to your immediate needs contacts you for information or to develop a story, you may not feel obligated to help. But if you don't, it may have an adverse effect on your media relations. You may need the publication one day, the publication may be important to a colleague, or the word may get around that you are uncooperative.

Let me emphasize again that the results expected should be reasonable. Sometimes both marketing and communications set objectives that are too high, too difficult. An appearance on the "Today" show or a story in *Newsweek* may be ego-building, but may not be the most effective way to reach the target audiences. Similarly, another exclusive story in the leading trade publication—following two last year—may not be possible.

Publicity should be held to the same accountability as any other form of communications or business. When this activity has to account for its actions, much of the mystique about it will disappear, and publicity will be an accepted business practice. And everyone will benefit.

Budget

This last item in the publicity plan is discussed in detail later in this chapter.

Other Planning Considerations

Role of the Agency

Your agency should be brought in early on these planning activities. Share your information with them. And be open to their suggestions and ideas on planning the future program. The plan should not be fixed until the agency has contributed its suggestions, and responded with a plan based on the objectives you have set out.

In evaluating a program presented by an agency, watch for the sort of vague generalities that are often included in a program but don't, upon close examination, make a whole lot of sense. They also call for mind reading by the client. Unless the objectives are clearly spelled out (they don't have to be in great detail), look with some suspicion upon phrases like these:

"Develop specific awareness of product benefits . . ."

"Publicize to the trade the company's commitment to . . ."

"Develop press kit" (without stating timing, effectiveness, reasons for this approach, etc.).

"Prepare multimedia show for press conference." (Again, what objective, what content, what audience?)

Commitment to Followup

No matter how the interest is generated, the marketing or sales manager should make a commitment in writing that qualified inquiries are followed up assiduously by the salespeople, as soon as possible after they have been identified. Inquiries that result from reader service inquiries or "bingo cards" can be screened by telemarketing.

All qualified leads generated by the program should be pursued and a report written on each call. Unless this is done, there is a good chance that there will not be any followup, and customers and potential customers will get a bad impression of the company. I once generated 512 inquiries from a case history story about a customer's business. Unfortunately, many of the inquiries were not followed up, even though they were qualified. The excuse was that the sales group did not have a big enough staff to handle the task. Before planning an action that may require extensive qualification and followup, make sure there are people who will do it. This is the one area that seems to get the least attention.

Effective Budgeting

Even if you have developed a workable publicity program, one that you feel comfortable with, one that you feel will help meet your objectives and fits well with the other elements of the communications plan, none of it will be worth very much if you can't get a budget approved.

In spite of the fact that marketing research shows there is a high return on investment when management is willing to spend money on communications to get a "dominant share of voice," advertising and publicity programs frequently are trimmed when there is a budget crunch. This is a very short-sighted approach to effective communications, but one that many communicators have to deal with just about every time a program is written and proposed.

Still, the total effectiveness of any plan cannot be measured unless the results are evaluated against numbers. If the budget is trimmed, or marketing management tells the communications group it has only so much money available for a program, the most effective means must be found to reach at least part of the objectives set out in the plan. A communications plan must be designed to reach the intended audiences.

The *wrong* approach is to allocate a fixed number of dollars to advertising, another fixed amount to publicity, and some for sales promotion. If advertising can reach the audiences best, then that is where the money should be spent. If publicity can be most effective, then that is where the emphasis should be placed. The program is developed on the best combination of *all* elements.

Ideally, the publicity budget should be zero-based.

Gather Your Facts

Before you start working on a budget, you have some homework to do.

1. Examine carefully the results of the past year's events, compared with the money expended to achieve them. Look at each element:

Expenditures on special events. Could a given event have been staged at a lower cost and still have reached the targeted media? Was it even necessary?

News releases. Are the mailing lists too long? Is there too much "slush" in them? Were releases mailed that were not targeted properly, or went to publications that had little or no interest in them? Will trimming the lists to only primary media achieve the same results? Postage, printing, and handling costs may appear to be small items. They are not.

Photography. Don't skimp on getting good photographs. But use them cost-effectively. Were photos sent to publications that did not use them? Were too many prints ordered? Were color transparencies sent to publications that do not use color? Were black and white prints made that weren't used or may never be used? If you order your prints from the photographer, rather than a color lab or print house, chances are you'll pay more. (As explained in Chapter 8, photography should be "work for hire," with the client owning all negatives.) Is the agency marking up photography it supervises for you, the client? Agencies should bill out-of-pocket charges at cost.

2. Check agency expenses. Are you calling too many agency meetings? Can consultation be done over the phone instead of in person? Is the agency sending three people to a meeting (two of them executives with a high hourly rate), when the account executive can handle the business? Should you visit the agency, instead of asking the agency to come to you for consultation? Are out-of-pocket costs reasonable?

3. Are you paying for clippings you don't need? Check your clipping instructions; if they are not followed, return the excess clips. You are paying a per-clip charge.

4. Are you, or your agency, spending too much on entertainment or travel? Has the entertainment been productive? Are you spending money on contacts that haven't paid off? Are you directing your media relations to the proper people? It is not necessary to entertain editors to have good media relations.

5. Are videotape or film charges too high? Although you are looking for technical expertise and dramatic effect, and while production houses should not be retained solely on the basis of cost, you may wish to get several bids for future projects.

6. Are the freelancers or other outside services costing you too much in relation to the material delivered? Is too much time spent on rewrite?

7. Is your own time or your staff time spent efficiently? How much can you delegate? How much should you be doing yourself?

8. Was the past budget overrun? By how much? If it was more than 5 to 10 percent, you should examine the reasons. If you spent only 90 percent of last year's budget, it's equally important to understand why. You may not get as much in your future budget as you had hoped for unless you can show substantive reasons why last year's expenses deviated from the year before, particularly if last year's expenses were *lower* than the preceding year's. (Perhaps an event was postponed, or maybe you found a less expensive way to reach editors or produce a TV news clip.)

The Annual Departmental Budget

There are two parts of any publicity budget. The first section is what might be characterized as the routine costs of doing business. This is your overall "department budget." It is not the total communications budget. It will change from year to year as demands on your time and the number of activities change. It can be driven by the life cycles of various products, by new products that may be in the offing, by agency charges and fees.

Items in this half of the budget include:

1. Office expenses. These should be budgeted first if it is your company's policy to show personnel and administrative costs on individual department budgets. Don't forget to include any salary increases planned for your staff or expected for yourself. Your company may not require that you show these items as part of a program, but it will give you an idea of the actual costs of your business. It's important to *detail* these budget elements as much as possible.

2. Cost of your agency (if you have one). Costs for agency support should be based not on fees, but on actual hours devoted to your account, with out-of-pocket expenses billed at cost, no markup (see Chapter 4). Agency costs can be considerable. A modest support program may cost $50,000 a year. A more ambitious one may cost $250,000 or more. Do not accept an agency budget that shows items such as retainers or fees for counseling. Pay only for the actual time to be spent, which is an average of the hourly charges for the people assigned to your account.

3. Clipping service. This is essential; in fact, you might need more than one. The normal costs include a monthly fee plus a charge for each clipping. This charge is higher if you have a broadcast program. If so, add a budget item for transcripts, recordings, and tapes of the television and radio shows that also might run information about your products.

Even though you have a clipping service, I recommend you subscribe to all the publications that now or might in the future run news about your company. Then you will not miss any news about your company in the key publications. (If a colleague asks if you saw the story in a certain publication, it's pretty embarrassing to have to admit you didn't.)

Try to estimate whether your volume of clippings will increase or decrease in the next budget year, and be sure to check with your services to see if they anticipate any cost increase. Chances are they will.

4. Distribution service. It often is less expensive to use an outside distribution service for your news releases than to do it yourself. If there are only a few publications in your marketing audience, and if you have a very limited publicity program, it may be worthwhile to maintain your own list. On the other hand, most services offer printing, photo print-making, collating, press kit production, and a number of other tasks relating to news distribution, frequently at a far lower cost than you can do it in-house. Check anticipated costs based on your assessment of activities. For the average two-page release, plus a photo and caption, sent to a couple of dozen publications, estimate $100 and up. Add the cost of the photo prints or duplicate transparencies.

Also check your agency costs if it is handling distribution. It is usually more productive and less expensive to handle it through a service.

5. The tactical elements of the program (if they are not included in your agency budget). These include news releases, case histories, backgrounders, literature releases, etc., that you produce with outside assistance, including the cost of freelance writers. Don't overlook such items as reprints of case histories or exclusive articles to merchandise through your salespeople.

Some company and agency budgets will often show a line item for a category, such as "Releases," with just a lump sum. Yet adding a photo to one release mailing can raise the cost a couple of hundred dollars. While you may not know in advance exactly what each release is going to cost, you and your agency should try to estimate the number planned, the number to be distributed, photo needs for each, and name each—"New Gizmo Improvement"—for the budget year. You are not going to be exact and come in at an exact number for a full year. But you can arrive at a close estimate that relates to the objectives you wish to achieve.

6. Other contracted work: printing or reprinting design of release letterheads, folders, memos, and so on.

7. Photography. This also cannot be budgeted to the exact dollar. But you can come close. If you are used to working with photographers, you will have a good idea of the local rate or what you might have to pay for location shooting. Consider both photos planned for a straight photo release and those that go with news stories. Photography handled by your agency should be a line item on the agency budget. And you should have an understanding with your agency on a limit on photography costs, unless checked with you first. Budget on the basis of half-day or full-day rates, film and processing charges, and travel expenses. Photography can cost a few hundred a day, for the average good publicity photographer, to several thousand dollars a day for the top fashion photographer and models. (See Chapter 8.)

8. Travel and entertainment. Include in this trips to meet editors and to attend trade shows. These are very much a part of a publicity budget. This budget item is not normally broken out for each activity, but careful planning is recommended. It's very easy to criticize someone for exceeding a travel budget, even if it was justified.

9. Movies and tapes in support of ongoing programs, including additional prints or tapes, and distribution costs and measurement. Add to this the cost of film and tape storage.

10. Mat and syndication services. Do you plan a program with one of these services, perhaps a seasonal story release such as Christmas gift ideas?

The Special-Events Budget

The other part of a publicity budget is for special events or activities planned for this budget year only; they may not be done on an annual basis. For instance:

1. A new product campaign. The first year's budget will likely be higher than succeeding years. It may be a three-month blitz to introduce a new product, with all the stops pulled. Or it may be the blitz plus a longer-term program.

Under this item include press conferences or staged press events and media tours. Add the support material necessary, including film clips and printing. Agency costs needed to support this effort also are important budget items.

2. Marketing research. You may want to determine how well you did with your product introduction. Or it could be a study of editors' attitudes toward a particular business, toward your company, or on a particular issue. Talk to your agency about some research on competitive activity, or how the market sees your company. The agency may be able to develop a program that goes even beyond product publicity, such as an attitude study.

3. More editorial contact. Is there a need to increase the amount of editorial contact because of a broader product line or a press event? Will these items affect a travel budget?

4. Trade shows. Is the advertising department planning additional show or exhibit participation? Either routine support or a special event may be needed.

In summary, research your activities over the past year—two or more if you are looking for a pattern. And be sure to look at your own office productivity, as well as your agency's.

It also is advisable to ask your accounting department to provide you with a monthly printout showing the status of each budget item. Adjustments can be made far easier month by month, and then you won't be shocked with bad news at the end of the year if you overran or came in under estimate. Both show poor budget management.

Effective Timing: Publicity and the Product Life Cycle

There are a number of tasks or activities involved in a publicity program. The ones chosen for a certain program and the time budgeted for them should be a factor of the position of a product in its life cycle. The following theory, developed by my colleague, Eileen Quirk, can be applied to a product or a group of products in a particular market, or to a particular audience. It can be used to plan and execute a publicity program for a product as it relates to a market segment of a business.

As we know, one product may be marketed to several different audiences or businesses. Du Pont, for example, has a manmade fiberfill product, "Quallofil," which is used in high-quality pillows and upholstery cushions, and also in outdoor wear. Each of these uses involves different audiences, so a communications program is developed for each end-use market. Another example is Kodak film; there are a number of different types of film for amateur and professional photographers. The same approach can be taken for virtually any product, from agricultural chemicals to clothing.

According to Eileen Quirk, the practice of product publicity can be summarized as the art of getting editors to publish or air material that relates the product messages to identifiable audiences. Editors, whether they are print or broadcast, are interested in "news," and the newsworthiness of a product is at its peak when it is *new* and declines as it matures over time. An example is a "breakthrough" product in automotive technology. This is news and will attract the high interest of a number of media. When the product has been around for a while, when it's in maturity or a decline, it's not very newsworthy—although it may still hold a high market share because of its value.

The problem occurs when marketing management tries to use publicity to turn around or slow down a decline in market share or interest. In fact, this is seldom possible.

It is obvious, then, that as a product's inherent newsworthiness declines, it becomes more and more difficult for a publicity person to convince editors to write about it, talk about it, or show it on television. The publicist must work harder and devote more effort to making the product newsworthy, and this becomes extremely difficult over time.

The relationship between inherent news value and effort is shown in Figure 2-2. Theoretically, publicity is most efficient and cost-effective during the introductory and growth stages. Marketing management may be loath to allocate funds to publicity at these stages because the product has not contributed much to earnings. However, it is precisely at these stages that an investment in communications is needed, to stake out a market position and gain wide interest.

At the end of the mature stage and when the product/market is in its decline, the effort required to create publicity can often be more than it is worth in terms of return on investment.

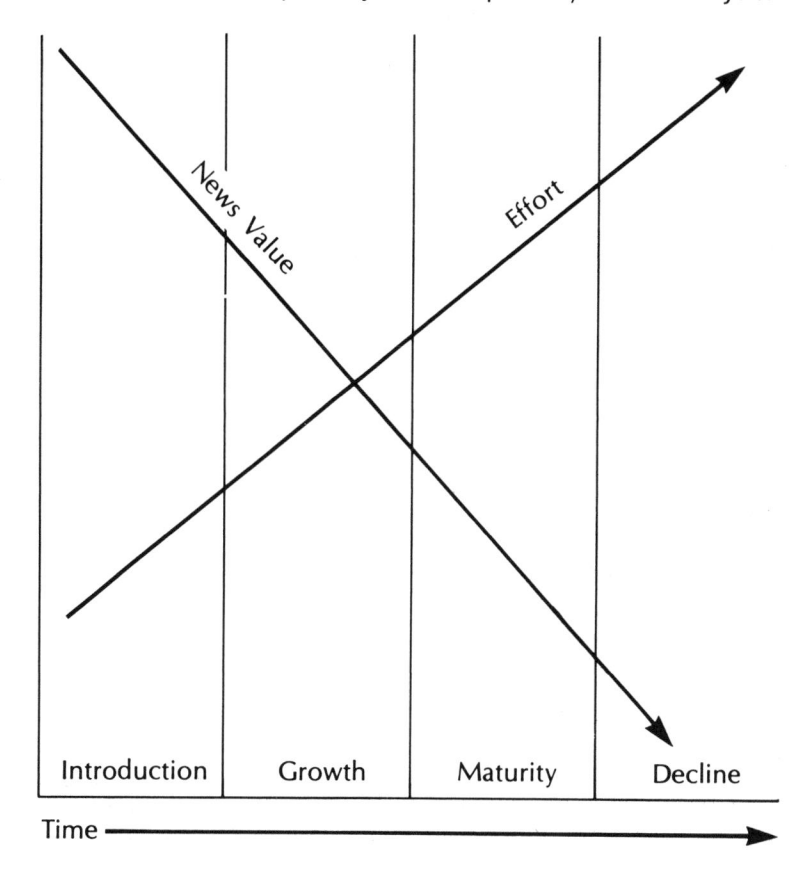

Figure 2-2. News value versus publicity effort for product/market life cycle.

News Value

Effort

| Introduction | Growth | Maturity | Decline |

Time ⟶

Publicity programs typically follow the curve shown in Figure 2-3. That is, the effort begins at a high level because a great deal of effort is required at the very beginning before a product is introduced. The effort level and time required rise as the product goes through its growth stages. It peaks at the late growth and early maturity stages, then gradually declines.

There can be blips and bumps on the curve. These are often caused by factors not entirely within the control of the publicist. Some can be negative, such as the case of a product recall or a negative report on its safety. A rather large blip involved "Tylenol," where a skillful and quick-responding public relations program finally overcame much of the initial negative press and rebuilt consumer confidence.

Publicity, of course, is not the only discipline in a well-thought-out communications program. It is most effective when it is used in conjunction with advertis-

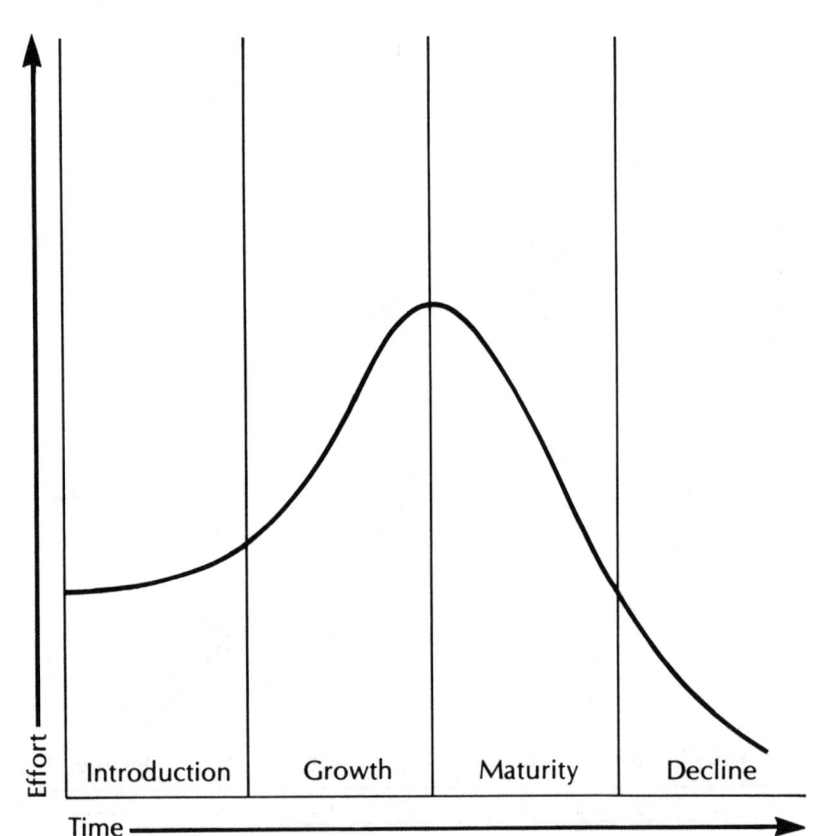

Figure 2-3. A typical publicity life cycle chart.

ing, direct mail, and sales promotion. All elements, in fact, will fit the curve. Advertising and sales promotion may very well continue to be used beyond publicity because these tools are not dependent upon the "news" value of the product.

Taking this one step further, Figure 2-4 illustrates the typical results from a given effort. The results curve resembles the effort curve and illustrates that the payoff of a well-structured publicity program will follow the effort.

Figure 2-5 takes the tools or tactics that are at the heart of a publicity program and groups them according to their effectiveness at the various life cycle stages of a product in a given market. Note that the most tools are utilized in the growth and maturity stages, thus indicating the greatest effort.

The tools or tactics most effective at the various stages of growth are at the top

Figure 2-4. Publicity effectiveness chart.

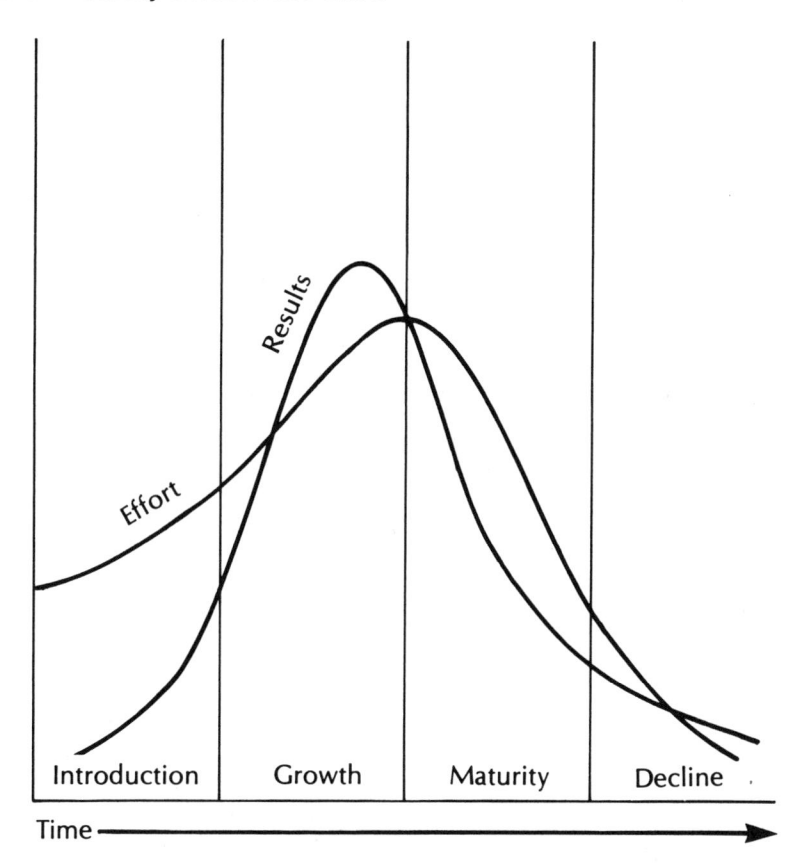

of each column, except in the late-growth and maturity stages, when the tools are all basically equal in effectiveness and choice should be determined by the particular situation.

Tools listed in the later stages can be used in the earlier stages but may not be as efficient or get the same results. Tools shown in the early stages that are not listed for later stages may not be effective at these times. As an example, an application release or a feature during the mature stage of a product development will probably not result in publicity. It is important to note that media relations and photography become more important and effective as the product matures.

The tools or tactics listed are general categories only; there are many variations of each.

These life cycle curves can be used as general guidelines in developing a

Figure 2-5. Publicity tools over the life cycle.

Introduction	Early Growth	Late Growth	Maturity	Decline
Release	Application releases	Technical articles	Media relations	Media relations
Press conference	Case history articles	Photography	Photography	Responses to requests
Product data	Case history releases	Media relations	Industry roundups	Roundups
	Technical articles	Trend features	Product changes	
	Media relations	Special mailings	Trend features	
	Trend features	Press events	Special mailings	
		Customer roundups	Special events	
		Product changes		

publicity program. They can help determine the appropriate level of publicity activity, and help identify the right tactics and tools to use at each stage of the product's maturity.

The publicity program must be developed and planned by considering each product or service, because each situation is different. The ultimate decision on the direction of a program must take into account the marketing objectives, the audiences to be addressed, and the best way all the communications tools—publicity, advertising, and sales promotion—can be coordinated to work together most effectively.

3
The Role and Responsibilities of the Publicity Manager

A product publicity program needs strong leadership, to encourage and maintain the most effective communications program possible. Important elements are a high level of quality of all material released to the press, and a high degree of professionalism in relations with the press. There must be as much emphasis on quality and productivity in the publicity function as there is in management, manufacturing, and marketing. Editorial relations should be treated with the same level of concern as customer relations, because editors *are* customers and the media are your market.

It is no exaggeration to say that the success of a product publicity program is tied directly to the skills and professional style of the publicity manager. And this is no less true when a company uses a public relations agency to conduct much of its programs. It is still the responsibility of the publicity manager to oversee the planning, to manage the program, and to monitor staff and agency work, all at the very highest level of quality. The publicity manager—male or female—is the key.

What is this person like?

A professional publicist must be creative, understand media, be able to write in a journalistic style, and have a good "news sense." He or she needs a good visual sense too, and must know and understand the needs of journalists, editors, and broadcast news and program directors covering the industry.

Most important is the ability to relate the marketing objectives to the needs of the media covering its products. The publicist must be a creative marketer, for adroitly marketing stories and story ideas to editors is the key to success.

Qualifications for the Job

1. The manager should have some background in communications and journalism—not necessarily as a working reporter or editor, but as an experienced public relations writer and practitioner, preferably with an educational background in communications from a university offering communications or journalism.

There was a time when most public relations people were hired from newspapers or other media because they understood news and were good news writers. Today, the communications industry—advertising and public relations—recruits from a number of disciplines, including business majors. But it is still essential that the publicity manager have a solid understanding of journalistic values.

2. The manager must have good writing and editing skills. Knowledge of journalistic style and the principles of good writing is essential if the company's communications are to compete for media attention. Any copy developed by a publicist, either one who works for a company or for an agency representing that company, still has to get past an editor. Copy is often not considered because it is poorly written.

The manager also must have an understanding of the writing style of the different media and needs to understand the differences between print and broadcast media, and where each is appropriate.

3. News judgment is very important. This means being able to spot news, separate puffery from facts, relate the facts to media, then develop the story for media. A proper presentation of the news story is what we mean by "marketing" your communications. It also means rejecting a "story" that has no relevance to media or audiences, or is only self-serving. And that requires a person with the courage and the authority to insist that all editorial material have a sound editorial base.

4. The best manager is a good all-around communicator. And this, according to Linda Pezzano, means "not only being able to write, but also being able to read. It means not only being able to speak, but being able to listen and hear." Because the manager has day-to-day contacts with middle management and often upper management, both within his own company and on the agency level, he or she has to be able to communicate orally and in writing with a high degree of skill and polish. It's an important part of the job, because these are the people who approve the budgets and judge the efforts. Verbal communications skills are just as important as the ability to lead and advocate.

5. A sharp, creative visual sense is also essential. Being able to identify a photo with stopping power and to couple it with a provocative head is an important quality—remember that the ad that is heavy with type or that has banal art seldom gets more than a passing glance.

Having photographic skills is not a criterion; what's important is being able to recognize good photos and knowing the best and most creative news photographers. A good publicist thinks cover or AP wire even with the most pedestrian-looking product.

6. Background and experience in marketing or marketing communications also can be very helpful, because most of the material this manager will review and counsel others on will be market-related.

Understanding the concepts of marketing can also help target news items to *interested* media serving the company's key markets. "Marketing" in this sense means that the publicist understands the various media and knows the audiences of each. It is impossible to communicate with an audience that has no interest in what you are trying to tell it. As a colleague of mine said, "It's like trying to sell diapers to women who have no children." An example of poor strategy in this regard might be to try to get a home hobbyist interested in building a 40-foot racing yacht in his backyard—what a waste of time and money! To publicize such a boat, the right media to reach the right audience must be targeted. Such an audience would include people who already have a yacht or, at least, have the money to afford one. Those who have a permanent or a summer home near a large body of water and who are interested in yacht racing would be part of the targeted group as well. The skilled publicist knows the media that reach the people his company wants to address and which of these media are likely to be responsive to story ideas and, in particular, to news of his company.

However, marketing publicity material, including ideas for news stories, is not "selling." Marketing is producing and adapting products to meet the needs of the marketplace. The manager must look at *his* markets—the editors and media audiences—in much the same manner.

7. The manager must be objective-oriented and must insist upon accountability and measuring successes (and failures) against objectives. The manager can be of great help in program development and in assuring that objectives are being met once the program is underway.

8. The manager must be a good administrator. There are a number of administrative functions, such as supervising media research and clipping and distribution services, that belong in this office.

9. Budget management skills are essential. The experienced manager will know what various peripheral services cost, and what constitutes reasonable charges from agencies and outside services.

10. The manager should possess an ability to research media and story possibilities (much as a reporter would), to focus the story, and to present material in an orderly fashion.

The talent for research and an understanding of the logical steps needed to develop a story also can help the manager provide precise direction to the freelancer or agency assigned to the task. The manager can then determine quickly where further research will help the story and make it marketable, or can recognize that the story has only limited value and either suggest another direction or abandon the idea entirely.

11. Personal characteristics are very important. Much of the manager's work involves dealing with creative people. Creativity is not a line item on a program or budget, and is something of value an agency can bring to a company. So this manager must be flexible, willing to listen and learn.

The publicity manager also must be able to move easily from a creative environment to one that is totally pragmatic and business-oriented. The manager may advocate projects and programs that have an element of risk, but he or she must be able to weigh the risks against the business objectives.

The manager should be able to deal with insiders and outsiders on all levels, and will be evaluated on the ability to work with and gain the confidence of top management.

12. The manager also must be flexible. Many media people do not keep 9 to 5 hours. It's quite possible that an editor will call for information after most other people have gone home.

Travel is an essential part of the job—to visit editors, to make calls with salespeople to learn what is really happening in the marketplace. Or getting a flight on a Sunday afternoon to get press material in the press room when an industry show opens at 9:00 A.M. Monday morning.

And one thing is certain: At some point, the manager will be unpacking boxes, stuffing envelopes, or using a copy machine.

13. The manager must believe in, and adhere to, professional standards. This may mean—but not necessarily—accreditation (APR) by the Public Relations Society of America (PRSA), the professional organization in the field. Any self-respecting public relations person will follow the ethical standards of PRSA, member or not. I am a member of the Publicity Club of New York, which I find to be a highly worthwhile—and fun—organization.

Areas of Responsibility

Quality Control

Whether the manager directs a large news bureau–style operation (such as the broad publicity program conducted by General Electric), has an in-house program staffed by professionals, works with agencies, or any combination of these, the most critical element is quality control. This is just as important in a publicity activity as it is on the factory floor.

Quality control is assured by using the office as a review point between the agency, staff (if any), and media, with enough authority to veto material that is not appropriate, not properly targeted, or not professionally written.

The manager's role as company "managing editor" is recommended for any type of business — small, medium, large; profit or nonprofit. A major part of the assignment is to assure that professional standards in media relations and practices are maintained.

The manager must understand publicity thoroughly, and must regard his or her position as much for counseling as for seeing that journalistic guidelines are observed and programs carried out properly. Something of a balancing act is required: Professional standards need to be maintained, but not overmanaged at the expense of professional pride or a stifling of creativity.

One aspect of quality control that cannot be overlooked (and cannot be overemphasized) is insistence on high standards of writing. The manager should be responsible for journalistic editing of all material directed to the media. This includes style, news value, technical accuracy, review of media fit, and photo quality. No material should be released without the manager's approval.

If it is understood by the advertising, marketing, and legal departments that a media "expert" makes the final judgment on the quality and appropriateness of editorial copy and oversees distribution, there will be less likelihood that individuals and agencies will be pressured to commercialize their copy. I have found that when it is clear to everyone in the approval chain that quality will be monitored, maintained, and upheld, it improves vastly. The responsibility for quality assurance and control rests with the company and is shared by the agency.

Program Development

A person who is in a position to see *all* the publicity produced by a company can recommend timing, targeting, common editorial tie-ins of events and product promotions. This kind of coordination is aimed at helping the publicity and agency staff reach communications goals set for marketing as well as overall company objectives. This helps a company develop its programs strategically — planned, rather than task by task.

Training

The professional development of people in the department should be very much a part of the manager's responsibility. Publicists are often overlooked when training programs are offered, even though many companies maintain continuing educational programs, either within their own organizations or outside. Because they work with marketing and management on many levels, including the very top, the publicity staff can profit from career development training both in their own professional areas and in marketing and management.

The American Management Association and the Association of National Advertisers, the Public Relations Society of America, the Publicity Club of New York, among others, conduct training sessions in public relations, product publicity, and marketing communications.

Communications Counseling

A source for communications counseling can be of inestimable value to a company. This may involve discussing a story and finding the right angle, evaluating the newsworthiness of material, looking at the right way to meet a marketing need, assessing target media, or finding the best way to approach an editor with a story idea.

It can be valuable to have a disinterested person as a sounding board and a resource to discuss problems and opportunities. Discussions among staff and agencies, either formal or informal, can help determine the direction of a program — from the press release to the press event, the feature, the interview, the television placement.

A disinterested person also is in an excellent position to help evaluate an agency's performance. This takes the direct responsibility for agency supervision from marketing and places it where it belongs — under a publicity professional. The manager's responsibility with agencies is to work closely with account people on programs, keep them on track, monitor the budget, and help them do their job.

Resource Management

The tools and resources that the publicity department uses should be centralized under the manager's control. (These tools are discussed in detail in Chapter 11.)

One is the clipping service, which can be better managed in a company media office than in the agency. Production can be monitored carefully and attention can be devoted to seeking ways to increase the clipping percentage rate.

The manager's office should maintain media directories, either in print, on a computer, or with computer access.

Source lists of freelance writers and photographers and their rates can also be maintained for staff benefit when the scope and nature of the assignment does not justify an agency. A central office is in a good position to act in a company's behalf on negotiating service rates.

Records of all news material should be kept in a central location, with work by each individual and by agencies and outside services noted. This type of record-keeping provides another way of measuring productivity. It also provides a running log of the status of each piece of news material.

Files of photos and of all released news material should be maintained in a central office. A well-maintained photo file is a valuable resource at any time, especially when products are in the maturing and declining phases of their life cycles.

A central office also can serve effectively as a traffic center for mailing and distribution. This is not only a convenience for staff, but a way to control timing so that a batch of news releases, for example, are not all going out at the same time to the same media.

A centralized office also can function as a *back-up contact* for editors, when staff people are out of the office, and as a central clearinghouse when an editor needs information but does not know who to contact.

Internal Promotion

One of the manager's most important roles is to be a strong advocate within the company for publicity.

The dilemma for the manager is that the value of publicity must often be sold to management; on the other hand, it can't be oversold. It is essential that it be positioned properly and its limitations understood clearly. A publicist or an agency can't work miracles. A company publicity manager can bring some order and reason to the publicity function, even in those situations that may not reflect favorably on the company.

The values of publicity are not easy to communicate or understand. A news story, a new product item, even a free brochure listing in a trade publication does not say "here courtesy of a publicist and the editor." Publicity requires constant explanation of its value to a business.

It behooves the person charged with the publicity program to promote the concept of publicity by showing how it contributes to marketing, how it works, and how it fits in the program (see Chapter 13 for ideas). It is a constant challenge to communicate the very basic advantages of publicity and position it as an important communications tool, because of the fluid nature of a marketing organization in which personnel move, leave the company, change assignments, and are promoted.

Good communications also means letting the company know what the media, the competition, the opinion makers think about a company, its products and services. This means the manager, the staff, and the agency should be good listeners, then very good at interpreting what they hear to make it worthwhile to management.

Scope of Authority

The publicity manager must be given full authority to edit all copy — and have the editing stick. All copy from an agency or freelancer should be reviewed before it is sent to anyone else in the company. Once it's been through the approval chain, it should be reviewed once more before being submitted to media for consideration. If it has been established that an "editor" has reviewed copy submitted for journalistic standards and editorial acceptability, there is less chance that those in the approval process will make frivolous changes.

The editor/manager assures that basic guidelines on style, presentation, and content (outlined in Chapter 7), are clearly followed.

Company staff writers will come to appreciate judicious editing. Some may balk at first, because of "pride of authorship" or sensitivity to criticism. But sound editing can help them become skilled in writing journalistically and in adapting their work to media expectations.

Editing should be done to bring order and clarity to prose, not just for the sake of change. The editor must be cognizant of the sensitivities of the writers whose material is edited. The editor also must be available to justify editing if the writers do not agree with the changes made.

The argument has been advanced that public relations agencies are retained because they have the necessary writing and editing skills and need little supervision. Or, at the very least, that a person at the agency is designated to review the material before it is sent to clients. Unhappily, this is not always so. There are many inconsistencies even with material coming from the same agency. Agency writers need guidance; because of frequent staff turnover and movement in agencies, many are new to assignments. Both internal review and review by a client manager are necessary.

By working with the company "managing editor," the agency and company can assure that consistent quality is maintained. The investment will provide a high return, as editors will come to expect and respect the quality of writing and the focus on the interests of the media.

Coordination with the Agency

Public relations agencies frequently bring to a company the ability to look at its business from another point of view. Their recommendations should always be considered — many are quite creative. But even the most creative agency does not have the authority to act independently if a contemplated action does not fit the communications plan. The publicity manager can act as a checkpoint for ideas and new proposals, help an idea along, or suggest another direction while helping to keep the agency focused on the marketing objectives.

No matter how limited or how broad the scope of the agency's services, the publicity manager must remain in charge. It's a little like the operation of a large cargo ship: A lot of people are involved in making everything work on the ship, and all their efforts are important, but there is only one captain, only one person making the ultimate decisions.

There are several reasons why having central authority vested in one person —the manager—is important. One is purely pragmatic: most editors (your customers) prefer one contact. And they would rather it be a company person than an agency person. Fairly or not, there is a widespread feeling among editors that the work of many agency people is mediocre; an astute manager must recognize this and be on guard against it.

Most editors don't like working through a go-between — which is how they think of agencies. Almost all editors say they can get answers to their questions faster from the company representative. As one editor commented, "They (agency people) tell us they will have to get back to us." They may or may not get the answers, and frequently don't follow through. An in-house person knows who to call for information, if he doesn't know himself, and understands the urgency of the request.

Company publicity people also are more sensitive than outsiders to company idiosyncracies, differences in personalities, and corporate policies. This is important in dealing with the press: getting the right person as the authority on a given subject, and understanding the kind of information that can be offered.

A business-to-business editor had this opinion of in-house publicity people: "Company people are very good. The majority of agency people are marginal. The good ones have looked at the magazines and know their markets and ours. The marginal ones ask us what we are going to do with a release they sent, when am I going to use it? Even worse, the head of an agency called me with the implied threat that the advertising depended upon our using the release. Or, we are planning advertising and we want you to run these press releases. Or, we sent you a release, why didn't you run it, because we think it is important. Then you ask what the release was about and he doesn't really know!"

Few editors will ever admit it, but the fact that your company is an advertiser in a given publication may affect the amount of attention your company receives from this publication or whether you get contacted when the editor is planning a feature. I believe that if your company is a frequent advertiser in a given publication, you *should* be contacted whenever the editor is planning a story related to your business or your products.

On the other hand, many editors have said that being an advertiser does not affect coverage. "It's like the separation of church and state." They say they will not cave in to pressures to run stories just because the company is an advertiser, or sacrifice the publication's editorial integrity to run puffery and pass it off as news. This is true. Although there is a tacit understanding among some business-to-business editors that advertisers will be given attention, the editors should not be pressured. The publicist should understand very clearly that the subject of advertising *should never be raised by the publicist seeking news coverage.* There is no quid pro quo assumed.

One last good reason for central authority is that the manager will know the marketing objectives far better than an agency account executive, if only because the manager is totally involved with the communications programs every day. There is more staff turnover in agencies, and even the account executive will seldom know a business as well as an insider.

In Summary

To be able to "market" communications effectively to media requires sound planning, knowing how to manage people and communications budgets, and setting clear objectives. The publicity manager is more than a public relations professional; the publicity manager is a sound businessperson.

The publicity manager is responsible for developing, executing, and preparing budgets for cost-effective programs that are fully supportive of business and marketing objectives. The manager must coordinate these plans with advertising and promotion activities with the objective of bringing to the company the most effective communications plan possible. The overall objective is effective marketing communications.

The manager must recognize the importance of establishing and maintaining a sound working relationship with the media relevant to the areas of responsibility. Responses to media requests about the products or services must be made promptly.

The manager must use good judgment in recommending press conferences and other special events. All programs must be consistent with agreed-upon strategies to reach program objectives.

Copy sent to media must be of the highest journalistic quality, and must meet company and media standards.

The manager must select only those agencies and vendors who can meet the company's high quality standards.

The manager must set only those objectives that can be measured. The manager must keep company associates in management and marketing fully informed of the progress of publicity programs.

4
Selecting and Working with Public Relations Agencies

In my 30 years in public relations, I have worked on the agency side, worked solely on publicity for corporations, worked with freelance help, and worked directly with an agency. Having had the experience in all situations, I have found the most effective way to carry out a program is with the help of an agency, preferably one that specializes in public relations as opposed to one that specializes in advertising and has a public relations division. Either way, it is essential that an agency have a sound appreciation for a true marketing communications approach.

The best time to use an agency is usually when programs have been developed that reflect the coordination of advertising and publicity—with marketing as the prime beneficiary. When advertising and publicity people think "marketing communications," it is often necessary to call upon the skills of an agency for special talents to support the businesses.

However—and this is to be emphasized—there is still a need for an in-house public relations professional to guide and direct the program—in-house, agency, or combination. The role of this person is discussed in Chapter 3.

It is not my purpose here to recommend any agency, although I quote some agency people, because I know them well and what they say makes sense. If you are seeking an agency you must make your own decisions, based on a company's specific program objectives and, in some cases, the amount of money available for agency services.

What makes a good agency? Linda Pezzano of Pezzano+Company says, "We think it's a special combination of creativity and talent mixed with professionalism and thoroughness.

"Creativity requires the willingness to be daring, sometimes even outrageous. Talent is the intuitive feel for what will work best. Creativity and talent give our programs the pizazz needed to set our clients apart from their competition by associating them with memorable communications.

"But even the best ideas lose lustre if they are not professionally developed and implemented with near-fanatical thoroughness. Professionalism means doing all that is necessary to understand a client's business. And using that understanding to guide creativity, developing concepts so skillfully that good ideas become great ones.

"Effective implementation of these ideas calls for a level of thoroughness that leaves no possibility unexplored, no opportunity that is not pursued. At the same time, successful implementation requires that budgets and deadlines are respected so that the only surprises are happy ones."

Pluses and Minuses of Agencies

The Benefits of Using an Agency

1. It permits the company communications staff to devote time to planning and supervising the total effort, while the agencies do the outside work.
2. It provides great flexibility. Your company doesn't have to add staff when the work load increases, and you can trim programs when necessary without laying off your own staff.
3. You can shift emphasis easily as the communications programs change.
4. It frees you to manage and direct your advertising and promotion programs as well as the one for product publicity.
5. An agency can bring special talents and new thinking to your program.

If you are planning a major event, such as a press conference, which also may entail customers and distributors, an agency can be of inestimable value, not just for the media contacts but for arranging and staging the event and handling all the detail work.

Some agencies specialize. For example, Jeff Blumenfeld and Associates, a small New York agency, has special talents in fashion, travel, outdoor promotions, sports and sports tie-in promotions. Blumenfeld fosters and maintains editorial contacts in these fields. Other agencies have specialists in such areas as food and nutrition, medical and health care, industrial (business-to-business), agriculture, electronics and high tech, among others.

Selecting and Working with Public Relations Agencies

Companies with a wide range of products and services may need more than one agency. Du Pont works with several public relations agencies, just as it does with more than one ad agency; so do GE and other major corporations. These companies also use outside support services and freelancers. There are a number of companies—small and large—that are staffed separately for publicity and public relations. That is, one group specializes in product publicity; the other in public affairs.

A smaller company may not need an agency full time, but can use its services for special projects, such as new product introductions or trade show support. There are few companies that *never* need an agency, even those with in-house advertising media buyers.

Few companies have the luxury of having broadcast specialists on their staff, so agencies are essential for broadcast publicity and very useful for the aid and ideas they can bring to special events, and for programs directed toward areas as diverse as the arts, sports, and health care. Their professional staffs are often made up of highly creative and enthusiastic individuals.

. . . And Some Drawbacks

My primary criticisms of agencies I have worked with and observed is that the writing is all too often mediocre; not enough attention is paid to needs of media; and pressure is placed on editors to use material because the agency account executive is trying too hard to please the client. Sometimes an agency is not realistic in analyzing a program and setting objectives. There must be a germination period, time devoted to understanding the client's own needs, and learning the marketplace as it relates to the client company. Too often the program is tactical, almost as if the actions were picked from a menu of things publicity people are "supposed to do."

Elsewhere in this book I have quoted or paraphrased editors' negative comments about agencies. These comments are valid and should not be minimized, because editors, whether print or broadcast, make the decisions on publicity. It is extremely important to understand fully the role of an agency and to take great care in selecting one to represent your company. It will often be your primary contact with media.

According to the many editors I interviewed, agencies need to examine their own relationship with the media they are contacting on behalf of their clients. The reputation of a company can suffer if it is not represented well and wisely by its agency. You can assume that the media the agency is dealing with on your behalf may have a jaundiced view of agency people to begin with. Because this is one of the reasons you are retaining an agency, you must have a clear understanding that any agency you will select follows the guidelines on developing and fostering sound editorial relations detailed in Chapter 5.

In all fairness, those agencies that have strong direction from a professional who understands the differences between advertising and public relations, will work with you far better than those with little or no direction or control, and you will hear few, if any, complaints from media.

Your Alternatives — Agency or In-House

Staff movement from agency to agency and even within agencies is frequent. This can create difficulties when the account representatives move or account supervision is changed. The corporate client has to take additional time to orient the new people to the business; in any new relationship it takes time for trust to be offered and confidence gained. Programs can often be delayed during this orientation process. But there are alternatives.

One alternative is doing publicity in-house. The cost of adding one or more company staff professionals may be less than an agency. But more than salaries are involved. Compared with advertising, publicity costs do not normally run as high because publicists do not buy space, air time, and production. But other elements cost money: time, travel, photography, printing, production and distribution, and entertainment. All these must be considered for effective program support, in addition to salaries and operating expenses. Think of publicists as members of the marketing team when budgeting is considered. No good marketing program comes cheap.

This assumes that you can afford the time to develop a team of inside publicists with solid backgrounds in public relations or product publicity, who can write, conduct interviews, maintain media contacts, and who are creative and intrepreneural. It also assumes that the company is serious about a communications program that includes product publicity and is willing to pay for the talent.

Now consider the flexibility an agency can offer, and base the decision not purely on cost. The actual dollar cost will probably be higher than with an in-house staff, but the return on the investment may be better in terms of increased productivity, better results, and more attention to the marketing communications programs and accountability. These will more than make up for any additional costs. It behooves the company, however, to be extremely careful in selecting an agency and, having done so, expect the same performance it does from its own staff. You are buying time, and time must be managed productively.

The Cost Factor

In most cases, two thirds of your budget for a publicity agency will be time only — actual agency staff time. There is no need to have a contract that includes retainers and contingency fees. The most effective use of the dollar is budgeting

Selecting and Working with Public Relations Agencies

and paying on an estimated hourly basis. You must insist that your agency keep and report to you accurate records of time actually spent on an account. Contingency funds are often suggested as part of an agency budget to cover unplanned-for opportunities. Look upon these with some skepticism; a well-planned program will not need a contingency element. The other third of the budget will be out-of-pocket, such as travel, entertainment, telephone, printing, and photography. You also must consider that agencies are in business to make a profit too. (Budgeting is covered later in this chapter.)

Your investment must be a wise one, and must be managed prudently. It is far more than handing an agency the key to the executive suite. Having worked for public relations agencies, and having been in a position to see them at work from a client's view, I believe the most successful programs are those that have clear direction, and with agency people who are part of the team.

I remain a strong supporter of the agency concept and the added value agencies can bring to companies of all sizes.

Selecting the Agency

A full-service agency should be able to handle any assignment—from industrial publicity to a celebrity media tour—because most are staffed with specialists serving a wide range of noncompetitive clients in a number of different industries.

However, many corporations may not need and may not be able to justify the cost of a full-service agency—a Hill and Knowlton, a Ketchum Communications, a Burson-Marsteller. Location has a lot to do with agency selection, although most major agencies with headquarters in New York have branches or affiliates in other large cities. It has been my experience that they work best for larger clients, which require more personnel and more specialized talents.

If you have a major account and your objective is to get major media coverage, including television, the larger agencies have the most resources, specialists, and media contacts. But this does not mean smaller, regional agencies lack the resources to handle major products or events. Most of them have working relationships with agencies in other areas.

The key to any agency-client relationship is picking the right one at the beginning, and supervising it properly.

Step 1: Goal Setting

Roy Alexander, head of one of the leading smaller agencies, says it quite succinctly: "Personnel departments write job descriptions before screening applicants. Go thou and do likewise. Know where you want to go before you hire someone to help you go there."

This means taking a very close look at your marketing and business plans, your advertising and promotion programs, and identifying markets you wish to reach through product publicity. Very likely they will be many of the same ones you are now reaching through advertising. Your objective with publicity is to increase the number of times you deliver your messages to your target audiences, make new impressions upon them, and develop in more detail the messages communicated. You also should be able to increase the number of media outlets delivering your message with a creative, journalistic approach.

So before you talk to an agency and ask it what it can do for you, be very clear about what you expect it to accomplish. Write down for your own information and for agreement by your management and staff the reasons you need an agency. Be realistic. And be astonished and very skeptical if your candidate agencies propose programs too grandiose or ambitious for your company.

Step 2: Searching

The next thing to do is develop a list of several agencies to look at. Here are some ideas:

- Call a couple of editors covering your business and ask them what firms they feel take a professional approach to publicity.
- Ask your business associates for recommendations.
- Check with members of your trade association, or its executive director.
- Ask the public relations person handling press arrangements at your industry's trade show.

It also would be unusual if you haven't already been contacted by an agency seeking your business.

You should be looking for an agency that has a commitment to and understanding of marketing. Agency people should regard product publicity as having the same importance to a corporation as its public relations activities—issue management, corporate interests, investment community and stockholder relations. These are heady topics, and many practitioners working in these areas tend to look down upon their product publicity associates. While issues affect a corporation's image, it is marketing and sales that are held accountable for earnings. The product publicist and the agency have equally important responsibilities.

After you have identified a few agencies that appear to have some skills in product publicity, you're ready to begin some additional research. Carol Jennings, senior vice president of Hill and Knowlton, supports research on candidate agencies, and offers some advice on how to conduct it.

Selecting and Working with Public Relations Agencies

"Find out what kinds of service they provide, and whether or not they have any conflicts that might prevent them from working for you, to avoid wasting your time and theirs."

She also suggests you review your own past agency relationships (if you have them) and try to identify the good and bad elements.

Try to identify your specific needs, "but don't eliminate the opportunity for the agency to think about them from a fresh perspective. Consider giving the agency a hypothetical assignment, rather than working on something that you really need to have solved. Chances of the agency knowing enough to solve your problems without in-depth backgrounding are remote." I second this, because it puts an agency on the spot and has an aura of not being quite ethical. If you have problems, give them to the agency you finally select.

"Share necessary and appropriate background with all agencies that you are talking to," Jennings says. "If necessary, you can request confidentiality agreements. Without proper backgrounding, you will be wasting your time and [that of] all the agencies."

Treat all candidate agencies equally. "Provide the same materials and briefing to all," Jennings says. "Allow a fair amount of time for anything that you may request by way of a creative or speculative presentation." The time will depend on the nature of the presentation, but two weeks to a month is about average. I also suggest you provide some guidelines on the extent of the presentation. You don't want a multi-media extravaganza when a simple, straightforward presentation will do. Offer to pay for it. As Jennings says, "Clearly identify a time and place for the presentation and work with the agency to develop an appropriate format for your company.

"Don't be clever and childish about this—trying to withhold information or teasing the agency to see if it can guess what it is you're after. You are about to begin a long-term business arrangement and you should treat all parties involved as adults."

I would add that it is desirable to share with the agencies what you hope to accomplish with a publicity program. You are not required to divulge highly confidential material, nor are you giving the agency information on your proposals in order to pick its brain. But sharing will give the agency people some needed data on what your program involves.

Identify clearly the audiences you wish to reach and the media you wish to use to reach them.

Ask to meet the account executives and supervisors who would be working on your account if the agency is given the assignment. It is nice to meet the top executives, but they won't be the people assigned to the account. One negative comment I have heard several times is that the client meets the top agency management at the presentation before the account is awarded and is assured that they will be giving it "their personal attention," then seldom or never hears from them again.

Jennings also suggests you consider whether the agency has experience in similar situations, not only in the specific areas of concern, but within the industry in which you operate and with the same types of distribution patterns.

Do they demonstrate a basic understanding of the business, or do they at least try to?

Is the chemistry right? Is there energy, enthusiasm, and commitment to your business?

Does the agency bring anything extra or creative to the presentation beyond what you asked for?

Was the presentation well polished and professionally done? As an aside to this, I find ad agencies give much better presentations than public relations agencies. They perhaps are more used to the razzle-dazzle presentations needed to get advertising accounts.

Does the agency specifically address issues such as pricing, administration, reporting, and measurement of results?

Are you assured of management contribution to provide quality control and appropriate staffing?

Jennings also recommends using a checklist to evaluate each of the points upon which you want to measure the agency. "Consider even a numerical ranking, if need be, so that if several evaluaters are involved, you can be quantitative about the process, as opposed to being completely subjective." I've played off Jennings's idea for a checklist, as follows:

1. Does the agency have an understanding of the markets your company is in?
2. Does the agency understand your industry? (For example, if you are in electronics, the agency should have at least a broad understanding of the field and trends within it.) Or do you suspect that agency personnel may not know as much as they think they do?
3. How do the people at the agency come across? Were they enthusiastic? Was there too much sell? Did you pick up on any note of insincerity?
4. Did they show you any creative programs they executed? And did they tie these in with measurable results—not just scrapbooks?
5. How does the agency bill? How much is charged (per hour) for management, account service executives, and the like?
6. Can staff members write?
7. Did you meet the people who might be working on your account? Or were you told by a top executive that he or she would be "supervising it full time, with some of my best account people"?

Don't set an unrealistic limit on how much you are willing to spend and hope the agency is hungry enough to develop some dazzling program for you. Or take the position that "if you do well with this, we'll discuss other business later." Let

Selecting and Working with Public Relations Agencies

the agency propose a budget and fee structure based on its response to your needs and, as previously noted, on hourly costs and estimated out-of-pocket expenses. Of course you should have a budget in mind, but budgets can be negotiated. Reach an understanding about how the financial arrangements will be handled when the decision is made and a contract signed. Then there will be no surprises later on.

And don't back away if the agency head and most of the staff are women. Women (including Barbara Walters, who began in public relations) have been in the business for a long time. Most of the best publicists I am currently associated with are women, including top agency executives like Hill and Knowlton's Carol Jennings and the highly capable Joanna Hanes, a Hill and Knowlton alumna who heads her own Washington, D.C., agency.

If you have an ad agency, you may wish to begin the search with it, if for no other reason than courtesy. Or your ad agency may already be doing some product publicity for you. Most advertising agencies are not staffed to handle a full-range product publicity program, even though you will hear of a "division" or "department" for publicity. Also, they tend to be tactical, not strategic. If your ad agency has not already come to you and suggested a product publicity program, it probably can't handle one now — although it may ask for the business, now that you are interested. While an agency may do great advertising and even public relations or publicity, unfortunately, many ad agencies' view of marketing communications ends with advertising and sales literature.

As I have said before, I believe that a purely public relations agency can provide better service than an ad agency with a public relations division, and I base this opinion on several years of experience working with both types of agencies. There are exceptions, agencies that can do both very well. However, if I were beginning a search for an agency to handle my product publicity, I would look only at public relations agencies.

Another point of view comes from Gerald Voros, president of Ketchum Communications. In an article in the November 1984 issue of *Madison Avenue*, he wrote,

> Not every advertising campaign can be strengthened with PR or vice versa. But the agency that knows when, how and why to use both can offer tremendous advantages to its client. This does not mean that every "total communications" outfit that offers advertising and PR plus other services has the most to offer to a client. On the contrary, it's just as important to know how to make the two disciplines work together smoothly as it is to know when to recommend one or both to clients. If the harmony is lacking, then a client may actually be better off using two separate agencies.
>
> However, when a marketing director establishes a relationship with an agency that does offer both disciplines, headed by managers that understand and respect each other's capabilities, he is fortunate indeed. Not only can he call on objective counsel for a particular problem, but on joint programs, he can

count on unified themes, complimentary strategies, and coordinated messages directed to the same target audiences.

There will always be rivalry between advertising and public relations as each tries to convince his client that his ideas are the best. This is as it should be, and usually there's a place for both. But once the plans are set, it's essential that the two teams put the contest aside and start working and living together. Better still, they should get married.

I would add that you should search for an agency that understands marketing communications. For openers, you might ask, "How do you feel about working with our ad agency (and/or staff) on a marketing communications program?" If the answer gives you the impression that the twain were never meant to meet, then look further.

When you have selected your agency, phone the others and give them the bad news in as positive a manner as possible. It may have been a difficult decision to make. Follow up with a short letter thanking them again for their time and effort. There's always hope at any agency that every presentation will bring a new client. Having been there, and having been disappointed, I know it's some consolation when the lost client has the courtesy to write you a nice letter. And, from a business point of view, you may want to go back to one of the losing agencies, if the winner doesn't work out.

Getting Down to Business

The first thing you should do after you have selected your product publicity agency is appoint one company person as the key agency contact, if at all possible. All directions to the agency and all proposals and work from the agency should go through this person. This way, the agency people will have a clear understanding of what is expected, they won't get conflicting instructions, and their work will be screened before going on to others for approvals. Many prefer to get their directions and make their contacts through one person with sufficient responsibility to make decisions.

Even though there may be a number of product managers in your company using agency support, the programs should be coordinated and managed by one person, if possible. In large companies, there may be more than one person to whom an agency reports, and perhaps more than one agency. One agency, for example, might be better equipped to deal with a particular market than another.

The *least* effective manager is a trainee or recent college graduate named the agency contact with the hope that this person can learn by working with the agency. This is a sure indication you have little respect for the agency and tells it that its role is delivering the message, not having any say in how the message is created and who will receive it.

Getting to Know the Agency

Introduce the agency account people to your key marketing and product people, technical experts, and R&D staff, so that they can become fully immersed in the company. The "member of the team" idea has been used so much in speeches and to rally the salesforce it's become hackneyed, but it may be the best way to describe how to work with your agency. Your contract should have a confidentiality clause and, if you have screened your agency carefully, you should have enough confidence in the staff to reveal the state of your business and plans for the future. Obviously, the agency should not be handling any competitive products either.

If they don't know where you are now, or where you plan to be, they can't help you get there.

If after you have oriented the agency staff, the account executive fails to impress your colleagues, it's normally because (1) it's not the same person you met when the agency made its presentation for the business, or (2) that person has left the agency. This has happened, and the best way to handle it is to ask for an immediate replacement. It can be upsetting, but it's not a time to waffle. Evaluate carefully the next account executive the agency assigns before taking him or her around to meet your associates.

Turnover is a problem with many agencies, although there's usually no relation between the agency's capabilities or reputation and the staff movement. There also is movement within an agency, so be prepared that your account executive may be given another assignment or promoted. Clients should not dictate or try to influence agency personnel policies. But they do have a right to have the very best agency representatives handling their accounts, and the best account management. If there is a continual failure to provide good account representation and solid account management, then it's time for a change.

Keeping a Good Thing Going

Carol Jennings adds some tips on fostering a long and fruitful relationship:

"Assume going in that the relationship will be a long-term one. Do not take the approach that 'churning' the agencies will get you better work.

"Recognize that the relationship is a partnership. The agency is not subservient to the client. Best results are achieved when both partners work together.

"Be honest in your relationships. You will both make mistakes and they can be more easily forgiven on both sides if honesty is the rule. As a corollary to that, be decent in your human relationships. If you have problems, say so. Try to be civilized to each other. Don't dictate or yell or threaten the agency. That does not necessarily produce the best work.

"Talk to each other often.

"Maintain relationships at all levels of the agency with all levels of the client organization.

"Be timely in your response to the agency.

"Schedule and hold regular reviews. Be candid with each other about shortcomings on both sides.

"Let your agency make you look good! Give credit where credit is due. If the agency did good work, say so. You can only gain by having been clever enough to select them."

Getting Organized

The agency was selected because you felt its proposal for your company made sense, was directed to helping you meet your communications objectives, and the return on investment looked promising. Now that your new agency people have met your marketing associates, it's time to introduce them to your advertising agency people, and all of you sit down and develop the plan and the media calendar.

First try to get an understanding of the amount of time each agency person will be devoting to your account. You can assume that the account executive will be spending the most time on your account. The account supervisor will spend less time, but the hourly cost will be higher. And you may need to charge only a few hours against your budget for the top agency brass, whose hourly time charges can run into the hundreds of dollars. Your budget, therefore, should spell out an estimate of the number of hours each is expected to spend on your account. Then you can develop a composite hourly cost, which becomes part of the contract.

By planning in advance the time spent on your account, you are forcing yourself and the agency to plan a program. You will expect the agency to look for new opportunities that may not be part of the agreed-upon program. Often these can be alternatives to programmed elements and not projects that will add to your publicity budget.

If there is a possibility of a new product introduction, but your research and marketing people can't give you a definite time, then it may be wise to write in a contingency amount to cover this—although a better alternative is to get assurances from management that should the new product or development come about and promotional support be needed, money will be allocated at that time.

Selecting and Working with Public Relations Agencies

Gale Johnson, public relations director for Rumrill-Hoyt, favors the planned hourly budget. He says it works well for his agency and clients, but cautions it must be carefully managed by both the client and agency lest unnecessary time be spent to fill in the estimated hours. The hourly approach is preferred far above the retainer arrangement, and I have found that even those agencies that work on a retainer with other clients will agree to work with you on a time-charge basis.

Out-of-pocket costs billed by some agencies are often marked up 15 percent. I disagree with this practice. The agency should submit monthly copies of all paid out-of-pocket charges exceeding $25. Expenses less than $25 can be listed or grouped, such as phone calls or taxi fares. Entertainment receipts should be checked carefully. There is no need to take an editor to lunch to discuss every story idea. All editors I have spoken to on this subject say they seldom have lunch with publicity people unless they know them very well. And twice a year is about tops, even when they do. One reason these editors give for shunning such lunches is they are quite busy. "What may be promised as an hour often turns into two-and-a-half hours," explains Gray Maycumber, an editor at the *Daily News Record*. Maycumber adds that it is more important for him to know the contact at the company from whom he can get his information than to have lunch. The moral is: The agency should use good judgment in entertaining. It's a necessary part of marketing, but it can be overdone or abused, and it is not an essential part of publicity. Question budgets that have several "lunch to sell the story" items.

I recommend that an agency contract contain the following items. These are not detailed, because they should be developed between a company attorney and the person to whom the agency will report, and reviewed by the agency's legal counsel.

1. Statement of agreement and purpose.
2. Statement of services to be performed.
3. Compensation details.
4. Statement that agency is an independent contractor.
5. Warranty, exclusivity statement.
6. Confidential information statement.
7. Use of work. The company has the right to the programs, materials, and so forth.
8. Statement of compliance with applicable laws.
9. Indemnifications.
10. Releases and warranties.
11. Force majeure.
12. Period of agreement and cancellation clauses.

The company and agency publicity plans should be attached to the contract.

Drafting the Communications Plan

The agency budget may not be firm, however, until the total plan has been developed. The basic plan is drafted by the publicity contact or manager at the company to whom the agency reports. While the agency may participate, this manager should have a clear understanding of the communications objectives and a complete marketing communications plan should already have been drafted. The first action between the agency and the client is to develop an agency communications plan that reflects the company communications and business plans. One way to begin is to prepare an agency briefing paper. (This also is recommended for existing agencies when new plans are developed.)

Agency Briefing Paper

1. Identify by name the products or services.
2. Provide a brief but detailed outline of the marketing purpose, the objectives outlined in your marketing communications plan.
3. Background: Describe in as few words as possible the product's market position, its market share, whether it's a new, mature, or declining product, and pinpoint some of the prime market areas. Describe competitive products, their market positions and properties.
4. Outline how you think product publicity can help the program. Include any other communications program (advertising, sales promotion) now or planned, and how you see publicity fitting into the program.
5. Identify your audience, and detail briefly who they are — designers, retailers, sporting goods dealers, equipment buyers, whoever.
6. Outline your communications objectives.
7. List in detail the products or services you wish the agency to devote its time to, and show the relationship between the products and the markets. List copy points for each area. Is there one common communications idea?
8. Briefly outline what you expect to happen as a result of your communications program. Will you increase the number of qualified inquiries? Will you identify some new uses for the product? Will your company come to be known as an authority in your business or market area as a result of the program? Anything else? When do you expect this to begin to happen and when will you begin to see results? Be realistic; public relations agencies are not made up of magicians. But once goals are established, results can be measured against actions.

Give this to your agency, let the people there who will be working on the account digest it, ask questions, and resolve the questions, then return with a plan that is directed to the objectives you set.

You need to leave some room for opportunistic activities. There are times when the opportunity for a tie-in with another event comes up, a good story possibility arises, or the agency has a flash of brilliance that will get your product wide exposure. There should be an understanding that each creative idea or opportunity that may be suggested during the course of the year will be considered seriously.

Agreeing on a Budget

Now comes the shocker: the proposed agency budget. It could range from $50,000 for a fairly simple support program to $250,000 or more for a sophisticated and complex package. A colleague of mine says he "expresses astonishment" each time he sees the new budget.

Assume there is some room for negotiation. The items to cut may include high management costs, programs not related directly to plans, and elaborate events. But if you must trim, do so realistically. The agency is a profit-making organization, not a charity, and has the same basic expenses as your firm. You will not get full support, creative thinking, or high enthusiasm if you are stingy.

One important element in any agency-client relationship is paying bills promptly. Agencies have only services to sell, and they need cash flow to stay in business.

A friend of mine, who works with a small agency, is very emphatic about this. He says that some small agencies "live off their American Express cards" and need the cash flow to maintain their business. Remember, too, that they are also paying suppliers such as photographers, who work indirectly for you, and who expect prompt payment.

Setting Realistic Schedules

Just as it is important to set realistic goals, it's equally important to set realistic schedules: to deliver copy for approval, to have trade show support material approved well in advance so that it can arrive there when the show opens or the day before a press preview, to have new product stories written so that everyone involved has time to check for accuracy—just general good-sense practices that make everyone's job a little easier.

The major complaint I have heard about agencies is that too much work arrives at the client's office at the last minute with a "rush" sticker attached. Having worked for agencies in New York, I can second this observation. There's an aura of tension, and everything seems to be held and done at the last minute, frantic and rushed. It's not all that way, but when I am a client and my agency gives me very little time to review its work, it's difficult to think otherwise. If everything (or almost everything) arrives on top of my deadline, it's difficult to ask others to review copy quickly, even when circumstances warrant rush treatment, such as the promising project that was unplanned and had to be hurried.

Developing a Media Plan

It is difficult for me to get excited about a publicity opportunity in a publication that my audience will not read, or an appearance by one of my experts on a television show that does not reach at least part of the audiences my company wants to influence. There may be some benefits, of course, but the agency's job is to represent my company, understand my markets, my customers, services and products—and show me results in the media we jointly have identified as primary. Every agency client has the right to insist that the program reach the target media, and must monitor agency production carefully.

A clip mentality, measuring results by tonnage, is not acceptable. I will "ho-hum" clips or TV reports shown to me from media not on my primary media list. I insist that the agency spend its time developing publicity that reaches my markets, and I will consider changing agencies that do not. This means the agency must maintain contact with and make placements in media that we together have identified as the most important for reaching our markets.

Honesty and Skill

Along with this, the agency should be open and honest with its client. For example, if the plan calls for three features with publication A (an important one to the client), and the agency believes that two is about the best that can be expected, then it should not agree to three. This is a little like the agency that pitches an account and wins it by promising to deliver a *Time* cover for the company president. Candor ("No, we doubt if *Time* will be interested in running your president on its cover because . . .") is refreshing, but more than that, it's good business.

The agency should be held accountable for maintaining a high level of writing that meets acceptable journalistic standards and needs little rewrite by the company contact or an editor. Some agency writers whose work I have reviewed cannot write a proper dateline on a news release. This is one way I can quickly determine whether the person has a journalistic background or education. I find it difficult to believe that the rest of the work an agency does will be good, if the writing is fair at best.

Reviewing Agency Reports

Because a contract is based on hours, accurate reporting of time spent on various client projects is essential. Reports should reflect actual time spent. This is

Selecting and Working with Public Relations Agencies 63

another reason that someone familiar with publicity should review agency reports.

If results are not forthcoming in a reasonable time, say six months after an agency takes on a new account, then all that time spent has been wasted. Be skeptical, too, when you get a report showing only editorial contacts and calls. The next report, or one soon after that, should show how these calls paid off in interviews and actual stories placed or set up in key media.

Question time spent on writing. It should not take 12 hours to write a simple two-page news release, even with account supervision review. Two hours for research, two to four hours for writing are all that a good writer needs. And it certainly doesn't warrant a discussion over lunch with an editor, which will be another two or three hours, plus expenses, charged to your account.

A good agency report might list the activities for a given month, briefly detail the actions taken, and report the staff time and out-of-pocket expenses. For example:

National Widget Company
June Activity Report
New Product Introduction

>Reviewed press conference plans with Joe Smith in Chicago. Discussed, researched and wrote press kit contents, confirmed dates, and checked Los Angeles office to confirm customer appearance at conference. Reviewed plans for laser show. Too costly. Will explore other means of staging event. Complete kits, plans, and budgets will be submitted [date].
>Staff time, $2,300. OOP, $314.85.

This format could be followed for each activity.

Once this is done, the costs might be entered on a form that shows each month and breaks out the costs for the account executive's time, plus the time for other management staff such as account supervision. The hours and out-of-pocket charges are then compared with the projects and authorized costs.

An agency will set up a diary showing the activities and the time spent and compare them with budget estimates or something similar to track the time and the costs. Agencies have their own ways of recording the activities, time allocations, and year-to-date charges. Because they are different from one another, I am not suggesting a formula or format; just suggesting that the company review how an agency keeps track of time and expenses, and that the agency understand that any projected budget overruns must be reported as soon as they are identified.

Careful review of budget allocations and tracking can signal a need to plan programs more carefully to eliminate unnecessary expenses such as messenger services and overnight air where MCI Mail or the postal service might have sufficed.

The agency also should not spend excessively on travel, and should follow the same practices as your company. For example, if your people fly tourist class, so do the agency folks. If you get a commercial rate in a hotel, then the agency should ask for your rate too. The only exception might be if an agency person is traveling with one of his client's top executives who flies first class. Then it is proper that the agency person fly with the client.

From the Client's Side: Typical Complaints

In interviews with colleagues, editors, and publicity and public relations professionals, several general complaints about agencies emerge. All can be corrected.

1. Poor writing. At the risk of being redundant, everyone working at an agency should know how to write properly. I do not believe that media experience necessarily makes better public relations people, but many agency account executives and their management could profit from a news writing course.

2. Lack of understanding of markets and the business climate. The client should not have to teach the account executive marketing communications and marketing principles.

3. Far too many wild ideas that don't address the markets. It is dangerous, of course, to criticize off-the-wall ideas, because there is a risk of stifling creativity. It is possible to be highly creative and still meet business objectives.

4. Little creativity. Using the same old tactics, the Chinese menu syndrome: one from column A, one from column B. Many program proposals take this approach.

5. Refusal to admit foulups. It happens to everyone. To be creative, to get the job done, requires risk taking. Not everything works. The press conference bombed because of a power failure, or there was a bus and subway strike. A major corporation filed a Chapter 11 and dominated the business pages. A key editor got the flu. The lead dancer in the show you were doing for press and customers broke her ankle. Or it was a great idea but just the wrong timing.

Candor is refreshing. "We just screwed up. Here's where we did it, and here's why it will never happen again." There is not enough of this from agencies.

At the very beginning, when the two parties meet, the agency should not have to assure the prospective client that there is no job it can't handle. There may very well be areas where its contacts are not all that good, or it has little experience, and it should be open about this. A client buys strengths. One of these strengths is that public relations professionals have the skills to make the necessary contacts and know how to work with editors on story ideas.

6. Another complaint is that the agency follows, not leads; or the reverse, takes its eye off the marketing communications plan, which it helped write.

From the Agency's Side: Be a Good Client

Having aired some complaints from the client point of view, it's only fair to cite agencies' wish lists and complaints.

1. The client does not define markets and objectives clearly. Not "I have a great ad program needing some publicity."

2. The client asks the agency to deviate from the plan. Or to run errands, such as getting theater tickets or ordering T-shirts for the company picnic. Agencies like to do things for their clients; it gives them a feeling that they are wanted. But too much and there's an uncomfortable feeling that "we're getting sidetracked and the plans are slowly going down the drain."

3. The client seldom offers any encouragement and support to the agency staff. Bring the agency in on planning, marketing meetings, make sure the account management knows when its account people are doing a good job, and support creativity. Don't shoot down the offbeat idea by blasting it out of the air. If it's not workable, there's no budget, or it won't get marketing support, encourage the agency to keep trying, and make sure it knows you aren't shutting off other ideas. And don't be afraid to go with one that just might pay off. Product introductions and special events can often profit from creativity that turns the routine and humdrum into events that will not only attract media attention, but get far greater coverage.

Right along with encouragement is constructive criticism. This goes both ways—client to agency; agency to client.

4. The client doesn't schedule work realistically. For example, the Spring Furniture Mart in High Point, North Carolina, is held at the same time every year. If you're in the business, you don't tell your agency at the end of February to get something ready for an April show. If there is a frantic rush to get everything ready on time and a couple things go wrong, then the client must take the blame.

5. Clients hold up their bills. Pay agency bills on time, if possible within ten days. Agencies must pay vendors, travel, entertain, make phone calls, and pay rent just the same as their clients. They need the cash flow just as any other business.

6. The client waits to bring up a problem until it's too late. Resolve any problems as they occur—the "One Minute Manager" lesson. Don't wait until the next meeting to complain or discuss a problem. Pick up the phone.

List review points, and others that may apply to your own business situation, and cover them when you review the agency program. You might set up a 1 to 5 rating scale for each, 1 being poor and 5 excellent. Ask your agency to rate your performance too, just as you will rate the agency's performance. Put both reviews in writing and exchange them a couple of weeks before the formal, sit-down review. Then you have an agenda for a good part of the meeting. If you have an open relationship, the agency will be honest and straightforward in its evaluation of you and your company.

An agency executive remarked that many of its clients stayed with the agency about two years then moved on to another agency. Knowing the reputation of this agency and how well it has served most of its clients, this came as a surprise to me. It suggests poor management at the client company. A relationship often founders because it was not as open as it should have been. Perhaps in some cases, the expectations of the client were too high. Perhaps the evaluation points suggested above were not considered; perhaps the fault lay in not "managing" the company side of the relationship, and not providing sufficient direction and supervision.

If there is a problem, it often can be traced to an account person. Better to make a change on this level than fire the agency. It takes far too long to orient a new agency—which may not last any longer than the first one.

Freelancers and Where They Fit

If your publicity program is limited in scope, it may be more economical to use freelancers or writing services, rather than retain an agency full-time. If your needs in some areas are only tactical, such as an occasional release or exclusive, then using a freelance writer is recommended. This would apply to product areas with limited budget support, or in a small market where there is little media coverage.

You might want to consider whether the entire program is manageable with just freelancers. In that case, a lot of the responsibility for developing story ideas, placing the story in the right media, and providing good direction, will rest with the company publicist or marketing communications planner. You'll probably still use an agency for special events and promotions.

Like agencies, if you find good freelancers that work well with you, you also will find that you'll need to devote less and less of your time to providing direction and supervision, and can spend more time on media relations. A freelancer also is less expensive than an agency—about one quarter to one fifth the cost per activity.

If your company has a marketing communications program, chances are you already have been contacted by freelancers. If not, call your local newspaper; there may be retired journalists in the area, or writers who contribute from time to time to area papers.

Check with the Chamber of Commerce, hospitals, nonprofit organizations, state or local business publications. Many publish newsletters or have someone doing publicity, but perhaps only part time. Call the mayor's press secretary for a suggestion. Think of all the organizations that might need publicity assistance, and ask for recommendations.

Choose carefully, however. Check writing ability first by reviewing samples of published work.

Selecting and Working with Public Relations Agencies

If your product is technical, you may need a writer with a background in the subject—engineering, physics, electronics, whatever. But be sure to get one that can write so that the copy is understood. A technical writer is not necessarily a good writer for nontechnical subjects. At the same time, a writer who specializes in electronics, for instance, will probably do a better job than one who doesn't. While much of the copy needed for electronics publications is not always technical, it is important that the writer know the media needs. The same advice applies to virtually any area in business.

If your subject is in some special area, and you can't find a good writer locally for that specialty, there is still hope. Two writing services, Creative Communications Services and Oesterwinter Associates, have good staff journalists and may be able to meet your needs. (See Chapter 11 for more information.)

Good journalists have been trained to be quick studies. They can write on a number of subjects with a little help. If you can provide the proper background, the right sources, and the right directions, a good writer will produce good copy.

Several of my colleagues use a number of freelancers quite successfully. Most of these writers have become experts in the areas they are covering after doing only a couple of stories.

One former associate of mine kept her writers so busy that she discouraged her colleagues from contacting them. Trusting in and being able to delegate assignments to freelancers gave her the time she needed to spend on editorial relations and planning.

Check writers' fees. They will be low relative to an agency because their overhead is much less. They may charge by the hour, the day, or the page. If they are to travel for you, be sure they follow your own company's travel policy. You go tourist; they go tourist. Travel time should be on a half day or day rate, not hourly, to protect you from excess charges if the flight is late.

Some agencies also use freelancers. If you suspect yours is doing this, you best have a chat with the agency management. There may be a legitimate reason: "It was far less expensive to hire a writer in Chicago to cover for us than send one of our staff from Mobile." That certainly makes sense. But if it's a Chicago freelancer for a Chicago agency, ask questions.

An assignment sheet should be provided for each freelance assignment (see Figure 6-4). It spells out the objective for the story, possible length, the audiences, media target, copy points to be emphasized, applications, and so on.

If writing the story will involve a customer, I recommend the company publicist make the first contact, and thoroughly brief the customer on the upcoming interview. The name of the freelancer should be provided and a date and time selected for the freelancer to contact the customer to make further arrangements.

The freelancer also may take pictures. If so, brief her or him thoroughly on the pictures needed. Good freelancers will spot photo opportunities. If the writer is not a photojournalist, make arrangements for photography the same day of the interview. Tell the photographer to get directions from the writer.

The company representative has responsibility for clearing the story with the customer, not the freelancer. Customer relations are better served when your company makes the contact and follows up than when this is done by an outsider.

Build a relationship with some good freelancers; it will make your job far easier, and greatly increase productivity. I've had some approach me with some good story ideas. This meant they had more work and my company got more coverage.

Freelancers are viable alternatives to agencies, but can't be used in place of an agency for an ongoing marketing communications program unless the publicist is prepared to spend a great deal of the time contacting editors and developing story leads.

5
Developing Good Relations with the Press

It is essential to know the media and the people in them who might write about or comment on your company. This will determine in a large part whether your publicity program is successful and whether you will reach your target markets with messages about your products and services. The most successful publicists are those who can "market" news material to the particular media that reach the audiences important to their marketing management and programs.

The focus of this chapter is on print media. While most of the principles and guidelines that relate to good editorial relations are the same for both print and broadcast—notably fostering and maintaining a professional relationship—broadcast is highly specialized and the approaches are different. It also is likely that a product publicist will have far fewer contacts with broadcast media than with print. Broadcast—television and radio—is discussed in detail in Chapter 9.

To achieve a worthwhile and productive relationship with editors, you don't have to be poker pals, golf buddies, lunch partners, or fraternity brothers or sorority sisters. But you *do* need to know who they are, and they should know who you are and what business interests you represent.

To have a successful and long-lasting relationship, trust must be earned. Once it is, the editors will come to respect your judgment. The material you send or the ideas you present will be seen as news, your feature ideas will be listened to, and the invitation to your press event will be taken seriously. The professional relationship may make a difference in the frequency and extent of coverage of your company.

Many editors base their consideration of a news release on the reputation of the company and the source. It is productive, therefore, when the editor spots the name of the company contact and recognizes someone who is known and respected and has a reputation for submitting material that is pertinent to the reader.

But there's another side too: If the material is consistently of little value, you may get a *bad* reputation, and whatever you send will be regarded with suspicion or ignored.

The person doing publicity must understand that this relationship goes in two directions. The agency or publicist sends material to the editor as "news." The editor also calls the publicist to obtain data or to speak to an authority who can provide facts for a story underway. The publicist must do everything possible to help, short of giving away proprietary or confidential information.

As I suspected, editors interviewed for this book, even those who get a substantial portion of the news they run from publicists, had mixed feelings about publicity people. Most said there were good ones and poor ones—not a very definitive answer. But the good ones had gained their respect and met the guidelines cited above. On the other hand, a number of editors, although willing to work with publicists, felt that many of those in product publicity were "mediocre."

An often-heard complaint is that publicists try to please their bosses, rather than the editors. Editors say that the "mediocre" ones have little news sense and don't relate their messages to the needs of the media. The publicist should realize that pleasing the boss is a good way to remain employed, but it doesn't mean answering "yes" to every request. When the boss understands publicity—and its limits—the publicist will be able to relate far more effectively with editors and the media.

Another complaint is that publicists continually call the publication to get their stories printed, or to find out if a release was received and would be used. But when the editors call to get more information or check some detail, these same publicists can't help.

In defense, I am sure that far too much is expected of some of the publicity people the editors are complaining about. This does not excuse unprofessionalism, but it may be that their companies or clients exert considerable pressure on them to get material published, even material of questionable news value. It may also mean that publicists have oversold their talents or promised something they could not deliver, leading company marketing people to believe their public relations staff or agency can work miracles without providing something of value or giving something in return. Or a marketing or management person, because he is so close to and intimately involved with a product, may have exaggerated the importance of its news value, or may have decided that an event, such as a branch opening, warrants a self-serving statement to the media. In such cases marketing or management expects the publicist to deliver because "he's the expert."

There are also times when a publicist cannot provide information to an editor because management won't cooperate. In some instances, this may be partly the fault of a publicist who has not briefed management on the elements of publicity or on the need to maintain good relations with editors. Or a publicist might insist on adhering to certain professional standards that do not reflect the wishes of management. The company may go so far as to switch agencies in the hopes that the new one can achieve miracles the past one could not. Most often, however, the results are no different.

I have observed that knowledge and understanding of public relations and product publicity are very limited in the business community. Publicists should work closely with management and marketing personnel to help them understand what can reasonably be expected from publicity, how to cooperate in the effort, and how best to evaluate its results.

One other common area of complaint from editors revolves around the question of whom they should be contacted by: company or agency. Given a choice, most editors prefer to deal with a company person, rather than an agency, because they feel they can get answers to their questions faster. Even if the questions can't be answered in time to meet the editor's deadline, the publicist—company or agency—owes it to the editor to let him know, not just fail to reply with any information. "I can't help because . . ." is a far better response than none at all, and far better editorial relations.

In defense of agencies, my experience has been largely positive. It's often a matter of making sure the right people from the right agency are working on the account. Yet complaints still persist.

An editor of a weekly business magazine says most agency people do not understand the needs of media and don't know what they are doing when contacting his publication about a story. He much prefers to deal with company publicity people and, unless they are uncooperative and can't or won't help him when he calls for information, he won't try to go around them and contact someone else in the company. In contrast, an industrial design publication editor says he likes most agency people. The difference in attitude may be that the agencies dealing with the design publications are more in tune with the publication's needs than those representing clients interested in publicizing what they regard as business news. I also suspect that editors can't tell sometimes whether the call is from an ad agency or a public relations agency. Most good public relations agencies have professional staffs.

From the Beginning: Identify Your Key Media

One of the first tasks for a person assuming a publicity assignment or setting up a program is getting acquainted with the editors covering a company's markets.

But before any contact is made, some research is needed. I usually break the research into five steps.

1. List every publication or news outlet that is of any importance to your

business. There is virtually no market or interest that is not reported upon by a publication. There is, for instance, a magazine devoted entirely to springs. There are publications for working women, health enthusiasts, oil drillers, furniture makers—whatever the audience you need to reach.

Standard Rate and Data is a good place to start. *Bacon's Publicity Directories* and *Working Press of the Nation* are other sources for publicity information. (See Chapter 11 for access information.)

If your company has an advertising program, check the publications on your ad schedule, because you, your ad agency, or someone else in your company has already done the proper research and decided that these media are important.

Another way to get the names of the publications covering your industry is to ask one of your company's sales representatives to check the publications in her customers' waiting rooms or offices. The magazine's space reps calling on you or your advertising people can help identify key editors too. Don't be afraid to ask. Just don't accept their help if they offer to give the editor your releases. This is very negative editorial relations; the editor may think you're putting pressure on him because your company is an advertiser, and may feel he's not very important to you if you are sending releases through a space rep.

2. Break out the list into its various categories. Start with *trade* (business-to-business) publications. These are publications that cover special industry areas—chemical, manufacturing, retailing, home building—more than 6,000 different publications. Then list *consumer* publications, which means those most frequently sold on newsstands. There are about 650 of these, and they run the gamut from computer and home magazines, through a number of women's and men's magazines. There also are *special-interest* consumer publications, which cover specific areas. Included in the consumer area are a number of publications devoted to people with *special interests.* These publications, which appeal to a specialized and sometimes rather small segment of the population, cover such areas as "popular science" (with the publication so named), photography, home computer, hobby, automotive, and outdoor sports. In the agricultural area alone, there are nearly 800 publications of this nature. Other consumer publications, which are departmentalized into various interest areas, are the news weeklies and the national and local newspapers. *Business and financial* publications are another media segment of interest to public corporations. These start with the business pages of the local daily press, and include the wire services, such publications as the *Wall Street Journal,* other nationally recognized newspapers, plus magazines such as *Forbes, Fortune, Business Week, Industry Week,* and others.

3. Learn the names of the key contacts at all the media: the editors of trade publications, newspaper reporters that cover your industry, television and radio news directors—whoever makes the decision about your story idea.

Most publicity directories list key editors and provide a brief description of editorial focus. Because of the frequent turnover in media, the directories may not always be up to date. If there is any doubt, call the publication or station and ask

Developing Good Relations with the Press

the person who answers for the name of the editor or TV or radio news director—a primary contact when you are getting acquainted. If you're on a new assignment, the person who held the job previously may be able to help, and also give some ideas on the editors' personalities.

There are so many departments and editors on most of the nearly 1,700 daily newspapers that it's hard to keep up with the changes. Unless your business is totally consumer-oriented, where newspaper contacts must be maintained (home pages, fashion, food, sports, business, and agriculture in some rural areas), don't develop these lists until you need them. The exception is the newspapers circulated in the vicinity of your plants and headquarters. Know these editors, because your top executives read their newspapers. And so do the company employees, people who are interested in the products because they make them. You don't need any more justification.

Don't omit electronic media. Television and radio programs also have a format, producers, and news directors, and you may find they often fit in quite well with your product publicity plans. Or you may want to plan an event especially because it offers publicity opportunities for local or cable TV shows. There is more turnover of both personnel and programs in television, so if these media are important, stay in very close touch.

4. Once you have your media lists, rank them by order of importance to your business. The primary media are the publications or news outlets you are targeting for your publicity program—the ones that talk directly to your marketing audiences. You should develop secondary media lists, but the measure of your success is going to be whether the primary media use news of your company and products, which you have developed for those publications or news outlets.

5. Now read *all* the publications carefully. Know their contents. Start a media profile for each. A media profile is a composite description of a publication and shows the basic information you need to know about the publication. It lists all the things you should be familiar with that can be important to your publicity program. This can be anything from a card file to a looseleaf binder (see Figure 5-1). For now, you should try to find out the following information; when you get to know the editors and have worked with the publication a number of times, you can fill in the rest of the information.

- What type of features are used: roundup stories (on more than one company), trend stories, case histories, or any and all?
- How are features treated? Are they staff-written, do they carry the byline of a technical expert, someone from a company, or combinations thereof?
- Are stories technical, semitechnical, problem/solution?
- Are there regular columnists covering special areas of interest? If so, note their areas of specialty. Columnists sometimes get stuck for ideas and welcome suggestions.
- Does it have a new products section?

Figure 5-1. Media profile.

Name of publication _____

Address _____

Phone _____ Editor _____

How frequently published _____

Circulation _____ Rating in field _____

Audience _____

Editorial direction _____

Chief competitors _____

_____

Editorial Breakdown

Type of material	Typical Length (words)	Method of illustration	Contributed text accepted	Editor responsible
_____	_____	_____	_____	_____
_____	_____	_____	_____	_____
_____	_____	_____	_____	_____

Products likely to be covered _____

_____

Placement/editorial relations assessment _____

_____

_____

Prepared by _____ Date _____

- Is there a new literature section?
- A news brief section? (Short, one- or two-paragraph items on news or trends in the marketplace.)
- How are company references used? Some publications severely limit references, especially any that are self-serving.
- Ditto on trademarks. One or two mentions are usually all allowed. But don't be concerned. Readers are smart enough to know what the story is all about.
- Are the stories short and punchy, or long and detailed?
- How are photos used? Color covers, color inside, combination of black and white and color? Getting photo coverage can increase your chances, so pay particular attention to how photos are used; see Chapter 8.
- Does the publication use cover photos from companies, or does it design or take its own? (Getting a cover photo is a coup.)

In short, know the *total* contents of the publications, issue by issue. Don Cannon, contributing editor of *Chemical Week,* recommends publicity people read the publication, "*all* of it, every issue—not just what's printed about your company, but what the publication says about other companies." The first reaction to this advice often is, "Of course I read the publications covering my markets." Not necessarily. Many ad people just read a publication for their own ads and those of the competition, and are less concerned about what the publication is saying to its readers. Actually *reading* the publication, Cannon advises, "will give you an idea of the audience and subjects, or how they are treated." He also recommends publicists read the circulation statement, "in fact, the whole media kit that your advertising people peruse. Especially, look at the Media Comparability Council data—as concise and hype-free a printed picture of a publication as there is available."

A good marketing communicator should know the contents and format of a given publication from cover to cover, and know the full format of all the national and local broadcast news outlets thoroughly. Also make it your business to know the personalities of the editors, including those who have very little patience with PR people.

Numbers are important, too—you should estimate cost per thousand and find out page rates and frequency and circulation figures. But the most important numbers relate to how many people buy the publication to read the articles and news selected by the editor. And don't forget about free publications. The debate will go on as to how many people read these "freebies," which often have a controlled circulation—that is, they are sent only to a specific group of people who are directly interested in them. Advertisers and publicists alike should ask questions about these publications: How many people are incorrectly categorized as being in the interest group? How often is the mailing list updated?

The Next Step: Know the Editor

Having researched the basics of the media, you're ready for the next step, which is getting acquainted personally with the people who will make judgments on your publicity material. Knowing editors is important; you must learn how they view the audiences reached through the media they control. Why? Because it is the editor's job to select news material that contributes to the knowledge of the reader, listener, or viewer, or provides a solution to a problem.

How each editor views the role and the media outlet managed can best be learned by knowing these people professionally and, in many cases, personally. This does not absolve publicists from learning as much as possible about a given medium so that they will not appear foolish when they do meet the editors.

It is the editors of the thousands of publications who make decisions on what goes in their magazines. It is seldom related to whether you advertise or not. There are a very few publications that cater only to their advertisers, and most of these are not worth knowing, because "news" should relate only to whether it offers a value to the readers.

If you have a PR agency, an obvious question is, "Why am I bothering with all of this? This is the agency's job." The answer begs another question: Who's in charge? The person to whom the agency reports has full responsibility for managing the function and the program. Retaining a publicity agency is not a turnkey operation. It requires as much control as an advertising agency—more, perhaps, in the area of editorial relations. The responsibility for knowing editors should be shared by the agency and the company publicity representative. You may retain an agency for its expertise and media contacts, but you do not give up the responsibility for maintaining good relations with key media.

If there is not a person at the company with publicity responsibility, the person to whom the agency reports directly—even if it's a product manager—should be introduced by the agency to the important editors at media serving the company's markets. This shows the editors that there is someone other than an agency person who can provide information when it is needed. Neither a company nor an agency can afford not to know editors.

Getting Personal

The first step is getting acquainted with the *primary* media people covering your company's markets and services. You must begin to develop the trust needed and to identify for the editor the company contact who can be relied upon for information. As Don Cannon of *Chemical Week* points out, "A company is the prime source of information about itself, and the publicist is the entree to that information." The publicist should know the products and services as well as his or her marketing counterparts (or nearly as well) and have ready access to the sources of company information.

Begin by assuming that editors want to know you. They are looking for a reliable company source from whom they can get information when they are working on a story that might involve your company or industry. A common complaint from editors is, "I don't know who to contact; you keep moving people around, and I am not kept up to date on the changes."

Keith Felcyn, chief of correspondents at *Business Week*, says McGraw-Hill is very open to contacts from publicity people. He uses as an example the publicist who called his Houston bureau and said that he and his company president would be in town and could they get together for lunch to talk on a background basis? The publicity person did not expect a story to come out of it. The bureau chief welcomed the opportunity to meet the company president informally, and a good contact was established. "Once the relationship is established, the odds are pretty good that something may come of it. It may not be a story in *Business Week,* but the president will be on the reporter's list to call, he may be quoted, a relationship developed," Felcyn states. That is good public relations. No specific stories were discussed, but the relationship began on a professional level and the odds are it would be profitable for both. It also emphasizes a point relating to publication groups that have regional offices. Deal only with the editors in the bureau nearest your business. They are equally as competent as the editors at publication headquarters, and have the responsibility for developing news in their area.

Gray Maycumber of *Daily News Record* tells about a business editor who joined a major daily newspaper in a southern city located near many textile manufacturers' headquarters. After seven years on the job, he had not heard from a single public relations person from any of those companies. The message is: Don't wait until you need something to get acquainted, or don't wait for a call from the editor. Also, if there is an accident or a disaster at your place of business, you have a better chance of having your side of the story told. You won't be favored, but you will be able to get the facts presented accurately.

Two people decide whether your news will reach your selected audiences: you and an editor. The editor knows his readers better than you do, and is always looking for stories that appeal to them. He wants to improve the editorial content to help increase circulation — which, of course, can enable the publication to ask for more money from its advertisers. The odds are the story ideas that will be considered come from someone or some company the editor respects.

A friendly editor may offer some suggestions to make your suggested features more pertinent to the publication's readers. If you have what you believe is a good story idea, call. If nothing else happens, you've made another contact. And the editor will become more familiar with you and your company and its products.

You are competing with many, many companies for space. An editor who knows the publicist and respects that person as a professional will more than likely favor his or her releases over the hundreds of others that arrive at the publication every day.

Editors also are very much on top of the markets they cover. After you get to know them, they may share information with you on what is taking place in your industry or business area.

A good way to begin to learn about the editor's personality is to read the editorial in the front of the publication. The person writing this may not be the contact for every story, but should be the person contacted first. The editorial will reflect the "tone" of the magazine and suggest directions, trends, or concerns in the business or among the readers. Knowing what the editor wrote in the most recent issues is a good way to get a conversation moving when you first meet, and a way to subtly flatter the writer.

The advice to know the publication's style cannot be overemphasized. Every idea discussed with an editor, every note written, should have some news value that relates directly to the format of the publication. Some have a problem/solution format; others use none or very few company references or trademarks; others run long in-depth pieces while some prefer shorter, punchier material. The first-time visitor or caller should be fully aware of the total format, even though he or she may not have any other information.

Don Cannon says the relationship between an editor and a publicist is adversarial. No doubt it is with the news publications, but it seldom is with trades and many consumer publications. However, as he rightly points out, the editor frequently wants more than a publicist or his clients are willing to give, and the publicist wants more from the editor than he is willing to cede.

Chemical Week, for example, is a *news* weekly serving the chemical and allied industries. If an editor doesn't get all the information he wants from a company, he will dig and probe elsewhere for the answers. Always be aware that there are other sources for news about your company—competitors, customers, government publications, security analysts, among others—and don't be surprised when a story contains information you did not provide.

The key to any relationship, adversarial or otherwise, is respect, and the publicist must earn it. It's earned by first knowing your company's business, your own business, and the business of media.

Making the Cold Contact

If you don't know the editor, start by dropping a short note introducing yourself and providing your address, product assignments, and phone number for his future reference. Most product publicists deal with trade media, so aren't likely to get a call at night when a reporter is putting together a story for the next morning's paper. Even so, it's a help to the editor if you also give your home phone number. You also might print and send Rollodex cards with the information.

Developing Good Relations with the Press

Include a backgrounder on your product assignments. (For details on backgrounders, see Chapter 6 and the sample backgrounder in Figure 6-3.) Don't send sales literature. The editor is not interested in buying your products, just your ideas, and wants to be able to identify a source if he or she is working on a story and needs information. You can send technical bulletins if they are pertinent.

Here is an outline of a suggested letter:

> Dear Mr. Editor: (If you don't know the editor, use last name. If it's a woman, use Ms.)
>
> I have been assigned product publicity responsibility for Product X. As you may know, this is used [follow with *brief* description of product]. I am enclosing a backgrounder that will give you additional information on the properties and markets of Product X.
>
> If you have any questions about Product X of if I can provide any information for a story you are developing, please phone me at [number].
>
> I look forward to meeting you. [If you plan to be in the editor's city or are attending a trade show that he might cover for his publication, it is appropriate to add:] I expect to be in New York in a couple of weeks. I will call you to see if it is convenient for me to stop by your office for a few minutes and introduce myself. [Or] I expect to be attending the National Housewares Show in Chicago in July. I'll call you in a couple of days to see if we can get together at the show.

Note that you didn't try to sell any story ideas in the letter. Your first objective is to let the editor know who you are and the products you handle. You also have subtly told the editor that you may be submitting story ideas, and are a source of information on your company.

Another alternative is to call the editor, briefly introduce yourself in the same way, determine if he or she is familiar with your products or services, provide very brief descriptions, and leave your phone number. Ask about a future meeting, then express thanks for the time. Always follow with a note and enclose the backgrounder.

There are two important considerations before any contact is made, written or oral. First, make absolutely sure you contact the proper person. If you find out after you introduce yourself that the person you meant to call has left the publication or, perish the thought, is deceased, you will appear foolish and unprofessional.

Second, don't call when the editor is closing the magazine (getting it ready to go to the printer). Check editorial closing dates in your media directory. It's one thing to contact a publication with an advertising question on ad closing dates (you're the customer), yet another entirely if it is on an editorial closing date (you're the seller).

How about direct mail? There have been some excellent three-dimensional direct mail programs used in advertising, some with gifts enclosed. They can work with editors too, just as long as the "gift" is not too elaborate or expensive. To introduce herself to editors, a publicist I know sent printed literature describing all the products she handled that could loosely be categorized as "rubber industry." They ranged from neoprene to special elastomeric products and covered a wide variety of industries and audiences. Along with the literature, she sent a peat pot that contained a zinnia seed. When water was added, the pot swelled and the seed started growing. The message, of course, was that she hoped their future relationship would grow and blossom. It was a clever way to get editors' attention to a product area. The publicist was recognized the next time contact was made because she was the one that sent the zinnia plant. Most important, it was memorable without being expensive enough to be regarded as a payoff for editorial coverage.

Sending a gift to editors, whether it's to introduce oneself or "wrapped around a release," is okay, according to many of the editors I interviewed, as long as it does not appear to be a ruse to get coverage or preferential treatment. If an editor thinks a small gift smacks the slightest bit of a payoff, it will be returned quickly. Another of my colleagues put together a press kit on products directed to the plumbing and heating industry and enclosed the kit in a tool box. All the editors who received it were very pleasantly surprised.

Many releases have been sent to fashion and women's interest magazines inside a wicker picnic basket luncheon complete with wine. This is a much-used ploy. And it may very well work sometimes. But in any case, good taste (no pun intended) should prevail.

There's a feeling among fledgling publicity people that the way to an editor's heart is through his stomach. Most editors eat lunch, but not all of them go out to lunch with a publicist. Don't be offended if you invite an editor to lunch and are turned down.

However the contact is made, the editor must get a strong first impression that you know your business, understand the media, and come across as a professional.

While you are in an editor's office, look around at the piles of mail received every day. One of the most sobering experiences is seeing the large number of news releases that arrive daily, and the heaps of them in the trash. It brings home the point very quickly that there is a lot of competition for the editor's attention.

Making Trade Show Contacts

Most industry trade association shows are well attended by the press, and often covered by the local media. Trade shows can be for industry only or open to the public. The consumer electronics show, for example, is covered widely by the daily and weekly news media because of the products being introduced, trends being discussed, and competition among products. Competition for the editors'

Developing Good Relations with the Press

time at this type of show is fierce. But there are hundreds of other trade shows attended by the business press (and sometimes covered by the local newspaper and television), and they are good places to meet editors, even when you have nothing new to discuss.

First, understand that editors attend a show for two reasons: The first is to develop information upon which they can write stories for their publications. The second is that many of their publications will also be exhibitors; the ad reps and publishers will be seeking new business and getting reacquainted with their advertisers. The editor may be involved in helping them on the business side too. Editors also will be invited to luncheons, dinners, and press conferences. They will be busy. But given enough notice, it is possible to get together with the editors

---

Dos and Don'ts of Editorial Contacts

DO	DON'T
Be brief, make your point.	Come over like a Broadway press agent. Try to hype a product, or sell a story that doesn't fit the audience or format.
Know your markets, market trends, and products.	Rap the competition.
Know the publication thoroughly. Read the last issue.	Start out by telling the editor you have a great idea for a cover story.
Offer assistance, but be concise about story suggestions.	
Read the last two editorials.	Disagree with the point of view of the editorials.
Know what has been run about your product in the past year.	Express ignorance if the editor asks you if you saw a recent story about your product.
Spend time productively.	Spend time on idle chitchat—sports, weather, politics. (There may be exceptions, when an editor you know well will enjoy a nonbusiness chat.)
Write a report on your visit.	Rely on your memory.
Write a note to the editor thanking him for the time; if you promised material, send it.	Overlook the common courtesies. And don't delay—get the material in the mail fast.

---

covering your business. Not every one perhaps, but a few who are important to your business.

It's to your advantage to have a reason to meet. This may be an offer to discuss industry trends, a new development in your industry, or some of the problems facing your industry. If you can't discuss business, simply state you'd like to have an opportunity to meet and ask if he or she has any free time for lunch or dinner.

The secret is to ask at least three to four months ahead of time. Get on the editor's calendar early. Follow with a letter confirming the meeting, then a couple of weeks before the date, phone again. Find out at this time the editor's hotel, and provide information on where you are staying. If you want to make a real impression, check in advance for the name of an excellent restaurant, make a reservation for you and the editor, and tell him or her of the plans when you call to confirm. If you have made specific plans, it is harder for your prospective guest to cancel. Make your reservations ahead of time too. The best restaurants in major convention cities get booked very quickly. Some, even during nonconvention times, must be booked weeks in advance.

Editors rarely stay at the publication's show booth. Most of their time is spent touring the show, looking for stories. If you didn't set up a meeting ahead of time, check the show press room to see if he or she has registered. Leave a message and maybe the editor will call you. Check the publication's booth. You'll probably be greeted by sales reps, but someone should know when your elusive editor will return or will take a message.

If, during your visit, you come across as a professional communicator with a solid background on your product assignment, the chances are the editor will voluntarily provide a lot of details on the publication. You also will get a good idea of the editor's personality. The editor may invite you to call in the future if you have any story ideas.

Unless the editor knows your marketing people well, it's best not to suggest a visit to the company suite. While it gives the editor the opportunity to meet your associates, it also gives them a chance to ask questions about why he didn't run a news release, or hear other criticism about his publication. You're better off meeting the editor where the two of you can talk privately, or possibly with one of your top management people.

Writing Visit Reports

Many salespeople write call reports after they've met with a customer. You may use the call report form shown in Figure 5-2 or write a brief report that includes the following:

- Editor's attitude. Was he friendly, hostile, open to ideas, what?
- Was he interested in your business?

Figure 5-2. Editorial call report.

Editor: _____

Publication: _____

Specific story(ies) discussed: _____

_____

_____

Any other products that could be involved: _____

_____

_____

General trends/important topics editor sees for readers:

_____

_____

_____

Problem areas/editor needs (Business info, photos, covers, tech papers, access to more spokespersons, etc.):

_____

_____

_____

Specific info/assistance needed: _____

_____

_____

Other comments, recommendations: _____

_____

_____

- Was he receptive to a story suggestion?
- Did he ask for a story, ask for a followup on an idea, suggest another meeting? Surprisingly, editorial visits often pay off with the editor asking for a story (assuming the publicist made a good impression).

Put the memo in a "tickle" file for followup. If it's not something you need do right away, file it for a couple of months; then when you call the editor (as part of your staying in touch program), you'll have something to talk about.

And whenever and wherever you visited or even chatted with an editor, drop a short note saying how much you enjoyed the meeting and hope you can work together on a story in the near future.

Whenever and however you get back in touch, offer some information or some bit of news. Make your editorial contacts think that you spend part of your day helping them develop stories.

When an Editor Calls: Five Basic Rules

One of the main reasons for making and maintaining editorial contacts is to open the lines of communications from the editor to the publicist. At the same time the editor has gained an impression of a publicist, the assumption can be made that he also has an impression of the company represented. The impression of both can be damaged, however, if certain guidelines are not followed when the editor calls for information in developing a story, getting additional information on a story submitted, or checking data he may have obtained elsewhere. You may wish to keep a log of all inquiries and calls from editors (see Figure 5-3). These can be integrated in your report to management and used as reminders to check the editors' publications for the stories that relate to the calls.

1. You will not lie, try to cover up, or fudge on answers to difficult questions. You will be factual.

2. You will return phone calls promptly. A major complaint from virtually every editor I interviewed for this book is that the publicist somehow feels it's all right to ask the editor for a favor or to run a story, but fails to provide any information when the editor calls.

3. You have a tacit obligation to provide as much information as possible within the bounds of good business judgment. The publicist who is forever mute not only does not have the confidence of the editor, but apparently does not have the confidence of the marketing or business executives he or she works with. This is basic: It is hard enough handling a publicity assignment, but even more so when the people you represent don't understand what it takes to make things work. If this is the case, perhaps some "marketing" of publicity to marketing is called for.

Figure 5-3. Editorial contact log.

Date	Editor/Media	Phone	Subject/Action/Deadline

4. Assuming a good relationship both internally and externally, you are not expected or obligated to answer every question asked, or put editors in touch with everyone they want to question. But if you can't provide additional information, or another source, you must be able to offer a valid reason. Even if the editor doesn't agree with your position, you will have gained enough respect that it will, in most instances, be honored. You may have to tell the editor that the kind of information he is seeking is proprietary and decline to answer questions about it. As much as you may try to please the media, there are times when you must place your company's interests first. The simplest advice is, use good judgment. You should not give share-of-market information if it will help the competition. You don't have to comment at length on a new product, if the introduction is six months away.

5. Nor are you expected to know everything, although you should as much as possible be cooperative and help the editor get the story written. You may need to put the editor off while you check for information, and set up a conference call with one of your authorities.

When the editor starts calling the publicist when another question comes up, that is editorial relations at their best. There may be editors who, having not gotten all the answers from the publicity contact, may contact others in your organization or company. You should have an understanding with your counterparts and your company "clients" that editors seeking information should always contact you first. It is to the editor's advantage because a good publicist knows where to get the answers fast. It also can help head off someone giving the editor too much information or someone else offering a "no comment." There will be few end-runs if publicists are like those Gray Maycumber of Fairchild Publications prefers to work with: "I like people who are enthusiastic and believe in what they are doing."

Not every situation is ideal, of course. There are some editors who will refuse to recognize your authority, who have little regard for "flacks" and "press agents." There is no good way to handle these, other than insisting that the editor observe your company's policies and being professional at all times, no matter how upset you are.

A very few editors are difficult to deal with. They may have in the past encountered a less than competent person from your company, have been "stonewalled," been promised something that was not delivered, or lied to. And some editors, like some businesspeople, just want to get down to business with no preliminary chitchat. A colleague of mine was taken aback by the apparent brusque manner of an editor who called for a photo and information. Because I knew this editor personally, she asked if he was this way all the time. Yes, I said, when he was working on a story. If you met him socially, he was totally different. Understanding all the facets of an editor are vital in the relationship.

A few journalists are biased, and there is nothing to be done about it except to be very straightforward and businesslike.

Adversarial, friendly, hostile, disinterested, interested in listening to ideas on the phone or prefers a note—all these facets of a personality and more should be noted.

Whether the editor is friendly or not, there is one question you *never, never* ask: "Did you get my release about our new widget?" Unless there was a total breakdown in the U.S. mail, of course he got it. Don't look foolish by asking such a amateurish question. Unless there are plans to use it, it was dumped in the trash. If the editor wants more information, you will be contacted. If it runs, you will probably receive a clipping from the clip service, or an alert space rep will send it to you. The editorial "Opinion" by Bob Donath, editor of *Business Marketing* (February 1986), offers some excellent advice (see Figure 5-4).

Some publicists are so eager to find out what happened to a release they call not just one editor but several at the same publication. They also send releases to all the editors, hoping, I suspect, that one of them might bite. Maclean Hunter is very specific (but polite) in its brochure, "How to Get Your News in a Business Publication." "Please do not phone editors to ask if they have received a release and whether they will use it. Some editors receive hundreds of releases each week."

If the publication is important to your business, you should be a subscriber, and circulate it among your staff. You never want to be placed in the position of receiving a call from management questioning you about a story you haven't seen. But don't *ever* ask an editor to send a tear sheet of your story, especially if this is a ploy to see if he is going to run your news release. Even if it's an exclusive, he will most certainly not be too keen on doing it, or may forget that you asked by the time the story appears. You might ask the person who calls on your advertising department for a copy, although most alert ad reps will make sure you get it without having to ask.

What About the Agency?

I've got an agency. Why should I be the prime editorial contact?

Because many editors feel that most agency people can't get the answers "right now," are reluctant to provide some information, and often have to check with their clients for permission and answers. A company contact is essential. You also have eliminated the possibility that an agency person will give out too much information in the eagerness to please an editor. Or, because an account executive may work on accounts in addition to your own, it is quite possible that the agency contact won't be there when an editor calls for information.

There are few editors who aren't in a hurry and working against a deadline. I can remember only one or two who could wait until the next day for the information. Most seem to need it within minutes of the call. Even if you can't get the information when it is needed—which sometimes happens—return the call and tell the editor you were unsuccessful. This is not only a courtesy, but sound media relations. Don Cannon also says that there are some things journalists should do for publicists. One is explain what they need. And, if a publicist helps out and it doesn't pan out, "we should tell you why because you're in the middle. Maybe you've pressed your management for cooperation and then the information wasn't used."

Figure 5-4. Advice from an editor.

OPINION / BOB DONATH

The Comment I Didn't Want to Write

Each month, one of the joys (or chores, in some months) around here is writing this column—the editorial that states the magazine's opinion of a subject presumably interesting to you readers. Usually we strive for (and if we're lucky, achieve) dispassionate comment—meaty without being, ahem, stuffy.

But this time, I'm annoyed. Sitting at the computer composing what's supposed to be intelligent writing is tough enough without constant and wildly inappropriate phone interruptions: namely, "Did you get the release I sent you?"

Please don't misunderstand. We know that the public relations and publicity function is as vital to the specialized business press as it is to the marketers who employ it. We editors and reporters, and ultimately our readers, benefit from having timely information about events and concepts within the industries we cover. And for every complaint journalists have about sloppy PR practices, PR people can complain about having to deal with editors and reporters who are too rude, lazy or sloppy. So carping about problems dealing with publicists could be disingenuous.

Except now, with the phone ringing ceaselessly and the assistant editor not around to answer it, I'm pushed beyond the edge of discretion.

PUBLICITY WHEEL-SPINNING

What are the sponsors, using PR to achieve a marketing goal, getting for their money when poorly trained beginners in the field waste their own and others' time? Not much.

Phone calls like this exchange over a routine mass mailing aren't uncommon:

Caller: Hello. I'm calling to see if you got our release on the enhanced XYZ widget. We mailed it two weeks ago.

Editor: I don't recall it. But we get hundreds of releases a week, and I can't read every one of them. Someone on the staff probably received it and will run it or not, or maybe call for more information.

Caller: Don't you read your own mail? We sent it to you personally.

Editor: So does everybody. I can only see personal correspondence. All those photocopied releases go to the staff. Incidentally, what's special about your enhanced widget?

Caller: I don't know. I was told just to call and ask if you got it.

The conversations get sillier when the alleged "news" is far distant from the type of stuff the magazine publishes.

Telling a PR person that he or she should look at the magazine before taking the time to telephone usually gets a shocked reaction, and at times a quick disconnection without so much as a goodbye.

The very nature of an editor's job makes him or her *want* to answer a ringing phone. It could be a news source on the line returning a call, it could be a writer with a question about an assigned story or it could be someone—even a PR person—with a hot news tip or otherwise important datum for the editor's readers.

Good publicity people know that, and respect their time and others' accordingly. They call editors only when they think they've got something of real interest to a publication's readers or when they want to do serious business, such as place an exclusive story. It's part of the editor's job—and a pleasure as well—to receive those kinds of calls.

WRONG SCENARIO

Far too often, however, the operating scenario seems to be something like this:

To impress its client, a publicity agency (in-house PR operations rarely operate as press release mills because they know their markets) mails a routine press release to names from a media directory. It doesn't matter if the publications might possibly have some interest. The objective is tonnage and a press list that looks good to the unsophisticated client.

Then the agency puts its rawest recruits on the task of following up even the most mundane mailings by phone, treating them to a PR version of boot camp.

Forcing tyros to call editors with silly questions and no helpful information just might, one supposes, separate the promising beginners from the pack, and steel them for a career of dealing with editors as adversaries.

It's a shame that the PR industry shoots itself in the foot by annoying, without good reason, the very people it is paid to entice. The unfavorable image that rubs off on the sponsor only hurts its marketing effort. ∎

From the February 1986 issue of *Business Marketing*. Used by permission of Bob Donath.

Editors, however, won't call you and tell you why they aren't using your releases. If a pattern (over a year, for example) develops that indicates one of the publications important to your markets never runs anything you send, it may be time to visit the editor and find out why. He may have been offended by someone in your agency or your company, may have been ignored when he asked for information, or a competing publication may have been given an exclusive he felt he should have had. You also may find out that he doesn't see any news value in the releases you or your agency are sending him. Whatever the case (and in rare instances it may be because you aren't advertising), find out. Then if he has a legitimate gripe, take all steps necessary to get him back on your good side.

It also may be difficult to know whether your agency is dealing with media in a professional manner unless you have a good knowledge of media and an appreciation for editorial relations. Don't assume that agencies always have the best people available on your account at any given time.

Learning about publications and meeting editors can be done in cooperation with your PR agency, but the responsibility for a program's success remains with the person managing and directing it.

Not everyone reading this has an agency or uses other services such as freelancers. Your program may be entirely in-house. There are advantages and disadvantages to each, which will be covered later. Whatever the situation, a successful product publicity program starts with good editorial relations, and runs far smoother when they are maintained. And one of the best reasons to foster and maintain good editorial relations can't be overemphasized: Most editors prefer a company contact and will call that person before calling the agency.

Developing Trust in All Directions

When there is a situation that requires an answer, but you cannot, explain your position. "I'm not in a position to answer that question now because . . . ." There may not be an agreement with the stance, but there won't be a feeling you are stonewalling, if you explain why you cannot answer. Mutual respect will be maintained if you have done your job in developing good relations with editors.

Editor Cannon recognizes that publicists are there to serve their employees first—to protect, interpret, and project a company's position. "We should let you do your job, let you get information from key people, let you set up interviews with your people. That means we should not insist on talking to everyone. That means we should not try to make end-runs if we feel we must talk to someone." He cautioned, however, that the possibility should be accepted that "publicists who are repeatedly ignored and circumvented by editors may deserve to be treated that way."

To avoid the end-run, you should develop a clear understanding with your inside contacts in marketing and management that you must screen any editorial calls. Editors may not like this policy, but it can work to the advantage of both the company and the media. You, as the company contact, are in a position to find a source for the information requested if you can't answer the questions yourself. You also are better able to find spokespersons who are able to speak with authority, are literate and articulate and, if it's technical, can answer in a way that is clearly understood.

If it is necessary to bring your expert together with an editor, be sure to listen in. Set these interviews up as conference calls. Most editors don't object if you interrupt when the situation gets touchy, a point needs clarification, or the interviewee muddles up the answer or gets off the track. A "do you mean to say . . ." often can help both parties. Or, "we can't discuss that because it's our company policy not to criticize competitors [or] reveal market share."

Plus, you are well aware of the executives in your company who won't speak to the press. Every company has at least one. (It also has one who may talk too much.) If an editor regards you as a prime contact, and the only one who can answer the question is the media-shy marketing person, you can get the answers from the latter and relay them to the former. In all cases, the person inside the company needs to remain in control.

You also may work with a sales manager who loves to be quoted, and thinks that because he met an editor two years ago at a trade show, he can call the editor whenever he has "a great idea for a story." Publicists have to deal with these people because many are working "clients." The publicist is looking for ways to develop leads for the salespeople, whether they're in packaged goods, chemicals, or intimate apparel. He can't tell the sales manager to lay off; maybe he *does* have a good story idea now and then.

Tact, diplomacy, and judgment come into play when the publicist is trying to stay on the best side of both the client and the editor. One way to solve this problem might be to ask the salesperson to discuss it with you so that it can be presented to the editor in the "best possible way." Another approach might be to wait for the right time, and ask the editor how he feels about getting the phone calls. He might not mind because the sales manager is giving him information he can't get anywhere else.

Another situation related to me by a colleague is that technical marketing people often become acquainted with the editors of technical publications and technical newsletters. The marketing people invite these editors to dinner at conferences, call them, and discuss developments without informing the publicity person responsible—sometimes with awkward results. With one salesman she made the tactful analogy that she would not think of calling his customers and making sales and technical arrangements. While she felt she could not flatly tell him to lay off, she did reach a diplomatic agreement that he would involve her and at the very least fill her in on any meeting so she could follow up.

The best policy in situations such as these is to have a policy to begin with—all editorial queries are automatically referred to the publicist handling the product or service. If the sales type persists and keeps the contacts to himself, it may be best not to offend him. Just hope he doesn't trap himself. It could be bad for both of you.

Of the more than 20 editors I interviewed for this book, all but one said he or she *preferred* to work through a company publicist when wishing to speak to a company executive. The one who said she would always call an executive directly was with a high-fashion publication. I can only assume that she had made several high-level contacts with executives in this rather special business, and felt free to call them.

The Payoff

The payoff of professional media relations is better acceptance of story ideas or a call when one involving your business is being developed at the publication. It may entail a request for an expert opinion from one of your company's scientists or "authorities," an interview, or a photo to illustrate a story.

If you initiate a story idea, do some advance research to make sure that everyone in your company will cooperate and that you have sources and information. Review the idea thoroughly with the marketing people who will be most favorably affected if the story is used, technical people for backup, and a person who can be used as the company authority. If everyone agrees with you, and you have facts and backup, then the idea is ready for the editor. Or, if you're just kicking around an idea with an editor, be sure it is understood that the extent of your contribution will depend upon how much valid information you can provide. The editor also may ask you to identify noncompany experts over which you have no control. Cooperate as much as possible and, if feasible, call the person (could be a good customer) and encourage his cooperation. This gesture could benefit the sales force too.

If it's an interview for print or broadcast, try to get all the information you can in advance from the medium on the specific areas of questioning. You may be told politely that the medium can't or won't provide advance details. Of course you know this, but there's no harm in asking, "Can you give me an idea of the gist of the questions so that I may make sure Dr. Smith has the information you need?"

You also may ask if the editor needs any special photos, and if there are specific data needed to support the story. Depending upon the nature of the interview, the editor may also be asked about his need for graphs, charts, tape, or other visuals for television. You may not get all the answers you want, but by asking a few questions in advance, you will have a better idea of the direction the questioning will take.

If it's a television interview, your expert must know how to handle himself. (See Chapter 9 for details.)

In a word, preparation is the most important aspect of good, results-oriented editorial relations.

A Final Quiz

Let's imagine some potentially sticky problems in media relations, and see how you would handle them.

- An editor calls you in your office in Chicago and asks about a product your associate Mary in Dallas handles. What should you do?

If your first response was "I don't handle that product; I think Mary Smith in Dallas does," you're only partly right. You also should get the caller's full name, title, publication, and phone number; give the caller Mary's phone number; determine the nature of the call and the questions; and tell him that you will call Mary and ask her to return the call. If she doesn't, the editor has her phone number and can reach her. Be sure to invite the editor to call you if he can't reach Mary. Every effort should be made to help editors, even when it's one that is not covering your markets. Someday you may need that editor's help.

People—and that includes editors, customers, consumers—outside a multiproduct or service company don't think divisions, they think company. The impression that everything possible is being done to help them is good *company* policy.

- You suspect the caller is not an editor, even though he says he is.

Get the name and number and tell him you'll call back. Most legitimate callers will provide this information, and editors are used to getting called back.

- A marketing manager suggests you call an editor about doing a feature story in an issue in which you are advertising.

If it's a special issue and one to which you can contribute, you already should have been in touch with the editor. If you have nothing to contribute, the editor will not run anything just because you're running an ad. This should be pointed out to your marketing associate as diplomatically as possible. Using advertising as a wedge just won't work.

You also might point out to the marketing person that you'll get better readership if you can place a story in another issue; then you'll be in two issues instead of just one.

- You learn from your advertising department that this same marketing manager has ordered cancellation of all advertising, because the publication ran a story that he thought was unfavorable.

The answer is in two parts: First, advertisers can't dictate what publications print. If they could, no one would read the publications except for the advertisers.

Developing Good Relations with the Press

Second, the publication was selected for the advertising program because it effectively reached your markets and buying influences. "If you want to stop reaching these people, then I'll pull the advertising. But it won't affect what the editor writes about our company or make him write something favorable about us or be critical in the future."

There may be a good reason why this marketing person reacted this way. Perhaps the story *was* unfair or inaccurate. It is the responsibility of the publicist to deal with these situations.

Whether you know the "offending" writer or editor or not, a meeting or phone call may be called for. Go well-prepared to discuss your side of the issue. Be quite clear that (unless it's a blatant error) you aren't necessarily looking for a retraction, but some type of clarification would be appreciated. The approach should be neither hat-in-hand nor hostile. It could be corrected as a letter to the editor, a "box" item admitting the error, or a more positive piece in the future. Or it may not be anything. But looking after a company's interests is also the responsibility of the publicist — and a part of editorial relations. Details on this are covered in Chapter 7.

- A space rep asks you for a story that he will pass on to the editor. (This often happens after you tell him you are planning some advertising.)

Don't give stories to space reps. Tell the space rep you prefer to deal with the editor directly. If the editor readily runs stories given him by space reps, reexamine your ad program. It may be a waste of money.

- A space rep calls you, says he and the publisher *and the editor* will be in town next Tuesday. Would you like to meet the editor?

Of course you would. Never pass up a chance to chat with the editor. And ask the ad staff to sit in for part of the meeting. Get the editor's views on how he sees the publication and the readers. It's one area many ad people fail to explore, and it's almost as important in planning advertising as circulation, cost per thousand, demographics, and all the other data weighed before an ad schedule is set.

- What do you do if, during the visit mentioned above, the editor asks if you can set up a meeting with one of your experts on a certain subject?

Do your best to set it up.

- The space rep asks if he can sit in on that meeting.

At the risk of offending him — which will be difficult not to do in this instance — tell him that you prefer discussions of editorial matter be between the editor and the expert. You do not want to give him any opportunity to pitch advertising to the marketing person, or to have the marketing person feel in any way that the fact that he is there is an endorsement of running advertising. Editorial and advertising must not be mixed.

There may appear to be a contradiction here. I've suggested that you meet the editor when he or she is traveling with the publisher and the space rep. This is sometimes done so that advertisers can meet the person responsible for the editorial side of the book. But when the editor asks to meet one of your experts (not necessarily a marketing person), I suggest excluding the ad rep. In the first instance, the primary topic is advertising and the overall thrust of the publication. In the second, the editor more than likely wants to learn something related only to editorial matter. That's the reason for the statement that the two don't mix.

• Your marketing manager asks why all the publications haven't run your latest news release. He suggests you call them and find out why.

If you have briefed your marketing counterparts well on publicity and how your stories are evaluated, how it's different from advertising, you may not get this question. Even so, it is often difficult to suggest on one hand that you are a marketer of news, as opposed to a buyer, and explain to a marketing person why you can't make a followup call. Where releases are concerned, it's a one-time call. If the question is asked a couple of weeks after the release was mailed, point out that very frequently publications work two to three months ahead on issues. Unless it's breaking news, it may take time before it is used, if at all.

In Summary

The practice of good editorial relations is the foundation of any publicity program. It is essential that you know the media and the people there that make the decisions about what the readers will read, what the listener will hear, and what the viewer will see and hear. Along with this is the development and nurturing of mutual trust and respect between the persons responsible for publicity and the editor, whatever the medium.

Stay in touch.

6
Getting into Print

It's highly likely that most of your efforts will be directed to print media. Because of the special nature of broadcast, radio and TV won't be used quite as often. The news release is the most common way to impart news to newspapers and magazines: That's why I refer to it as the ubiquitous news release. Releases aren't the only means; there are a number of ways to develop features as well as other methods for being included in stories that originate with the publication.

The Ubiquitous News Release

Before you sit down to write a news release, look at your profession from the editor's side of the desk.

Picture yourself trying to meet a deadline but having to deal with 100 or more pieces of mail every day, most of which is irrelevant, and taking innumerable phone calls from people trying to sell you something that seems to have little or no value. Not to mention people waiting outside your office, also with something to sell. You also have on your appointment calendar a number of special events you plan to attend and invitations to many others in your wastebasket.

If you weren't a person of strong physical or moral fiber, you would probably spend your declining years — perhaps sooner — in a room with rubber walls. But you are a magazine editor, and this is a typical day. It's a fact that publications receive hundreds of releases a week, thousands a month. And if you think that you have problems, think of the television and radio news directors. Not only do they have to read copy, they also have to listen to it.

A news release is certainly one way to release "news," but only a few ever see print — a humbling thought for the publicist. How much chance does a release have? Very little, if it is sent to publications that have no interest in your news.

More, if you understand the objectives of news releases and follow some essential guidelines.

Don Cannon of *Chemical Week* calls releases the "most overused, and in some respects, the least satisfactory communication between publicists and journalists. In fact the flood of releases is so great that editors are dying to find ways to ignore them without running the risk of missing something. There are simply too many poorly conceived, dreadfully dull handouts. We become numb, deaf. We get about 3,000 releases a month and use only a handful." Even publications that have extensive new product and new literature sections can't honor more than 50 to 100, tops. So the communications barriers releases face are awesome.

The word most commonly used when editors are asked whether the releases are seen at a publication is "skimmed." And skimming can be done very quickly. One editor places the daily pile of releases on his desk and a wastebasket between the desk and the credenza behind him. Most end up in the wastebasket; those that make it as far as the credenza are "considered."

How to Win the News Release Game

The news release may indeed be the most overused tactic of a product publicity program, as Don Cannon says. However, it is an essential element of any marketing communications program, and one of the most common ways a newspaper, trade, or consumer editor gets news.

Obviously, news releases that offer news backed up by facts, that are relevant to the publication's readers, and that are well written and properly presented stand the best chance. Don Dreger, an editor at *Machine Design,* says he often finds releases useful for news or even for development into feature articles. He also says that if he knows the company and knows the publicist, releases stand a better chance of consideration. "With someone we've worked with or someone in the company, there's a sort of unconscious increase in attention." Writing is good and bad: "The bad ones tend to use obscure jargon, which may be unique to a company or industry," one editor said. "The language is too flowery," said another. "They need to be more factual."

We can summarize all that good advice about press releases into two simple rules:

- Make it pertinent.
- Make it good (in both style and content).

- *Make it pertinent.*

News releases are used to deliver a simultaneous message to more than one publication that may have an interest in your company, your product, or your service. The number of publications may run from half a dozen to hundreds, but the message must be relevant to all who receive it.

One of the editors' most common criticisms is that publicists send them releases with information that is of no value and has no relation to their audiences. Bill Tortolano, an editor at *Design News,* says that only 40 to 50 of the 2,000 releases received are pertinent to the magazine's audiences.

The target publications that reach your audiences are the only ones that should be receiving your releases. Sending a "broadside" of news releases to media that "might" have an interest, with the hopes of hitting one or two, is a waste of production money and your time. Not to mention the editor's time to scan releases that turn out to be worthless. And if you waste his time you may also have used up some of your good will.

An editor knows at a glance if your news will interest his audience. And so should you. Because you should make it your business to know exactly who his audience is. Are they consumers, retailers, merchandisers, manufacturers, shippers, distributors?

And of course you should know exactly what groups you want to reach with your message. Is the product positioned for high-income singles? High tech? Is it of interest to only special segments of an industrial market? Who in these industries makes the buying decisions?

Knowing the two — your markets and the audiences of the magazines — you can target your releases very specifically.

An item about a new machine part may be of interest to only a few publications covering a specific type of manufacturing industry, and possibly to publications read by industrial designers. A story on a new style trend may be of interest to multiple audiences: the women who may wear garments reflecting it, the mills that might weave the cloth, the retailers and wholesalers who might sell the garments. And they can be reached through multiple media: fashion magazines, retailing and fiber industry trade publications, and newspaper fashion editors.

Specific releases should be angled for each audience. The fashion magazines would be interested in photos of the garments, styling "statements," news trends, and stories about the designer. Retailing trade publications would be interested in the same, plus the price range in which the garments will sell. Fiber industry trade emphasis would be on fiber content, colors, and mills, as well as the fashion statement. Newspaper stories would have a fashion angle and should be localized to include the names of the retailers in each city that will be carrying the garments. Newspapers in your head office city or plant community also are interested in new product news; if it could affect earnings or employment, there is a business story as well.

Here's a story about an attempt at localizing that didn't work. A beauty pageant publicity person had each state winner pose as if she were reading every newspaper in the state, in the hopes that such a gimmick would provide a local angle. That's a lot of newspapers in a state as large as, say, New York. The publicist tried to localize the story in a contrived way, to an extreme, and was not successful.

- *Make it good.*

Don Cannon advises that publicists give publications "hard news, news of significant change, and make its significance apparent. We tend not to get excited about what appears to be just another grade of something, a slightly different formulation, a little better this or that *unless* that little something extra is more significant than would appear at first glance. That first glance, I would add, may be all your press release is likely to get.

"So make sure the press release spells out what's important in an announcement: its context, how it fits in the company's activities and strategies, how it relates to the market, to the competition — and to the world outside the industry, if that is appropriate. If this seems obvious, I have seen hundreds of press releases in which the single most significant fact has been totally obscured by a lot of repetitive, historical, congratulatory stuff."

In summary, editors are pleading for information that:

- Really relates to their audience.
- Answers the questions the audience (and editor) might ask.
- Is accurate, clear, noncommercial, and free of gobbledegook and unnecessary superlatives.

Successful news releases are factual, to the point, and answer the five W's and How.

Who: Who is the authority, who is making the announcement, who supports the claims made? "Who" can be a company or individuals.

What: What is the subject of the news release? "What" needs to be described in a way that the editor won't need to ask for additional information.

Where: Where did this, or will this, take place? If a new product is being introduced at an electronics show in Las Vegas, that's a "where," and where the product is manufactured also is a "where."

When: News is usually immediate. Be specific. Sometimes you can get by with "recently," but it's far better to pinpoint a date. In any case, date the release so the editor has a reference as to when it was sent.

Why: Detail the why's. They can be the most important elements in a release, because they should back up your reason for sending a release in the first place.

How: Details again. How does the subject of the release work? How did the event come about? How is the subject of the release going to fit into the market, and how are you going to get it there?

If the release provides details and attributions, and numbers where appropriate, if it is a total package, it will be much easier for an editor to use. You can't assume that editors are able to read between the lines — or will even bother to try. Many are generalists, and don't have the background. Give them as many facts as

Getting into Print

you can. Provide quotes with attributions. This not only gives the story credibility, it provides a source for any editorial followup.

When to Use the News Release

It's tough to catch attention. As Don Cannon says, hard news sells, image-building doesn't. He considers safety, training, energy conservation, environmental protection, equal opportunity, and management changes as image-building. There is a place for stories like these, but it's in the publications that cover those subjects, not news publications such as *Chemical Week*. For product publicity, these are the most common types of releases.

1. *New Products.* When a new product or service is introduced that is expected to have a major effect in its markets, a news release is generally part of a press kit. (See Chapter 10.) It is the most important piece in a press kit because it factually and succinctly details the new product introduction, and is the one element of a press kit an editor is most likely to refer to or use.

2. *Improved Products, New Markets, New Applications.* A press release can be used to introduce or announce an improved product, or new markets for a given product. Does the product have a new look, a new package design? Is it being shipped in a different manner? What are the benefits to the customer, the user? Is there new technology involved to make it better than before? Have new markets opened up or are they predicted? News that affects a consumer or industrial market gain will get attention from trade publications. A press release can describe the discovery that a product provides new solutions to old problems: the better and more sophisticated mousetrap.

3. *New Distribution.* New distributors, new outlets for both consumer and industrial products can be announced by news releases. The news can be of interest to the industry, but will usually only get a few lines and possibly a small photo. Write these releases tight, short, and very much to the point. A statement by the company's marketing manager on how pleased he is (and of course he is) will be regarded as self-serving. Write no more than one page.

4. *New Literature.* Most trade publications run very short items on new product and technical literature. *Short* is the key word here. No more than a page, with a very brief description of the literature, including how a reader can get it. Many publications use reader service numbers under the items, so be sure to include an address to which publications can send inquiries. Many publications also run photos of the cover of the literature. These should be black and white, tight, vertical 8 × 10 head-on shots. Don't do a fancy layout. No tilting, no open pages, no exotic lighting. Also send a copy of the brochure with the release. The editor may want to keep it for background information.

5. *Awards.* A press release is used to announce that your company or a person in the company has won a prize, an award, any type of honor or recognition. Send

a short release, a bio, and a 5 × 7 head shot of the individual. The subjects can be of varying importance — a local good citizen's award for an employee, or a major award for a scientific accomplishment.

6. *Special Events.* If you are planning a special event around a trade show, such as a musical presentation or laser show, a release to the appropriate media might be considered. But if you plan a "by invitation only" event, don't publicize it, or you will get freeloaders and bruise some egos. A follow release on the event is appropriate, however. Get the story — the number, mix, important people such as industry leaders and top executives, cover the five W's and How, along with some good photos — and it's a natural for the trade publications covering the show or the trade dailies.

7. *Speeches.* Important speeches by important executives are often used. An example might be one given at an annual convention or industry meeting. If it is delivered in the evening, a copy of the speech should be given to daily media that morning or the afternoon before, so that the story can be prepared and ready for the next morning's editions (assuming it's important enough to cover). You can help media a great deal by providing a short release, two to three pages, outlining the important points made in the speech. In speeches, unlike releases, the most important point is often near the end of the presentation for dramatic effect. A release based on the speech does not follow its format, but puts the most important point first, in the lead paragraph.

Speeches that comment with wisdom on subjects of some controversy, clarify how events are affecting the health and economy of a particular industry, or offer some predictions for the future, may also be used as subjects for editorials in business-to-business publications. Editorial coverage of a speech may reflect favorably on a company and help position it as a leader in its field.

8. *Special Interest.* Releases often describe the use of a product in an inherently interesting situation:

> There has been an increase of 20 percent in the number of women baking bread since Fleischmann's introduced a yeast that was 50 percent faster acting that its previous one.

> The longest bridge in the world rests on bearing pads made of Teflon fluorocarbon.

> The Monsanto Company has introduced a new herbicide for cotton growers that takes less than a teaspoon an acre to be effective.

How to Write the News Release

The way the release is presented can help get it attention and make it easier for the editor to scan if it looks interesting at first glance.

Getting into Print

A news release has a headline, a lead paragraph, and body copy. It must be double spaced, and it must be dated so that editors can tell whether it is current "news." See Chapter 7 for details on these elements, and Figure 6-1 for a sample.

The release is written in an *inverted pyramid* style, because editors normally cut from the bottom (see Figure 6-2). Consider how much most people read of a newspaper story—often just the first two or three paragraphs. That's why the first one or two paragraphs should contain the important points. If the editor has to cut, the main message will still be there. Once the key point and important

Figure 6-1. Sample news release.

UMBRELLA DESIGN OF DU PONT "ZYTEL"
STRONGER, TOUGHER, MORE DURABLE

A new design using Du Pont "Zytel" 70G43L nylon resin produces a stronger, tougher, and more durable umbrella frame.

When the Nihon Umbrella Company Ltd. of Japan tested the nylon ribs it was considering as replacements for the steel ribs in its colorful "Moonac" umbrella, it bent the unfolded end ribs nearly 30 degrees until they were parallel with the umbrella handle. It took 1.2 to 1.3 kilograms (2.65 to 2.87 pounds) of force to make the bend. That came as a bit of a surprise to the testers, because steel ribs bent with only 1 kilogram (2.2 pounds) of force.

The ribs also quickly recovered their original shape thanks to Du Pont "Zytel" nylon resin, reinforced with 43 percent (by weight) glass fibers.

While the three segments of a nylon rib must be riveted together in much the same fashion as steel ribs, there are only three assembly steps following its emergence from the molding machine, compared with approximately 35 processing steps for a steel rib, including shaping, bending, and plating or painting.

Light weight and molded-in color are two additional benefits provided by the glass-reinforced nylon resin. Available in blue, green, yellow, red, and black, the rust-free ribs can be used to coordinate or contrast with many different fabrics. Integrally molded attachment points allow umbrella cloth to be sewn directly to the rib, eliminating the conventional metal rib caps that have an annoying way of pulling free and rendering an umbrella ineffectual.

Figure 6-2. Inverted pyramid.

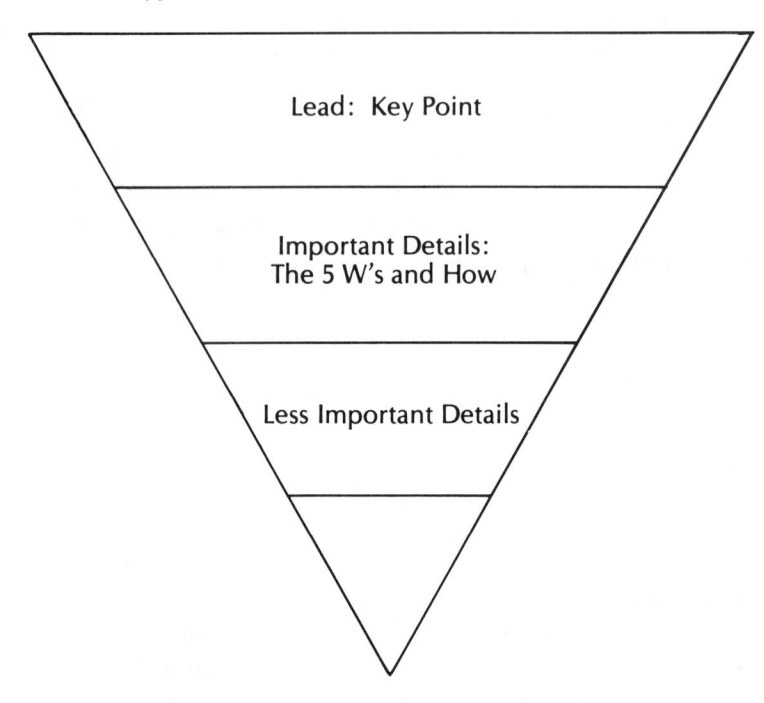

```
Lead: Key Point

Important Details:
The 5 W's and How

Less Important Details
```

details have been covered, the rest can be deleted, if necessary, without losing the meaning or failing to deliver the primary news.

Some release letterheads virtually shout at the reader, with a multi-colored banner and the words "NEWS RELEASE" written in such large and bold letters as to suggest that all editors are myopic and can't figure out that the latest unsolicited missive from a company is a news release.

The design, style, and format of the letterhead can be modest. It is not sales literature, the medium is not the message. A fancy one is not what is going to convince an editor to use the information written on it. Certainly the company color, company logo, and the simple statement "News from XYZ Company" in tasteful type are appropriate. When the Carl Byoir Agency was in existence, it used to send releases on plain paper, and editors recognized the name and read the agency's releases just as they did the others they received. The agency did, however, use a client letterhead when requested. The only time agency letterhead should be used is when a company is not well-known, has not had an active publicity program, and the agency enjoys a good reputation among media. Then it is appropriate at the beginning of the program, at least, for the agency to use its letterhead.

It should have a return address; the editor must know the source of the release and the name of the person who sent it.

Provide a contact—"John Smith/302-000-000"—so the editor reviewing the release can call for additional information. News material provided by an agency should carry two names as editorial contacts: the first is the company person; the second the agency account representative. If it is released to a daily publication, home phone numbers should be added, in case an editor working late in the evening needs more information.

Date the release, either at the top, or at the bottom of the last page. There rarely is a need to put an opening dateline on the release, unless it's used in conjunction with a major announcement and the city of origin and the date are essential. Earnings statements, corporate shifts, and other corporate-related news usually carry datelines, but this is not product publicity. But if one is needed (for example, in connection with a trade show event or press conference), it should be written properly; see the Associated Press style manual and also Chapter 7 in this book.

Contrary to many publicists and agency people, I do not believe it is necessary to use "For Immediate Release." There's a very good chance that if an editor decides to use the story, it will be in the next issue. Editors also agree that "immediate release" has no effect on their decision to use or not to use. If publicists believe that it will somehow make the editor think it's news that can't be ignored, they're wrong.

"Hold for release (date)" won't have much effect either, although one editor said if a company had a good reason to ask that a release be held for a particular date, he would consider observing the "embargo." I know this editor personally and if he asked to see some material in advance of a press conference, for example, I know he would observe a release date. But I recommend against asking just any editor to do this. I know others who will not observe release dates. I tend to agree with them. If they have a release in their hands, and they deem it newsworthy, they should not have to wait to print it. So treat everyone equally—except for *Women's Wear Daily* and other Fairchild publications, which will not print *anything* from a press event unless it is delivered the day before.

Rarely are releases filed away for another day, but it has happened. I have seen releases appear in trade publications six months to a year after they were sent. Either the mail was slow, or the editor saved the story until there was a hole in the layout that needed filling, or the information in the release related to a story that was under consideration. Some releases are collected if an editor is following a trend and may at some point decide to write a story. But this is rare.

Timing

Timing involves two factors: 1) moving news at the proper moment so that it is timely (seasonal items, for instance), and 2) getting the material to the media so that they can get it out in time.

It may seem elementary, but if you send a news release about a garden product in March, it's too late. Publicity must reach gardeners through the garden columns about the same time the seed catalogs arrive and the gardeners start to think about spring planting—late January. That's the seasonal aspect. To accomplish this target date, your story must be written and submitted to the trades in late fall to give them enough lead time to pull their publications together. The newspapers would need your story in January or early February. Don't send the story to the papers at the same time you send it to the garden publications and trades. Two or three weeks' advance is all that's needed for a newspaper column.

Timing is important even for routine stories. For example, a release announcing participation in a trade show should still arrive at the publication at least three months before the show date.

Fashion, agriculture, travel, trade shows, exhibitions, sports, plus many other areas of activity, are seasonal. The best time to promote tennis apparel to consumers is not in the fall, when many tennis players have put their racquets away, but in the spring when they're thinking it's almost time to play tennis. Aim to get publicity into professional agricultural publications to reach farmers right after they've reaped their crops. The other prime time would be during the late fall or winter when they're reviewing their successes and failures and deciding what crops to plant next spring and what equipment and chemicals they'll need.

Hitting the wrong audience at the wrong time is watching the boat sail off from the pier. Timing is critical in most areas of publicity.

Mailing

It is not necessary to send news releases to a particular editor by name. Personnel turnover in media is frequent, and in any case there is always someone on the editorial staff who opens the day's releases. You can simply address everything to "The Editor," or to specific department editors, such as fashion, women's interest, business, gardening. All releases will be evaluated for "news," and those of particular interest will be passed along.

A Word of Caution

Don't pay for editorial coverage. If you haven't already, you will at some time get a letter from a publication indicating that your release has been found "acceptable for publication" and requesting payment ($75 is the average rate in 1987) for reproducing the illustration, setting up the release, processing reader response

Tips for Success

Here's some advice on releases:

1. Follow the 5 W's and How.
2. Stick to the facts—no gobbledegook or self-serving statements.
3. Use the inverted pyramid structure.
4. Send your release only to those media that reach your markets.
5. Make it timely:

   - Give your release time to clear.
   - Make sure it will come out at the right time of year or season.
   - Get it to the editor in time for him to use it.

6. Write like a journalist, not an ad copywriter.
7. Don't call and ask if the editor received or will be using it.
8. Send eye-catching, interesting photos to help ensure that the release will be used.

---

cards, and so on. Your material should be evaluated on its news value and its interest to readers. The final judgment on use should always be based on editorial merit, not ability to pay. I question the value of any publication that uses only paid-for editorial material. When I want to advertise, I will select publications that do not earn money by selling editorial, because they can't be very good if they do.

Summing Up

Think through a release—why it's needed, where it fits, and what kind of information it can convey. There are a number of ways to do a release, and a number of practices to avoid. "Market" to the media for results.

The Feature Story

News releases may be a way to get news to target audiences through media, but they are often edited or cut. And there is good chance they won't be used at all. Successful placement of an exclusive or feature story can often mean far more to your publicity program than a couple of paragraphs in the new-product or literature-offering section.

Features are what carry a publication. Although some trade editors would disagree, I believe features are the best read part of the magazine. Those editors who think otherwise feel that their readers turn first to the new products section. (In fact, some have even moved the new products section from the back of the publication to the front to make it easier for readers to find.)

Features give a publication its own character, position it in the marketplace, and set it apart from its competitors.

The advantage to the publicist is that a feature provides the opportunity to present a detailed exposition on a given subject—but the discussion must be complete, objective, and free of commercial puffery and self-serving statements. Features that an editor requests of the publicist or agency, even if the idea was proposed by the publicist, may be subject to rewrite. But if they hold reader interest, are highly believable, and not full of commercials, features are seldom trimmed and, best of all, get high readership. Without good features, month after month, most publications will perish.

Features Fundamentals

Features that result from an action taken by a publicist are *exclusive:* They are proposed, discussed, and, if all goes well, placed with only one publication, no more. And they often discuss one product or service exclusively. But don't forget: a good feature is presented in a way that does not smack of commercialism—just well-backgrounded facts, authoritative statements, figures, and validation by experts. A story also should be well illustrated, either with clear photos that support it, or drawings, charts, or graphs that do the same. Excellent photography can make a good story better—and may even turn it into a cover story.

The publicist must understand the needs of her markets, and the publications and other news outlets that serve them, before attempting to market an idea or a story.

Before any feature is discussed with an editor, you should evaluate the publications that reach the market, rating the most important, the second most, and so on. The objective is to deliver the message to the target audience in the medium that reaches it best.

You must develop the story idea based on the format and needs of the *best* publication. If you can't work something out with the first publication, go on to your number two.

Good relations are important in working with editors on exclusives and features (see Chapter 5). If you don't know who to contact, call the managing editor.

Fortunately, a number of publications use features submitted by publicity people, and most of the others are receptive to feature suggestions. Those that use material written by publicists or agencies are primarily business-to-business, technical, or special-interest publications. This is in part because there are often fewer staff editors to write all the stories. Some editors will be receptive to feature suggestions and work with a publicity person, but may assign a freelance writer to do the story. Editors of staff-written publications are receptive to ideas from publicists.

There are many ways features are developed, but the key to success with these media is knowing the markets and being able to target the feature to the right publication. No two publications are exactly alike. There may be some similarities when publications are competing for the same audiences, but each is seeking to position itself in the markets it serves.

Consumer editors are receptive to ideas for features, but story ideas should be discussed with the departmental editors or columnists (rather than the chief or managing editor); they are constantly looking for ideas or feature material in the market or consumer segment they cover. These include the "standing" columns in many publications such as interior design, beauty, fashion, travel, and cooking magazines. They also include the newspaper editors who select the products to be featured in the special home sections, such as the Thursday *New York Times*.

One consumer magazine publisher told me that his editors are the source for "99 percent of the news in the magazines." I do not question this, but suggest that these editors also are being fed story ideas and leads from publicity people. Often working editors may not act on a story idea right after it's discussed, even if they see merit in it. It may be filed away to be developed later, or used as background for another story such as a roundup or trend piece.

Bull's-Eye Targeting

As we said, similar media compete with one another for the same readers. The most apparent ones are in the women's markets. The high-fashion segment is one obvious area; the "homemaker" segment another—*McCall's* and *Ladies Home Journal* have been battling for several decades. Even here, the editorial emphasis is shifting because of the growing number of women who are working and bringing home a second income, or are independent. It pays to keep up on how the publications are structured and how they see themselves. The cliché "You can't judge a book by the cover" applies to the fashion publications in particular, where the covers are very similar.

The name of the publication may be misleading, too. For example, in the business-to-business area, two "design" publications use feature material suggested by or developed with publicists. *Machine Design* focuses on the technical aspects of design and thus uses technical articles, either staff-written or contributed. It has 17 editors working with corporations and research institutes such as Battelle on stories of interest to design engineers in industry. Don Dreger, an editor at *Machine Design*, deplores the fact that there are not enough people in product publicity who have sufficient technical background to work with him and the other editors in developing stories tailored to his readers. There may never be enough technically oriented publicists to meet the needs of this publication. For *Machine Design,* a publicist must be sufficiently conversant with the technology behind a development to relate it to the magazine's specialized audience. *Design News* also covers the technical side of design but is more open in format. It has a staff of artists and illustrators who create exciting and often striking layouts and colorful illustrations. Its editors also expect that publicists know the business, but they need not be as technically oriented. Thus, two publications with the same name in the title may have different audiences and different editorial needs.

The point is that every publication is seeking to identify with its own audience, or relate better to its audience than its competition. Some of those publications that reach essentially the same audiences manage to co-exist — *McCall's* and *Ladies Home Journal, Vogue* and *Harper's Bazaar. Cosmopolitan,* in contrast, has created its own niche and audience. *Outdoor Life, Field & Stream,* and *Sports Afield* have had a loyal following of outdoor enthusiasts for many, many years. *Sports Illustrated* has little competition, even among other sports-oriented publications. Even the rash of computer and high-tech publications — many of which have failed — try to segment their audiences and often bump heads with each other when doing so.

The major business publications — *Business Week, Forbes, Fortune* — are very tough to crack. But if your target audience is upper middle and top management, these are the publications that reach them. Product publicity has a fit in business publications, although this is not their primary focus. But as James Warrilow, publisher of Canada's highly respected *Financial Post,* says, "We pride ourselves on an extensive library system at the *Post.* When doing a corporate profile we would use this information as background for our questions." When asked if he would run a story on a new advanced typewriter, he answered, "Probably not." However, he said editors would consider it if the publication were compiling a special report on the office. "As a weekly, we like to develop our own stories and not repeat what the readers already know from their daily newspapers." His publication is receptive to new ideas and "relies heavily on long-term relationships with companies to best understand their industries."

Financial and business publications are receptive to story ideas, but you have to understand the rules and how they structure their coverage. A *Business Week* editor told me that he far preferred to deal with company publicity people than with agencies. He felt they had a much better understanding of the needs of his publication and could get him in touch with the right people far faster.

The message is clear. Before approaching any business publication, be well prepared: understand the needs of the audiences of each. Each area is different in each publication.

Different Types of Features

The Case Histories

The case history story is the example most cited when a purely tactical publicity program is discussed, as in "Send a release and do a case history."

In its simplest form, a case history consists of a noncompany expert, frequently a customer, relating her successful experience with your product or service. Or it may be a report on a study by a scientist, or a semitechnical article, again with an expert relating his success with a product or service.

Not every publication uses the case history, and even those that do ask tough questions:

1. Does the story offer something to the reader? If it's an unusual use of the product, it may get a short mention in a news column, but it's not case history material. If it can't help the readers, it's not likely to be run.
2. Does it relate a problem and offer a solution? Again, this must apply to the majority of the publication's readers, not just a few.
3. Does it show and back up benefits such as cost reduction, manpower reduction, energy savings, higher productivity, higher quality — those benefits just about every company is seeking?
4. Is it straightforward and noncommercial? Has the writer stepped away from the subject and placed himself in the position of the editor?
5. Is it timely? Or is there another product in the market that does the job better than yours? Don't try to fool an editor by recasting or rehashing old material, no matter who your spokesperson is.

You are not expected to discuss competitive products in your own story, but be aware that the editor may include your competition in the story. If you are asked to comment on the competing product or the company that makes it, you should decline. Stress the major advantages of your product. If comparisons are necessary, do not mention the competition by name. It's bad manners, it's unprofessional, and it might get folks taking sides on the pages of a magazine. If the competition is strong, the best approach may be a story that positions your product in relation to the competition, and shows where it functions best in a given market area.

The Roundups

Roundup stories, most often written by a publication, show the activities of a number of companies and products in a given market area. They may take the form of an annual review of developments—the special issues. The annual trade show issue is also a roundup. A well-known example is *Sports Illustrated*'s annual bathing suit issue. It's annual, and a "roundup" of trends in swimwear. It's also a publicity person's delight to have one of a client's bathing suits pictured.

Most publications print editorial calendars that outline the upcoming special issues, explaining the general emphasis on the stories and features planned, and the special areas or industries to be covered. These are made up a year in advance, but other roundups may be done that are not in the media calendar. (These calendars are available from space reps or the publication.)

Bacon's Media Alerts, from the same firm that publishes the much-used *Publicity Checkers,* is updated every three months as changes in emphasis or new information become available. This publication is helpful in advance planning so that editors can be contacted with enough lead time—at least three months—to have your company included if any stories are being planned that relate to your products.

Many publications have a theme or a business area they feature nearly every month. Everything from high fashion to spring planting is covered in roundup stories and special issues. Several agencies also track special issues so that they have advance notice on possible feature development for the clients. Rumrill-Hoyt has a highly sophisticated computer program that helps the agency plan and time editorial material and advertising for a total marketing communications effort.

There is another type of roundup story that can be developed. If your company is a multiproduct organization serving a given industry, it may be possible to develop a story showing the overall contribution your company is making and the influence it has. If the story has a solid base and offers something new, not just puffery and a laundry list of products, it may be acceptable.

Then there are the roundups that are not planned; an editor may identify something taking place in the market and call a few of his publicity contacts. If it looks as if there is some movement in the market—a switch away from one type of product to another, new equipment, a fashion fad sweeping the country—he'll develop a feature. And he'll round up a number of opinions, quotes, and data from his contacts in writing the story. These are often called trend features.

Trend Features

This particular type of story can be found in virtually every media area. It may be about one product that is setting a trend, such as a fashion item or a toy, or about a group of products that are indicative of a trend. The trend story is closely related to the roundup; in fact it is sometimes hard to tell them apart. A feature may be a combination of both. The differences are subtle.

Trend stories may be developed with no consideration for the calendar. The sharp publicist or agency may be in a position to identify a trend taking shape that is related to a product or service and convince an editor to cover it. Trends develop as an industry moves from using one product to another, as the economy changes, as environmental regulations are enforced, as hemlines go higher or lower. They can be subtle and have little direct effect on the public, as with a change under the hood of an automobile, or more profound, when a particular social group starts buying a particular brand of automobile.

"Trendy" pieces often reflect the upwardly mobile generation, whatever they may be called at a given time. Close tracking of the market can help identify trends that can be turned into features and exclusives.

Application Features

Application stories show how one or several products are used in one or more industries. Again, relate the application to the reader of the publication, just as the editor will. Can the information in the story be used by readers of the publication? If not, there is no story. If it's a new application of a product, the publicist may decide to develop it with one publication rather than announce it to several through a news release. Because an exclusive often gets more space than a release, using this type of exclusive feature when appropriate is worth considering.

Technical Articles

Technical or semitechnical articles are developed as exclusives. Technical articles are often written by research scientists for presentation to a professional society. The society publication then has exclusive rights to the "paper." How well-read these publications are or whether the information is of any value beyond the scientific community is debatable in most cases. But it is worthwhile to review them to see if they can be rewritten for a broader market audience. Where this is possible, and where a rewrite will be understood by a more general audience, there may be opportunities to place it in an industry publication. But first consider whether the rewrite and possible publication will help market the product or establish the company as an authority on the subject. If in doubt, don't waste the time.

Chemical Engineering, a McGraw-Hill publication for chemical engineers and related technical people in the chemical processing industries, published a guide some years ago, titled "How to Write for Chemical Engineering." The advice on what the reader wants could apply to any number of publications: "Practical information. The individual (reader) wants concise information that aids in solving real problems. Such a person does not look to this publication for abstract theoretical treatises, vague general discussions or reviews of previously published material, or papers that promote only one of several options."

The guide lists several criteria for articles. They should:

- Appeal to at least one third of its readers.
- Impart useful, *impartial* information.
- Be timely or interpretive rather than just a rehash.
- Help someone become more conversant with the subject, rather than being written for another expert.
- Help readers make decisions in technical administration or policy formulation, and enable readers to accomplish their professional development.

These guidelines are a strong statement of a publication that has its readers very much in mind. The publication stresses that whoever develops the story angle and approach for a given target publication should know that publication's needs as well as *Chemical Engineering* expects its contributors to know the needs of its readers. My colleagues who work in the chemical processing field tell me that it is very difficult to place stories in *Chemical Engineering,* but that when stories have been developed, the payoff for marketing—interest and inquiries—has been excellent.

Roundtables

Roundtables are used to develop exclusives. For a roundtable, experts on a given subject—technical, research and development, marketing, management—are brought together with an editor who has shown interest in developing an exclusive that he agrees is important to his readers. Just *one* editor—this is an exclusive. The experts are not necessarily all from the company; outside authorities may help validate some of the points made by company people.

A roundtable discussion lets the editor question the panel in depth. The publicist has briefed the experts on the story line, and has tried to anticipate questions as much as possible. Areas that shouldn't be discussed or are proprietary are made clear in advance to both the editor and the participants.

The Backgrounders

This has been left until last because a backgrounder is not a feature in the sense that it is sent exclusively to one publication. Nor is it a news release: Most of the information in it is not news, just detailed information. Its description fits better here because a backgrounder can run several pages, while a release is usually only two or three pages. Also, editors have occasionally run backgrounders as feature stories. It doesn't happen very often, but it has happened to me and many of my associates.

A backgrounder can help sell a product for a feature. It is also used in press kits, to accompany a letter introducing yourself to an editor, or as a leave-behind

Getting into Print

after an editorial visit. A backgrounder can run as long as a dozen pages or be as short as one page. The length is dictated by the depth and amount of information it contains.

It should be tailored to the particular market the product serves and discuss applications and uses of the product in that market. It should be a very detailed history of the product and should highlight its scientific and technical development, where applicable. If appropriate, technical data should be included.

It should not be a rehash of sales literature, but a piece that is editorially acceptable to a publication as is — no commercial emphasis, no hard sell, no gobbledegook, no puffery. Backgrounders are a capsule history and explanatory dissertation on a product or service, tailored to a market segment. They should be high on the list of needs when any publicity program is undertaken.

Here's a suggested format. Open with a brief statement summarizing the product benefits.

Follow with information on when it was invented or developed, what markets it serves, then detail its properties — strength, weight, taste, heat resistance, health benefits, shelf life, feel — as they apply to each market.

If markets are limited, detail where it was tested or tried, results of the tests, and where it is expected to be used. Detail each and, if possible, outline its advantages over in-kind generic competition.

Add a brief section on the product's history, and on the people responsible for its development.

Along with the backgrounder, provide a selection of excellent photos of the product in use. These can be reproduced right on the backgrounder itself, if they can support the text. In any case, offer prints in a note to the editor at the bottom of the last page.

A sample backgrounder appears in Figure 6-3. Note that it contains many of the elements I have described here. The first line of the backgrounder specifically targets its market — original equipment engineers and manufacturers. The next few paragraphs provide a general view of what Du Pont has to offer its targeted audience and a brief history and description of its facilities for product development. Finally, the backgrounder concisely relates the characteristics of each category of products, pointing out what advantages each has to offer.

Placing the Story

Situation: A sales representative calls you and suggests a story be developed with one of his customers. It is a combination case history and application, and may indicate a trend beginning to take shape in the marketplace.

You get the data, develop a story angle, and call the customer. You discuss your approach, she agrees to cooperate by providing the information and allowing photography, and then you must make a decision.

Figure 6-3. A sample backgrounder.

DU PONT: A MAJOR RESOURCE
TO THE OEM DESIGN ENGINEER

Original equipment manufacturers and their vendors often turn to the Du Pont Company for a wide range of materials and parts to help engineer and design functional, marketable products at competitive costs. These materials and parts include engineering polymers, engineered parts, industrial polymers, high-performance films, and specialty materials. To help industry take full advantage of the value-engineering potential of Du Pont materials and parts, the company annually commits millions of dollars to provide comprehensive technical and customer service from initial design through full-scale production.

Du Pont's direct link to the OEM is its staff of more than 100 sales engineers assigned to OEM products and market segments. This technically trained sales force works closely with OEM engineers and design teams, consulting on design, materials, and production alternatives that can lead to higher quality, lower cost end products.

Du Pont's customer-oriented, market-driven effort in technical service and application development has its roots in 19th century America but began to take its present form in 1954 with the opening of the company's 100-acre Chestnut Run Technical Service Laboratory near Wilmington, Del. Now employing some 2,000 people, Chestnut Run is one of several Du Pont laboratories dedicated entirely to customer service and assistance. The company's new Automotive Development Center in Detroit brings technical and marketing resources to the front door of the automotive industry. A development center for the electronics industry opened in the Research Triangle, N.C., area in February 1986. Moreover, the company's commitment to OEM markets is global in scope, with major technical service facilities located throughout Europe and Japan.

These facilities are equipped for a wide range of tasks related to product engineering and design. A full range of test capabilities — mechanical, electrical, chemical, weathering — is available, including microstructural failure analysis, an advanced method borrowed from pathology. To assist customers in designing parts and tooling, the latest technologically advanced, computer-aided engineering methods are used. Computers also are used to estimate costs of alternative designs and manufacturing methods.

Major products for OEM market

Du Pont products with particularly wide applications and potential among OEMs fall into these broad categories:

— Engineering polymers
— Engineered parts
— Industrial polymers
— High performance films
— Elastomeric drive tape and seat-support fabric

Engineering polymers. Du Pont engineering polymers are a wide-ranging family of high-performance thermoplastic materials running the gamut from tough, rubber-like elastomers to strong, rigid structural plastics. The members of this engineering polymer family are: "Bexloy" automotive engineering resins, "Delrin" acetal resins, "Minlon" engineering thermoplastic resins, "Rynite" thermoplastic polyester resins, "Zytel" nylon resins, "Hytrel" polyester elastomers, and "Alcryn" melt-processible rubbers.

Engineered parts. Du Pont engineered parts are custom-fabricated, high-value parts offering ultra-high performance in plastic, metal, rubber, and composites. Products in this category include "Vespel" polyimide parts and "Kalrez" perfluoroelastomer parts.

Industrial polymers. Du Pont industrial polymers are a broad family of high-performance materials ranging from durable, high value-in-use, lightweight plastics to tougher, stiffer, more temperature-resistant materials. "Surlyn" ionomer resins offer versatility in processing for endless possibilities in part design. "Surlyn" HP high-performance ionomer resins combine toughness, stiffness, and cost efficiency for quality features that outperform ABS and polycarbonate.

High-performance films. Electrical insulation, flexible circuit substrates, release film for composite part production, and molded and shaped parts are just some of the applications design engineers have found for Du Pont "Kapton" polyimide film and "Teflon" FEP and PFA fluorocarbon films. These high-performance films are used primarily where extreme temperature resistance, chemical resistance, dielectric characteristics, and other high performance properties are needed.

Special products fill special needs. "Dymetrol" elastomeric mechanical drive tape provides a flexible, durable way to design for movement. For seating support systems in the automotive and furniture design areas, "Dymetrol" fabric offers a slim, lightweight alternative to spring supports.

Do you ask the editor if there is interest in the story before you write it, or do you go ahead and write it and then try to find an editor who may be interested?

Both approaches work. If you have a solid story, the chances are good it will be used. (Yet another possibility is that the editor assigns a staff writer to cover it.)

What the Editor Needs

Every time editors consider a suggested feature, they think: Will it be well read by the subscribers, and will it enhance the reputation of the magazine for delivering to its readers the information they need or find useful? A rule of thumb for trade publications might be: Does the story appeal to at least 60 percent of its readers? For consumer publications, it should be more than 80 percent.

Publicists must use the same guidelines when developing the ideas, preparing the proposal, and marketing it to the editor. This applies to an idea about a new hair styling trend for a high-fashion publication, or a story on how a newly designed steam trap helped a small manufacturing company reduce energy costs. Whatever the subject, it must relate to the people who buy the publication. Unless it does, don't bother an editor.

How to Make the Approach

The rule for suggesting features to media is: *Always* write a brief note outlining your idea, with an emphasis on how it relates to the publication's readers. Every single editor I interviewed when preparing this book preferred a brief note outlining the idea. Many will discuss a feature idea over the phone with a publicist whose judgment they trust, but still like to see a brief outline. With all the calls they receive every day, it is far easier to remember a phone conversation if it is followed up by a note reviewing the call. A note often will provide additional information (include a backgrounder).

Frequently, an editor will want to discuss the idea with colleagues or superiors; a written outline makes this far easier. Many trade publications have small staffs, and the written suggestion may be discussed with only one or two other people. But writing the idea down and presenting it this way makes the publicist think it through, and gives the editor a written summary from which to make a judgment.

There is no hard and fast rule on whether you should call before you send the outline or write first and *then* call. I've done both. For those people who don't have much experience dealing with editors, I suggest a written outline, followed no more than two weeks later by a phone call in which you ask for a response. I always call first to try to arrange for a quick reading for my suggestion. But I also have better luck in getting an answer if I already know the editor. Either way, there will be phone contact between publicist and editor at some point, and the written document will be useful no matter how the approach is made.

You must be thoroughly prepared before you make the first phone call or write the first note. You, or your agency, must research the story as if you were the editor or writer. Don't call with just a germ of an idea and expect the editor to find a fit and come up with some way it can be developed.

Find an angle. Start with how your product affects other businesses positively, how it offers a value that can be communicated as a feature, how it made a difference to the economy or a segment of the economy, how it has solved a problem, or how it may be seen as a "breakthrough" product—its position in a market area from a national point of view. If the product will not be of interest in New York, Dallas, Minneapolis, and San Francisco, it is not a candidate for coverage in a national magazine. "Interest" can mean current interest or future interest. If the latter, you must convince the publication that it will have an effect on the readers in some way. If that particular editor doesn't agree, your alternative is to look into other publications. If it's a good story, you should be able to find a home for it.

Don't try to sell the same story to more than one publication as an "exclusive." If you succeed with more than one, you do *not* have an embarrassment of riches, you have big problems, because you have misrepresented the story as an exclusive. Editors seek exclusives and are delighted when someone comes up with an idea for a good one. But they don't want another publication to have it.

When the Story Is Already Written

If you have done a good job of selling, and the outline describes a story that seems likely to fit readers' needs, an editor will ask to see it.

Write a cover note, referring to the phone call and recapping your pitch, and send the story and photos. Ask for consideration and note that you will call for an opinion in a week to ten days. Don't time the story to arrive the week before he is closing the publication. He has enough to do.

Be sure to call when you said you would.

If the editor is still indefinite, or has not read the story, make a brief pitch for it again, and ask when he might make a decision. If you can determine this, call back then. Just like the sales representative in his territory, you are going for "the close."

There are few *good* stories that can't be placed, provided the readers' and the editor's interests are uppermost in mind when the story is researched and written.

What do you do if the editor keeps putting you off? It is unethical to try to market the story to another publication while the first one is considering it, but it is proper to call the editor if after a few weeks he hasn't made a decision. Tell him you need to know because, frankly, both the customer and your clients (the marketing department) are asking questions. The editor should understand this. It is also proper, if the editor can't make up his mind, to pull the story and try to place it elsewhere.

If the editor assures you he will run it and if you know him and can trust his judgment, wait. Especially if it is the leading publication in your marketing area. I once waited 16 months for a story to run, all the while fending off negative remarks from my boss and clients. But the wait was well worth it. Other associates have waited longer. (You normally should not have to wait *that long*.) The decision is yours. One way to perhaps move up the publication date is to provide new information and make the story more timely.

When the Story Is Not Yet Written

Another approach is to sell the story before it is even written. There is no absolute guarantee it will run, but if the idea and outline get high interest before it is written, it can be developed to reflect the style of the magazine and the angle agreed upon by the publicist and editor.

If the editor has confidence in you and respects your judgment, he may spend some time discussing the story with you to get the right angle and the proper approach. At this point, you don't want to report to your clients that the publication *will* run a story, but you can report that it will be considered seriously and ask their cooperation in getting it approved to meet the deadline.

And meet the deadline you must. There are no excuses. You can change an ad insertion order, but you cannot miss an editorial deadline. If you do, the editor will lose confidence in your judgment and will not work with you in the future. Your releases may be dropped in the trash.

What Are Your Chances?

It is becoming increasingly difficult to place case history stories. Not all publications use them, so before you suggest one, read through the feature stories in those that reach your markets to see how they are structured. Do they focus on one "expert" or include the comments of a number of them?

Also be sure you know the publications' policies on accepting articles written by publicists. Many of the larger publications, both trade and consumer, use only staff-written material. Others, primarily trade publications with small staffs, assign articles to well-established freelancers and accept contributed exclusives from publicity people.

With just one exception, I know of no editor on any publication who will not at least *consider* story ideas from a publicist. It can't be overemphasized, however, that you must know the publications thoroughly to be able to make the proper approach. If you know the editors and have built up a professional relationship, your query may get a more sympathetic ear, and the editor may take some time to help you develop the story if he likes the idea. Note the qualifier: "may."

It is not *essential* you know the editors. Everyone in publicity begins by getting acquainted. If it's a solid story possibility, you may be assured it will get consideration; it just may take a little more time to get your foot in the door, and the editor may be somewhat skeptical about dealing with you.

The toughest features to place are with the major daily newspapers, wire services, leading consumer magazines, Sunday supplements, major women's and fashion magazines. Don't bother to call the dailies or the wire services unless you have a solid story idea, or can relate it to a strong trend or a current news development. These editors are deluged with story ideas daily.

If the story angle or approach captures the editor's imagination, you may have a chance. There is no time to send an outline if your idea is related to breaking news. But a note outlining a feature idea is important in most other circumstances. If you believe there is a germ of a story that has possibilities, it may be enough to interest an editor. Editors have a lot of news columns to fill, and may just welcome your call. But think it through carefully before calling.

The special-interest publications are not as difficult to approach as the news or business publications. There are a multitude of them, covering just about every interest area—from model railroading to gardening and wooden boat building. It's worth a check of media lists to see if there is a fit for your product.

Business publications are difficult, the news weeklies even more so. The key word for both is "news." The criteria include trendiness, timeliness, and the ability to move quickly on the story once the decision is made. Be sure you have a strong story angle, have all the facts assembled, and have your experts well primed. Be prepared to answer questions about the competition, negative aspects of the product (if any), effect on earnings, and social or environmental implications. Assume that the reporter covering the story will be calling other sources for comment, including the competition if you share the market with other products. This should be understood by everyone in your company before a story is proposed, even for an industrial or trade magazine. What started out in your mind as an exclusive on your company could turn into a roundup article involving others, even though your product may be the principal subject of the article.

If there is local or regional interest for any one of the many city, state, and regional publications, there may be more opportunity for placement. The editors are no less sophisticated than those working on national business publications, so the same news and interest criteria prevail. These media include business, state, and city publications. Most are staff-written, although some local business publications accept contributed bylined articles. There also may be opportunities in the business-to-business media covering your markets.

Writing the Story

Developing the Ideas

Good features start with good ideas, and for that you need good leads from reliable and dependable sources. Your first source should be the salespeople. They are in daily contact with customers and should have a good handle on where and how the products are being used and by whom. But don't expect that the sales staff will understand the value of publicity or necessarily go out of their way to help you. They may need some briefing on what publicity really is and what benefits it can provide, including great customer relations.

If you do get case-history story ideas that are not good enough to merit editorial attention, print them up anyway and distribute them to the sales force as a selling tool. The customers will be flattered, even if you couldn't find a home for them.

Marketing people often can suggest story leads. "Marketing" is used here to mean those people who are not supervising or direct selling, but monitoring and planning marketing programs—the strategic side of sales, as opposed to the tactical sales force.

Sales reports are another source. Check call reports or periodical reports from sales managers. Read the summaries of marketing meetings. Better yet, attend them if you can. You may learn something, and you may have something to contribute.

If your company has a technical service or research group that calls upon customers when they have problems, check them. Problem solving is an excellent basis for the problem/solution story approach. You can learn a lot about your product's performance in the marketplace, even on a supermarket shelf, by getting to know the people who troubleshoot or solve problems.

Then there's the sales pro who's been around the company since the day the accountants sat on high stools and used real ink instead of ballpoint pens and computers. A few minutes spent with him, just letting him reminisce about the "old days," can often turn up some good story leads. If you learn about a company that has been using your product for a number of years and has been profitable and successful with it, that is a story possibility.

Whatever you do, be sure your sources understand you can't *promise* a story in their favorite publication. The best you can do is consider it seriously.

Before you set out, consider where you would like to see the story appear. If the story looks good, go for the top publication in the market. Failing this, go to number two, and so on.

Getting the Interview

There are two ways to get the information: Interview the customer or authority in person or over the phone. This can be done either by the publicist, a freelance writer, or an agency person. It should not be left to the sales representative, technical person, or anyone else in management. It should be done only by someone with some skills in interviewing, and only after thorough preparation.

Before you send someone out to do it and, most important, before you query an editor, you need to screen the interviewee. First, write down everything you

Getting into Print

must know in order for the story to be salable. If the person won't reveal factual information about your product or his business and responds in generalities, such as "We like your product, but . . ." you don't have a story. If he will agree to discuss in detail the subjects you have told him you'd like to cover, schedule a couple of hours for an in-depth interview.

To prepare for and conduct a successful interview, keep these ten points in mind.

1. Write down all the questions you want to ask. Review the list with the interviewee and consult the list during the actual interview. If the contact will not discuss some key elements necessary to make a good story during your first discussion, very politely inform him or her that you are not sure the story is complete enough without the answers to those questions. If you can't get it, you may still save the situation by developing the "case history" sales literature suggested earlier.

2. You have planned to communicate, through both advertising and publicity, key points about your product. Keep the copy points of your product very much in mind when you are developing your story. Your objective, after all, is to deliver these points to your audience.

3. Try to hold the interview in some location other than the person's office, perhaps a nearby conference room, so the person is not interrupted by phone calls or visitors.

4. Make sure you are interviewing the right person. If you are told you should contact Mr. Smith, the vice president of manufacturing, talk to him. If he suggests you talk to Jane Doaks, the director of research, speak to her as well.

5. If the person you are interviewing tends to stray from the subject, you may need to bring him back into focus. But be careful. He may begin talking about an aspect of his business that is news to you, and may be even better news for the publication. If the conversation is heading in this direction, encourage and help him along.

6. Look at the person you are interviewing and show interest in what he or she is saying. The more relaxed the interview subject is, the more likely you will get all the information you need.

7. Be prepared. If a salesperson is involved, you should have already discussed the customer with him or her, and reviewed the nature of the customer's business. Interviews work best when the salesperson is not present, but this is not always possible. If the salesperson feels it is important for customer relations to be present, then there is no choice.

Direct your questions only to the person you are interviewing, but be prepared for the salesperson to answer the questions. I once traveled to Washington with a salesman to interview some naval architects for a story he had suggested. It was not highly technical and I had prepared a list of questions I planned to ask. The salesman answered every one of them. The best I could do was ask the architect "Do you agree with that?" and "Did you have anything to add?"

One way to handle situations like this is to tell both the salesperson and the customer before the interview starts that you don't know as much as they do about the business and that you may ask some "dumb questions," but that is the way you learn and the readers of the publication will learn. Then the salesperson will not interrupt you with statements that he thinks the question is irrelevant or tell the customer he will fill you in later, or just look at you with an expression that suggests "Who is this idiot?"

8. Always have your audience in the back of your mind. That means thinking of the information you need to gather that is in your best interest and the best interests of the audience.

9. Take notes and use a tape recorder. Tape recorders today are small and unobtrusive. Just be sure you have permission to use the tape recorder before the interview starts. If there is any question, you can respond by pointing out that you want to be sure that the information you get is accurate. After a few minutes into the interview, the tape recorder will probably not be noticed. Check it frequently to make sure the tape hasn't run out or the batteries died. I always take more tape cassettes than I need, and extra batteries.

10. Plan ahead for photos, ask the interviewee to send you photos (if he has any) of the subject of the story. You should take your own, but those supplied by the customer can help you plan the ones you will take. If you are going to visit the subject, meet the photographer at the site *after* the interview; an unplanned photo opportunity will probably occur to you during the course of interview. Also, be clear about the photos you can't take. There are probably secure plant areas and you should know ahead of time what areas to stay away from. If all you are able to take is a photo of the front of the building or the sign on the plant gate, reconsider doing the story. Most features need photos. Don't forget to clear your photos when you clear the story.

Another approach is with a telephone call. It often works just as well as an in-person interview. You also can set up a conference call and bring in one of your experts (*not* the salesperson) if he can contribute anything.

Getting It Written

The above assumes *you* are going to write the story. But there are three alternatives: your agency can do it, you can hire a freelancer, or it can be written by the editor or a staff writer.

If it is to be done by the first two, you must provide detailed information about the objectives for the story, the product, the customer, and the publication to which it is directed. Less information, of course, is needed if your agency is handling it, because you can assume that the account executive is familiar with the product. The objectives and media target should be spelled out, however. You will need an assignment sheet (see Figure 6-4), where everything is spelled out clearly,

Figure 6-4. Format for an assignment sheet.

> *To:* Agency, freelancer
> *From:* Name of company contact
> *Date:*
> *Working Title:*
> *Products/Services:* What product(s) or service(s) is involved? Attach backgrounders, technical data sheets, brochures, and other printed matter that can help the writer understand the product/service in preparing the story.
> *Type of Activity:* Case history, exclusive, technical article, roundup, or release.
> *Outside Contact:* Name, position, address, and phone of person(s) to be interviewed. Attach background on customer and company when appropriate.
> *Objectives:* Why use this approach? What will be accomplished? How does this activity relate to marketing objectives?
> *News Angle:* What is the key copy point that must be conveyed?
> *Other Copy Points:* List other benefits of the product or service you wish to cover.
> *Deadline:* When must story be submitted to company? When must all approvals be obtained? What is the editorial deadline?
> *Photos:* What photos are needed? Who is the contact for photos? Color or black and white? Get photo releases.
> *Audience:* What is the target audience?
> *Target medium:* List media to which this story is being written or will be submitted.
> *Restrictions:* Any areas, topics to be avoided? Any customer sensitivities?

including copy points to highlight and targeted medium. Such a sheet is used to provide agencies and outside services with the who, what, why, where, when, and how of a news story you wish them to develop. The format guidelines are generic. As you prepare the sheet, use the terminology appropriate to the type of story planned.

The first contact should be made by the publicist, who can tell the customer or interviewee that the writer (give name) is preparing a story for you, or Mr. Smith from Foghorn Communications will be calling to set up an appointment for the interview. Or that Editor Samuels will be contacting him. Learn as much as you can — as if you were going to conduct the interview personally.

If you have presold the story and the editor plans to do it, you also want to contact the customer with this information and provide the editor with extensive background information on the product (an editorial backgrounder, technical data sheets where appropriate, but no sales literature) and on the customer. It may not turn out just exactly the way you want it, and the editor may contact other sources — such as your competitor — for additional information, but the odds are that it will be favorable and very much the way you hoped.

Will the editor send it to you and your customer to check? Perhaps so, but only for technical accuracy. You can ask to review it on this basis, but you may be refused. Don't make the story conditional on your reviewing it, however. I have never seen a story that I have developed with or suggested to an editor turn out to be a disappointment. However, I have seen stories sent to me to check for accuracy ruined and killed because they were "rewritten for clarity" by a marketing or technical person and turned into one long commercial pitch for the product. Make sure the story gets back to you after checking and not sent directly to the editor. It may be saved if you catch it first. If it gets back to the editor greatly rewritten, it will surely raise some hackles and run a great risk of never being published. And it may mark the last time you get a story idea accepted by that publication.

If the story is to be sent to the customer for checking, be sure to impress upon him the need to meet the deadline, and avoid the panic a friend went through when the customer kept delaying the return of the story to the editor. In this case, the editor had written the story, selected a photo from the story to use on the cover, made room for it, and was kept waiting until the very last minute by the customer. The editor could have run the story without the customer's approval. After all, he wrote it. But the editor did not want to do this because the customer was important to my friend's company. It all turned out well, thanks to a frantic call from the publicist reminding the customer of the importance of meeting the deadline. Had it been otherwise, it would have adversely affected the relationship between editor and publicist, and the chances of working with the publication on another story would have been very dim.

If the publicist writes the story, there are two benefits. One, a *company* person is making contact with a *customer,* and two, the company person is getting valuable market information by getting out into the field. (Take every opportunity to make sales calls. It's an excellent way to see how your business operates and how the marketplace regards your company and its products.) Lest I be accused of disliking salespeople because I prefer not to have them around when I'm conducting an interview, they are often essential in helping to develop leads for stories and putting you in touch with the subjects. I just prefer to do interviews without them.

Of course, it may be far more economical to have it written by a freelancer. Some tips on hiring outside services are in Chapter 11. Suffice to say, you won't have to pay overhead. If it's done by an agency, the actual cost will be more, but if the agency is under contract, the agency should handle all of the business, not just bits and pieces.

Recycling to Get More Mileage

There is a possibility that the story can be developed as a feature for another media category altogether. A consumer feature might be adapted for a trade or business-to-business publication. Or conversely, a trade story might have a consumer angle. For example, the manufacturing process for a plastic part might be of interest to the plastics molding industry; the part might be a key element in a consumer product and make possible a better quality or longer-lasting product.

Once the story has run — and never before — it can be rewritten and mailed to other media of interest as a news release. The angle may need to be changed, it may need updating or some additional information, but it often can be an effective news release.

The feature also can be highly merchandisable: reprints can be used by salespeople, for direct mail, information kits, background information. And it's an excellent way to further customer relations.

Going for the Big One

Here is an example of how preparation paid off on a program developed by Du Pont for "Kevlar" aramid fibers. The prime media target was *Fortune*. The publicist working on the product believed a story could be developed that was strong enough for *Fortune*. Miller Communications of Boston was retained for this project, because both John A. Miller and Frank Morgan, agency principals, had worked as editors with business media and knew how to structure a presentation on a story for business media.

Tips for Success

Of course, your feature or exclusive must fit your communications plan and meet marketing objectives. With those as givens, here's some advice:

1. Be well prepared. Know your subject thoroughly before you contact an editor or ask a publication to run a story on it.
2. Get your company associates to sign off on the idea. Make sure they agree to be interviewed.
3. Get your outside experts in agreement, too.
4. Use only quality photos and artwork.
5. Go for the best on all counts!
6. If the feature runs, merchandise the results internally and externally.

The objective was clear: Reach major management in *Fortune* 500 companies about the benefits of Du Pont's aramid fiber. Get them and their companies interested in its benefits and teach them more about the technology.

Here's how the project was handled. First, theme outlines for proposal to media were developed. The first theme was marketing, which included the product's fit in a growing market and its competition, with reference to a recent capital investment in new plant facilities widely reported in the daily business media.

The second theme was innovation. Reference was made to the fact that the United States was losing share in some areas of the economy, but that this product, reflecting a commitment to developing new proprietary products, was contrary to the trend. Examples were given.

Then a brief summary reflecting marketing plans, markets, and product benefits was put together.

The client (me) was given for approval a copy of the letter to the target press and a list of major press to be contacted, with *Fortune* at top, and other second-tier publications for followup stories.

A complete backgrounder was developed and submitted for approval. It included product features, uses (more than ten were detailed), properties, history, and a glossary of terms used by people discussing its invention and manufacture.

Coincidentally, one of its inventors received a professional society award. The fact that the honoree was a woman, Stephanie Kwolek, who had been with the company for a number of years, focused even more attention on the product, and provided a human-interest angle.

Finally, a list was drawn up of all the people who might be interviewed (and were), and each of them was thoroughly briefed on questions they might be asked.

Figure 6-5. This photo proved to be so interesting that *Fortune* magazine selected it from a brochure.

Getting into Print

Photos were submitted to the publication with the cover letter and detailed information.

The letter was followed up by a telephone call from the agency, and a meeting between the agency and the publication was scheduled. Later, a number of editors at the publication met and a decision was reached to go ahead.

Fortune sent a photographer for additional photos at a laboratory, and also used two provided by the company. Interestingly, one company-provided photo, that of a "strong" man sitting on a swing suspended from the side of a tall building (see Figure 6-5), was taken from a product brochure. The rope was "Kevlar" and the photo dramatically demonstrated its high strength. Even more interesting than the fact that it was a brochure photo was that *Fortune* used it and photos from other features in its own advertising.

The results were positive. The product was positioned better as an example of a highly engineered and highly useful polymer, with growing use in everything from police body armor to aircraft composite structures.

Several other stories were developed with noncompeting media using a similar approach.

7
Getting It on Paper

Writing a news release or feature takes far more than sitting down at a typewriter or word processor for a couple of hours. The first step is planning. Chances are the story didn't just develop by itself. The new product or service was planned, the brochure was planned, the technical data bulletin was planned, the trade show was planned. And in just about every case, the news action—a release or feature story—was also planned as part of an overall strategic program.

Sometimes, of course, an unexpected story opportunity does occur—a company or person receives an award, a new use is discovered for a product, a customer is uncovered who is willing to discuss her successes with your product for a case history or feature. But even that takes planning. Before you sit down to write it, it must be researched, the facts have to be assembled, people interviewed, the key copy point identified, the angle figured out, the story laid out in a logical, sequential way, and the audience and media matched.

Format Basics

There are some format guidelines that apply to news stories in general, whether they be news releases, general-interest features, folksy farm stories, case histories, or technical articles. Following these guidelines can help you organize the material and present it in a solid, journalistic manner.

Headline

The headline is always written in the present tense. It is a capsule summary of the story and can help convince the editor that what follows is worth reading.

Getting It on Paper

When an editor is scanning hundreds of releases a week, yours will stand out if the head stands out. (Note that in a newspaper or magazine article, headlines are used to attract readers to a story and to tell them, in a second or two, what the article is about.)

The objective in writing good headlines is to provide one that the editor will use almost as is, with only minor editing. An editor has to fit the head in a column or two, so keep it short. Try to get a key product benefit in the head. And relate it to the company. The headline should urge the readers to keep reading. Sounds easy, but it's not. Most headlines are far too long, and try to say too much. It takes discipline and work to write a headline that is pithy and to the point.

A news release headline should be about eight words long, no more than twelve. A good style is a two-line head: Type in all caps, flush left to the margin, no space between the lines, and underline the second line. One line shouldn't overrun the other on the right side by more than one or two letters. *Try* to have a verb or preposition begin the second line (you won't always succeed). It is not essential to have the company name in the headline, but if it fits logically, use it. If a head just won't work on two lines, one line can be used. But keep the head short. And if a number is used in a head, it's always a numeral. Example:

IBM INTRODUCES 3 NEW PCS

Normally, the release headline does not have a subhead. Save that for the feature, if you feel it will work.

Here are some examples of heads, some better than others, but all acceptable and all on the same subject:

"MYLAR" ADOPTED   NESTLÉ ADOPTS "MYLAR"
FOR CHEESE PACKAGING   FOR CHEESE PACKAGING

"MYLAR" INCREASES   NESTLÉ PICKS "MYLAR"
PACKAGING SPEED   FOR CHEESE PACK

"MYLAR" SPEEDS
CHEESE PACKAGING

Now here's an example of a head that needs improvement:

NESTLÉ COMPANY OPTS FOR "MYLAR"
TO WRAP ITS CHEESE:

Faster Than the Present Process.

At first glance this head might seem okay. It spells out the reasons why Nestlé switched to "Mylar" packaging films. However, it goes against some important rules for good heads. For example, it's too long and wordy.

For a feature head, you still want to be imaginative, but it is not necessary to include the product name or company. But the headline should focus on the end benefits, uses, and applications. Read the lead paragraph for a feature story on page 132. An appropriate head for this story might be:

LONG BOAT TRIPS MAKE HIM SEASICK
"FEELS FINE" SINCE SWITCH TO CHOPPER

Humor, alliteration, poetry, or other devices to attract attention seldom work. Newspaper sports editors sometimes try to use humor, particularly when a pun suggests itself. Avoid this style, even when your release is sent to sports editors. Good examples abound elsewhere in a newspaper. Follow their example so you don't need to get cute to attract attention. Also read weekly news magazines for headlines, plus all the publications that reach your markets.

A basic rule of headline writing is that in it you should not state anything that is not fully justified or substantiated in the rest of the text. You can earn quicker editorial black marks with misleading headlines than almost any other way.

Preparation of a pithy headline often helps clear your thoughts for writing the rest of the story. But if you have trouble writing the head before beginning the story, leave it and come back to it after you write the release.

Subheads

Subheads are sometimes used by publicity writers and editors to flag upcoming sections (just as this one). The problem comes when they are used in a news release. Because a release is short, subheads tend to make the presentation choppy. In defense of some writers who use them, there is some value because it permits a busy editor to scan the key elements of the story quickly. But, in general, I don't recommend them.

Subheads are very useful in a long feature, but don't use them as a crutch to make a transition from one paragraph to another. In summary, for a simple news release, a subhead is usually not necessary. A subhead may help a feature story, but the headline style doesn't change.

Text

Everything following the headline is double-spaced. Pica type is preferred for editorial copy, because it's easy to read and it's what editors have had on their typewriters since the old Smith Coronas. If the release is done on a word processor, it still should be in pica type, and be alert to big gaps of space at the bottom of pages that computer printers sometimes leave. *Always* prepare copy on letter-quality printers.

Datelines

Most product publicity is sent from the company's home office and does not need a dateline. (Your return address is on your stationery, and most product stories are not breaking news.) But there are times when a dateline is needed: news is announced from another city, for example, and it is important enough to be used by daily media.

A dateline suggests immediacy. Don't send a release dated May 8 on May 10.

One way to tell if someone has attended journalism school or worked as a journalist is to see if he or she can write a dateline properly. Many public relations people can't, and many agencies and companies send out releases with unnecessary or improper datelines.

Here are some tips: The dateline appears before the beginning of the lead paragraph, and is indented. The city of origin is in all caps, comma, followed by the state (abbreviated the way we did it before the post office changed to the two-letter style), comma, followed by the month in upper- and lowercase and date (long months are abbreviated, short ones are not). Follow this with two dashes.

SYRACUSE, N.Y., Sept. 30 --
SAN FRANCISCO, Oct. 12 --

The state designation was left off San Francisco because we all know it's in California.

Leads

The lead paragraph of a news release gives the key copy point in a straightforward manner. Just the facts, no hard sell or ad copy. However, for the writer with advertising background, a good way to identify what you plan to present in the lead is think of the most important benefit you want to convey about the product.

Don't let the lead get drowned in irrelevant, hard-to-believe details — or read like ad copy. Give the lead extra attention, rewrite it two or three times if necessary, then polish it some more. Read *The New York Times, USA Today,* the *Wall Street Journal* — any good newspaper — and see how leads are written. A good, solid, punchy lead will get you good marks from editors, too.

Leads for features must ask the reader to read on, but can begin to set the stage for the story before getting right to the point.

For example, suppose an all-weather helicopter has been developed that will operate at zero visibility and in winds up to 60 miles an hour. Its first use is to get crews safely to and from offshore oil rigs. It is expected to replace crew boats as the way to move people back and forth. Let's compare a release lead and a feature lead. First, a release lead:

> An all-weather helicopter has been introduced by Igor Airlines that can fly 23 passengers safely in winds up to 60 m.p.h. and at zero visibility. FAA certification is expected within six months, after which the aircraft will begin ferrying crew members for Down Deep Oil Company between its drilling rig 60 miles out in the Gulf of Mexico and Grand Pass, La.

Now, the feature lead:

> Pierre Boulangerie used to get seasick every time he made the two-hour trip between Grand Pass, La., and his job on Down Deep Rig No. 3, 60 miles out in the Gulf of Mexico. It didn't matter whether the seas were calm or choppy, Boulangerie still became nauseous.
>
> Now the 37-year-old rigger arrives on the rig "feeling just fine," thanks to his company's replacing the crew boat with an Igor all-weather helicopter. The trip, which once could take as long as two hours if the seas were rough, now takes about 15 minutes, in good weather and bad.

Style

It is obvious that the news release wastes no time getting to the point. Just the facts. The feature, on the other hand, uses another device to get the reader's attention.

Sentence length is difficult to prescribe. Strive for simplicity. For a release about a new product, long sentences of more than 35 words may be far too complex and difficult to comprehend. Some writers use the two-line rule: A sentence running more than two lines of copy is considered too long. This doesn't necessarily apply to features, but even there try not to get ponderous or long-winded.

Brevity and unity go hand in hand. A single sentence contains a single thought, or a *related* sequence of points. Paragraphs contain related sentences. The copy should be well-organized and written in logical, orderly sequence. There should be a smooth transition between paragraphs.

The active voice should prevail. It is usually more alert and vigorous than the passive. For example "I shall always remember my first visit to New York" is much better than "My first visit to New York will always be remembered by me." Specific guidelines on writing style appear later in this chapter.

Getting It on Paper 133

The Editor's Role

An editor edits not only for style but also for fit. If you are working with an editor on a feature, she will be saving space for it. Together you have already worked out the length.

But news releases arrive unexpectedly, and there's no guarantee about final length. Out of the many releases she receives, an editor may find 15 good news stories she wants to run in the new products section. Not everything sent is going to be used, because it just won't fit in the space available. She may keep two paragraphs from four releases, three from two others, and so on.

The point is, she is going to have to cut and invariably will cut stories from the bottom. So remember the inverted pyramid — the most important information at the beginning and the least important at the end. (See Figure 6-1.) If, for example, the person you are quoting wants to make a self-serving statement about how important the company is in its industry, put it near the end. Or if you need to detail all the other uses of the product that have no real relevance but do provide some background about the subject, put this at the end too.

The common function of editing is to improve on style — tighten, simplify, clarify. Here are examples of releases that were improved by some minor editing.

JOHN DOUGHNUT MANUFACTURING COMPANY
<u>ANNOUNCES NEW FRANCHISE PROGRAM</u>

    The John Doughnut Company, East Lynn, MA, has announced a new franchise support program as a part of an aggressive effort to expand the sale of their unique doughnuts into new markets.

    The new program contains four basic elements: price reductions to franchisers, extensive training, comprehensive new selling aids and product literature, and increased customer service offered at the local level through the divisional office.

    "Our reputation for high quality, highly edible doughnuts has earned us a leadership position among suppliers of doughnuts. Capitalizing on this position, we want to greatly expand our market share for these doughnuts by competitive pricing and giving our franchisees the knowledge and tools they need to sell our doughnuts," commented John B. Hole, president.

Comments:

- The headline is okay for this type of release.
- The lead could be improved by changing *unique*, which will surely raise an editor's eyebrow, to *unusual*, and changing *they* to *it* (a company is an it, a singular entity).
- The state designation should be Mass. and the flow would be improved by writing "*of* East Lynn, Mass."

- The second paragraph can stand some tightening: "The new program has four elements: price reductions, extensive training, comprehensive selling aids, and increased local support."
- Eliminate the next paragraph; it is self-serving. If the president insists on using it, relegate it to the end of the release (inverted pyramid).
- The release also needs a paragraph briefly stating the number of current distributors, where they are located, and the number (if any) of company-owned units.

Here's a poor release:

FOR IMMEDIATE RELEASE

Joe Dokes Tool Company Announces a Breakthrough in Kitchen Fans

    Anytown, Delaware, August 19, 1987. The Joe Dokes Company of this thriving communitity have announced that they have developed a unique fan that is guaranteed to keep smoke out of the kitchen, because its made with a impact resistant polyethyleen that won't burn, and collect soot.
    The fan has been approved by the Underwriters' Lab and meets their V-O standards for flamability.
    If you are interested in learning more about this breakthrough product, write us at:

Comments:

- The typos and spelling mistakes are obvious, and are typical of many releases.
- "For immediate release" is not necessary.
- There is no editorial contact.
- The head is too long.
- A dateline is unnecessary. The letterhead gives the full address, including the city of origin. The release needs a date, however. This can go at the bottom left corner of the last page: 8/19/87.
- Third person should be avoided.

Here is a better way to write the story:

                                              Contact: Jim Smith
                                              302-111-2222

TOUGH APPLIANCE FAN
MEETS V-O STANDARDS

    When it comes to manufacturing fans, Joe Dokes Company of Anytown, Del., believes if a fan can't stand the heat, it shouldn't be in the kitchen.

Dokes has developed a low-torque, 5-inch fan molded of a tough plastic that meets Underwriters' Laboratories V-O standard for flammability. The fan has increased heat deflection temperature and has better impact resistance than the flame-retardant material used previously.

(And so on with facts in order of importance.)

Here's one of my favorites. It was released some years ago by a professional society. I *think* the point of the release was to generate requests for copies of its publications catalog.

FOR IMMEDIATE RELEASE

PDQ BOOKS ZOOM
330 STORIES HIGH

DETROIT, Michigan -- John Doe, president of the PDQ Society (PDQ) headquartered here, reports that in the last nine months PDQ has sold approximately 35.5 tons of books, based on an average weight of two pounds per book.

"If we stacked these books one on top of the other, we would have a pile 3,698 feet high based on an average height of 1.25 inches per book [sic]," Doe said. "As a building," he continued, "it would be 330 stories high, or three times the tallest building in the world, the Sears Tower in Chicago."

Doe calculates that if all the pages from the book were a single sheet, it would be 27.50 square miles in area—enough paper to cover the city of Dearborn with 2¾ square miles left over.

And if all the pages were placed end-to-end, there would be a train 1,126 miles long—the approximate distance from Dearborn, Michigan to New Orleans, Louisiana, with enough left over for a side trip to Baton Rouge.

In the next paragraph, the release finally gets to the point: It mentions a publications catalog, what is in it, and gives an address that a reader can write to for a free copy.

A sharp company editor will pick up some minor errors in the text. An editor's reaction to all the statistics would be "Who cares?" Someone went to a lot of trouble to estimate all the useless information. The release should have been two paragraphs: one a brief description of the society, the other giving the free catalog offer.

Some Writing Guidelines

It is difficult, if not impossible, to teach writing in a book. But some guidelines on good writing can be suggested. Writers and editors, including publicity people who will be assessing the work of freelancers and agency people, should read and reread *The Elements of Style* by Strunk and White.

As I mentioned before, the Associated Press stylebook is highly recommended and should be placed right next to the dictionary. AP also publishes *The Word*, a superb guide to writing and style.

Italicizing & Capitalizing

Names of newspapers, periodicals, and reference books that are constantly used are written in caps and lower case but not in quotes or underlined. Don't underline in body copy for effect or emphasis. This indicates italicizing, and that is an editorial decision. If a writer has to rely on an underline to make a point, the sentence may need to be recast. This goes for exclamation points as well. They imply astonishment, and should be used very sparingly in editorial copy.

Follow the current newspaper style for capitalizing titles of individuals: Use caps if a title precedes a name, but not if it follows. For example, "John Jones, chairman of the board, said . . ." but "Chairman of the Board John Jones said. . . ."

Normally, names of corporate departments, groups, and divisions are not capitalized. Major divisions may be and Board of Directors and Executive Committee always are. When written alone, the words *company, division,* and so on, even though they refer to a specific group, are lower case in both releases and correspondence.

Word Usage

Use superlatives such as *first* or *biggest* only if they are justified. Avoid overused phrases such as *high-tech* or *state-of-the-art*. Don't use hard-sell words such as *breakthrough,* which should be reserved for military actions; *amazing,* unless you're describing a magician; *revolutionary,* a great favorite of ad copywriters; *sensational,* ditto; or *unique*. When *unique* appears in a release or story, red flags pop up in front of the editor's eyes and the reaction is "prove it." *Unique* means one of a kind. Don't overstate the product benefits just to justify the word *unique*. Your story will be more believable if you don't use it. Find another word. *Unusual* is one; there are others in the dictionary.

Be factual. For example, using phrases such as "works faster," "is more heat resistant," "is better," "lasts longer," leaves editors asking, "Than what?" Answer the questions in the story and it will be far more believable.

Avoid the phrase "saving time or money" whenever possible, although "saving money" is often used to mean reducing costs or buying something for less than it normally costs. Instead state that you can *reduce costs,* in dollars or percent,

---

Reference Books for Publicists

The following books should be in every publicity manager's reference library:

American Heritage Dictionary of the English Language, New College Edition (Houghton Mifflin Co., Two Park Street, Boston, Mass. 02107). Also good is *Webster's New Collegiate Dictionary.*

Associated Press Stylebook and Libel Manual (Associated Press, 50 Rockefeller Plaza, New York, N.Y. 10020). The stylebook most widely used by print media.

Theodore M. Bernstein, *The Careful Writer, A Modern Guide to English Usage* (Atheneum, 115 Fifth Avenue, New York, N.Y. 10003). Answers most questions about word usage. An excellent and witty reference.

William Strunk, Jr. and E. B. White, *The Elements of Style* (Macmillan Publishing Co., 866 Third Avenue, New York, N.Y. 10022). If the choice ever should come down to one book as a guide to good writing, this is it.

The Word (Associated Press, same address). This is an excellent guide to good journalistic writing. Gets right to the point—as should any news writing.

---

from what you were paying previously. To show that something takes less time now than it did before, say that you are *reducing* rather than *saving* time. And strive to indicate by how much you are reducing everything.

When supporting facts in news material, it is appropriate to compare. According to *The Careful Writer*, by Theodore Bernstein, when the purpose is to liken *two different things* and put them in the same category, use *to*. Example: "The economy can be compared to a runner who is coasting to get a second breath." If the objective is to place one thing side by side with another and examine their differences or similarities, use *with*. Example: "Compared with linoleum, the new types of tile wear about 30 percent longer." Uses calling for *with* will vastly outnumber those calling for *to*.

Abbreviations

Unless you're writing about IBM or NATO or some other very common organization, don't use abbreviations or acronyms. The military is not the only place that loves to use these. Nearly every business or profession has its own favorite set of acronyms. They are now very much a part of business lingo, and may be an omen for the language of the future, but that is no excuse to use them editorially. Those that are unknown or known only to the few insiders will muddle a story. It's best to spell out.

If you work for an organization that prefers to use initials rather than spelling out its name, you're stuck. But if you're not as well-known as GM or GE, don't abbreviate in news writing. You can't assume everyone knows who you are, much less editors. If your company makes chocolates, for example, you're better off identifying yourself as International Chocolate Company than as ICC. You probably won't be mistaken for the Interstate Commerce Commission, but spelling out the name will, at the very least, tell the editor what business you are in. There are some exceptions, and these can be found in the AP stylebook.

I also take exception when an organization is spelled out and then followed by an abbreviation in parentheses. Example: "The Brotherhood of Fiction Fanciers (BOFF) is holding its annual meeting in. . . ." This little device is supposed to educate me so that when I see BOFF later on in the story I will know what it means. But I never heard of it before, and being like most folks not blessed with an indelible memory, by the time it is used again I have no idea what it is.

Quotes

There is a vast difference between oral communications and the written word. Clean up the grammar, even if it is a direct quote. Chances are when you run it by the quotee for comment, he or she will say, "That's exactly what I said" or "I couldn't have said it better myself." Using vernacular is fine for fiction, but not for publicity. Consider the writer who wrote a lot of farm case-history stories. He thought it would help the stories if he made farmers sound like the stereotype—the guy in overalls sucking on a wheat straw. It didn't work. Farmers are businessmen, not hayseeds. Some farm stories can be folksy, but too much can be insulting.

There are differences of opinion on the style to use in quoting a source. *The New York Times* always uses a title—Mr., Mrs., Ms., or Miss—when referring back to a person. The Associated Press uses last names only after the first reference. There is a temptation to refer back to women as Ms., even when you're referring to men by last name only. Don't be sexist; use the same format for both. Another good rule, which is an option call, is to use "Dr." only for medical practitioners. Treat academic "doctors" like everyone else.

The first reference to a person should spell out his or her full first name and middle initial. Unless the person really is named Billy Bob or has always been known as T.J., don't use nicknames or initials.

Buzz Words and Other Gobbledegook

The editor of a leading business-to-business publication says the worst writing comes from the federal government—"the gobbledegook that they put forth in their news releases." Unfortunately, too many corporations pick up and start using the same lingo.

A recent release across my desk read "allows a larger process window for extrusion." What this meant (I think) is that it is now easier to process this plastic than it was before. The *window* use is another example of a military term ("window of vulnerability") that has crept into our language. The best advice is to stay away from these open windows in writing.

Parameter is another one of those words that snuck into writing. This is often misused to mean boundaries or fixed limits. (Some might even mistake parameters for windows.) A parameter is a variable or arbitrary constant appearing in a mathematical expression, each value of which restricts or determines the specific form of the expression.

Impact is frequently misused when the writer really means *effect* or *influence*. *Impact* may have an impact in writing, but use it sparingly. It is government lingo. *Effect* is a far better word—or *affect* if you should (shudder) be tempted to use *impact* as a verb.

Host is a noun, not a verb. Shun phrases that state that someone or a company is hosting an event, even though the Phillies may be hosting the Cubs this weekend, according to your favorite TV sports reporter.

Said, said the editor, usually says it best. Many publicity writers, when quoting someone, shun the word *said*, which is indeed what the person did. They don't like to be repetitive. But words such as *asserted, indicated, observed, stated, noted, stressed, averred, explained,* and the like, are no substitute for *said*. About the only acceptable substitute is *added,* if there is a rather long quote; even that should be used sparingly.

Feature style should not deviate too much from the *"said* says it best " rule. But features may be more descriptive. For example, if the rigger who always got seasick when he went by boat to the oil rig said, "I don't get seasick any more since we started going to the rig in the helicopter," it might be appropriate to end the quote with "he said with a smile." Not, however, just "he smiled." You can't "smile" words, you can only say them. And if indeed one stressed a point, or explained something, then it is logical to say so. But the other substitutes are seldom necessary, and much overdone.

Let me repeat, because this error is so common: A company is an *it*, not a *they*. There is a temptation to refer back to a company as *they*, but the singular *it* or "the company" is correct.

Style Considerations for Foreign Countries

It is obvious that releasing news to media in Central and South America requires translation into Spanish and Portuguese, but not so apparent that there are both English- and French-language media in Canada, a bilingual country. Don't insult French-language magazines or newspapers by sending them news in English.

The same applies to the rest of the world. Releases must be sent in the proper language. In Europe alone, many companies translate a single release into six languages.

Further, when writing English for Canada, the U.K., and most other English-speaking countries, use the Queen's English: *colour* for *color*, *theatre* for *theater*. The *Oxford Book for Writers and Editors* and *Newsman's English* by Harold Evans are good references.

Another tip: Most editors of European journals dislike quotes in product releases. They consider them a form of false pride and puffery. Therefore, unless the person is saying something very original or very important, it is preferable to paraphrase.

The Use of Trademarks

One sure way to commercialize a story is to overdo trademark or brand name references. One reference per page is sufficient. Loading a story with frequent trademark references can cause two things to happen, neither of which will get results. One, the editor's first impression will be that the new material is too commercial, and it will get rejected; two, the editor will delete every trademark reference and, if it is used at all, you may be left with a generic story. So, instead of using a trademark, substitute "it," the generic term, or "the product." This technique can help a good story, increase its chance for use, and prevent it from appearing too commercial. The fact is readers are smart enough to know the subject of the story once the brand name is mentioned. They do not need to be reminded of it constantly.

There are some editors — fortunately very few — who refuse to use *any* trademark reference. This makes no sense at all. The readers should be let in on the subject of the story. Because newspapers are now devoting more attention to business and have reporters with business backgrounds, there are more opportunities for *news* coverage of a company. Most business, news, and business-to-business publications do use trademark or brand name references.

Trademark Misuse

Unfortunately, some publications do not use trademarks properly, which can rile company lawyers, and has compelled major corporations such as Coca-Cola and Xerox to run space advertising in media trade journals to remind editors that a company's trademark is extremely valuable, and asking their cooperation in protecting them. But the best a publicist can expect a publication to do is to treat it as a proper noun and use an initial cap.

Getting It on Paper

To protect your company's trademarks, as a publicist you should observe certain style guidelines:

1. Precede the trademark with the company name at least once, use an initial cap, and set the trademark off in quotes: Du Pont "Dacron". A comma or period next to the trademark is set outside the quotes. This looks wrong and is wrong in any other quote mark/punctuation usage. But it is proper usage here because it is another way to distinguish a trademark.

2. Follow with the generic term at least once every page or two. For example: Du Pont "Dacron" polyester fiber. That establishes "Dacron" as a trademark of the Du Pont Company and relates the trademark to the generic.

3. When you spot a trademark misuse in a news clip or story, call it to the editor's attention. The most common errors are treating trademarks as generics — using it all lower case, as a modifier, or as a possessive. Most times, it's not intentional. Even if it is, don't let a company lawyer write a chastising letter to the offending publications. The publicist is responsible for editorial relations, not lawyers. Letters from lawyers are seldom cast in the most diplomatic language.

The most effective way is to call the offending editor, pointing out the misuse of your company's trademark. Explain you appreciated the coverage given your product in the story on page 17 of the October issue, but he used your trademark incorrectly. Because your company has an enormous investment in its trademarks, you are going to send "the letter" pointing out the proper use of your company's trademark. Be diplomatic. Also point out that you are not expecting a "letter to the editor" appearance but that you would appreciate that it be used properly in any future news of your company the publication may run, and that the letter is necessary to have in your files to show that you are duly diligent in protecting your trademark should you ever be challenged in court. Then write a letter like this:

Dear Mr. Editor or Dear ——— (first name, if you know the person well)

This will follow up on our telephone conversation today about the misuse of our trademark "Ippy" in the story, "How to Keep Warm in the Yukon," on page 17 of your October issue.

As you can appreciate, Zippy Company has a considerable investment in its trademark and its misuse may suggest that it is a generic term. I would most appreciate it if in any future references to our product, use an initial cap, set it off in quotes, and follow at least once with the generic term. For example, hot water bottles of "Ippy" polyurethane.

Thanks very much for your understanding and cooperation. If you have any questions, please phone me at 098-098-0988.

Now you are on record as having contacted the editor and pointed out the error of his ways. There is a slight chance it might run in the "letters to the editor" column but it's highly unlikely. He may even throw the letter away. Every editor I have dealt with this way has been cordial. There are no assurances every one will be in the future, but it is far better editorial relations than having an editor angry with you because a lawyer jumped all over him. Don't expect an editor to comply with your every wish, however. If he uses the trademark with an initial cap, never as a modifier, and always as a proper noun, you have succeeded. Editorial trademark usage is covered in the leading stylebooks.

Dealing with Errors

Editors pride themselves on objectivity and getting the facts straight, but sometimes errors can creep into stories that may upset you and your marketing associates.

First off, the publicity person should deal with it, not the marketing person. Some marketing folks may take the error too personally and overreact.

The first thing to do is determine objectively whether it is indeed an error, an expression of an editor's opinion, or information obtained from another source. It's possible the trouble can be traced to not providing the editor with enough information in the first place, or not providing additional information when she called for it.

Don't start a feud by writing a chastising letter, no matter who is right. A phone call to set up a meeting is a far better approach — if the situation is serious. Even if you fail to change the editor's mind, you have become better acquainted, have heard her point of view, and may learn how to avoid such situations in the future. And you may even have reached an agreement on a positive story on your product in a future issue. At no time should you threaten to pull your advertising, as an irate marketing person might suggest.

You have several options.

1. Do nothing. If it is a minor error, it may be best to ignore, or perhaps mention it in passing to the editor if the opportunity arises.

2. If it is somewhat serious, a polite note may be in order, perhaps preceded by a phone call tipping the editor off to the letter and indicating it will spell out your points in more detail and help assuage marketing's feeling too. Don't ask that it be run in the letters to the editor column, although it might very well be. The letter always should be sent by the publicity person.

3. If the problem is even more serious, write the letter and *ask* that it be used in the letter column to set the record straight. You need to have all the facts to back up your statement, but keep the letter short. Letters to the editor seldom run more than three or four paragraphs, and editors have the right to edit and cut them, just as they do news stories.

4. If it is a *very* serious error, you may ask for a formal correction. Normally, this would be a statement of the error followed by the correction. Be warned, though, that the editor might follow this statement with a critical one of her own.

Whatever the degree of seriousness, never threaten legal action. And don't have your letter signed by a lawyer, although you may want to have it reviewed by a lawyer to make sure your facts are straight and you are not putting your company in an untenable position. Don't let your legal counsel recast the letter in legalese.

DOs and DON'Ts of Press Releases

DO	DON'T
Give the lead paragraph extra attention; rewrite it two or three times, and then polish it some more.	Let the point of your story be drowned in irrelevant detail.
Use superlatives like *first, biggest, only,* but only if they are justified.	Use "hard-sell" words like *breakthrough, amazing, unique, revolutionary, sensational.*
Keep the headlines short: 4 to 8 words is good, up to 12 is acceptable.	Try to be funny or clever in a headline — or anywhere else in the text.
State only facts.	Give opinions or try to pass opinions off as facts.
Keep the text short: There is no merit in a long release.	Editorialize (i.e., avoid writing "readers should . . ." or "users are advised to. . . ."
Avoid flowery language.	Announce every event or product introduction. A statement should stand on its own merits without the aid of such props.
Substantiate claims made in the headline or lead paragraph.	Start release with a negative statement, a quotation, or a numeral.
Use trademarks and brand names sparingly.	Overdo trademark use; once a page is enough. Also don't set it in all caps, or use asterisk, footnote, or ®.
Use sharp, well-cropped photos.	Use retouched photos, or ones that do not show the dimensions of the subject clearly.
Keep the needs and interests of the editor and the readers foremost in your mind.	Try to pass off advertising copy or technical or promotional literature as editorial material.

Correcting Your Own Errors

If an error gets by on your end, don't blame the agency or the nearest secretary. It should be the responsibility of the company's publicity supervisor to double check all copy to make sure the facts are presented correctly.

If a release goes out that contains an error, but it is detected quickly, a phone call (if only a few publications are involved) is recommended.

If the error is not caught for a week or more, phone calls to all the publications receiving the release are still necessary. You can only hope that the editor will still have time to make the correction, if he has decided to use it. This may be a situation where you're glad the editor tossed the release, if the mistake was a dandy.

One kind of error is inexcusable: typos or spelling errors. Proof all copy before it goes to the printer. Word processors have spelling checkers, which can help identify errors and typos, but are often useless with homonyms.

A good way to proof is to read it through, word by word, to pick up goofs and make certain it is sensible; then read it backward, word by word. It won't make any sense, but will force you to concentrate on the spelling of each word.

Observing these guidelines on writing and style can be helpful for almost any type of news writing. The only exception is technical writing. A writer should always strive for clarity, but the best guidance will come from the publications themselves, because of the many different levels of technical writing and the various audiences.

Being on Time

Any good communicator meets deadlines, whether they are advertising closing dates, deadlines set by an editor, or internal objectives.

Figure 7-1 is a typical timing schedule for story preparation and approval. A feature or case history story might take several days longer to clear because of outside sources and confirming technical data.

Figure 7-1 probably reflects the least amount of time you can expect to take to move a story from conception through completion, if it's sent through the post office or company mail. Overnight air and messenger service may be needed to meet a deadline.

Speeding Up Approvals

Here are some suggestions on how to move material quickly through the approval process.

Figure 7-1. How long does it take to do a story?

Action	Time*
1. Research, interviews, gathering data	3–5 days
2. Writing, editing	1–2 days
3. Photography	
Studio product photo	½–1 day
Location	1 day (travel extra)
Processing, selection	2 days
Prints	1 day (not including mailing)
4. Approval	
Marketing	2–3 days
Technical (if necessary)	2–3 days
Legal	2–3 days
5. Rewrite	1 day
6. Distribution	3–5 days
TOTAL	16½–27 days

* Some of these steps may take place simultaneously, including the photography and in-house approvals. If customers are involved in the process, it's best to wait until all company approvals have been obtained before sending the story on to a customer. Customer approvals may take anywhere from three days to two weeks.

- The copy should be as close to perfect as possible: all the facts included, points in order, sound journalistic style, and clear, error-free copy.
- Have a clear understanding of the people who *must* approve. There are frequently people in the approval stream who do not *have* to see news material; they are there for vanity reasons only. Try to get clear directions from management as to who must approve. The product manager and his boss, for example, should be at the top of the list. But you shouldn't have to have a news story approved by the advertising department. You might, however, put the department on your notification list so that your counterparts will know when it's mailed to media.
- Releases should be cleared with someone from your lab or technical service to make sure any claims made can be supported. In fact, you should designate

someone in the clearance chain who can confirm that there are data to back up any claims made, including any that may reflect upon your competitor.

- Have an understanding with the company attorney that you promise not to ask to edit his legal briefs if he promises to confine his comments to legal points only. There are more frustrated editors in the legal profession than in most others. You also might ask your legal department for guidance on what types of news material must be reviewed by an attorney. Probably not everything you release needs legal approval, but that is a decision you and your attorneys should make together.
- Once you have the direction as to who must see the copy, impress upon the approvers that news releases are *news* and need immediate attention. If someone travels frequently, ask that an alternate be designated.
- If outside approval is needed, have a polite understanding that it is to check quotes and technical accuracy only. An understanding that copy will receive immediate attention should be reached when the interviews are taking place.
- You may wish to add to the chart people's names and, in an adjacent column, the dates by which they have been requested to submit their approvals. Some of my colleagues find this a useful approach.

The ideal world would have a short approval form, a short approval cycle, and a story that zips through with no changes. But we are talking about the real world. Because changes are bound to be made in copy—many with good reason—plan for this so that there is not a last-minute rush or a panic two days after approval deadline has passed.

Approvals are important. There can be a lot of grief when a story proves to be inaccurate because the proper person did not review it. To make sure you get them all, use an approval form like that in Figure 7-2.

Try to keep the number of approvals to a minimum. Review your procedures with top management to help you obtain approvals more quickly than you are getting them now.

There are no agency personnel listed in the approval form in Figure 7-2. If an agency is preparing copy, make sure its review process is in place so that the copy is checked for style and accuracy before it is sent to you.

The names of the people who must review copy are to be added under press manager. These would include staff from the marketing and legal departments and, when necessary, technical people as well. I suggest that the first name listed below the press manager be the person who submitted the copy, so that he or she can clean and neatly type it before routing it on. I've found that people are less likely to change copy when they know the clean copy they are reviewing has already been carefully edited by a press manager.

One of the people in the review process should have an asterisk placed next to his or her name. As the footnote at the bottom of the figure shows, this person is responsible for confirming that any claims made in the news material can be verified.

Figure 7-2. Press material approval form.

```
From: _____

Date Routed: _____ Date Needed: _____
```

	Approved	
Route in turn to:	Initials	Date
Press Manager (Preliminary Review)		
Press Manager (Final Review)		

Subject _____

Products or Services _____

Communications Objectives _____

Media/Audiences _____

Photos or Illustrations _____

Distribution _____

* Claims verification: I certify that the facts and claims stated in the attached editorial material are accurate and that necessary supporting data are available and in our files or those of our consultants. At final approval, we will have a statement from any outside sources mentioned giving us permissions to use their names and statements attributed thereof.

Figure 7-3. Press release checklist.

	YES	NO
Headline Criteria		
1. Headline has sufficient news value to attract editor's attention.	——	——
2. Headline is concise.	——	——
Lead Criteria		
3. Lead is easy to understand.	——	——
4. Lead sentence is concise (15–35 words).	——	——
5. Contains key copy point.	——	——
6. Invites one to read further.	——	——
Body Copy Criteria		
7. Body copy is well organized; information appears in logical, orderly sequence with adequate paragraphing.	——	——
8. Overall article uses active voice and direct construction.	——	——
9. Technical terms are in clear, easily understood English.	——	——
10. Article (if applicable) follows newspaper style (inverted pyramid) with the least important elements at the end.	——	——
11. Writing is tight and factual; sentences and paragraphs are kept short.	——	——
12. Article is proper length; provides enough detail so editor/readers are not apt to have questions.	——	——
13. Attribution is credible and makes the point.	——	——
14. Link between company and brand names or trademarks is established.	——	——
15. Trademark usage not excessive.	——	——
Photo Criteria		
16. Photo is clear and well cropped.	——	——
17. Photo illustrates product use or application and features or benefits.	——	——
18. Photo has visual impact.	——	——
19. Photo caption is brief and explains features, benefits.	——	——
General Criteria		
20. Editorial contact and notes to editor (when needed) are included.	——	——

Getting It on Paper

After the story has been seen by everyone on the list, it is freshly typed and sent back to the press manager for a final review before distribution.

Summing Up

In this chapter I have provided you with many hints on how to write an effective press release. The press release checklist in Figure 7-3 covers many of my points and will be helpful to you after a draft of the release has been completed.

To reiterate, a news release runs from 1 to 3 pages; a feature might run as much as 15 double-spaced pages. Features are written to length set by the editor and the publication. They should not be padded with superfluous detail.

Good photos are essential for any type of news material. A story almost always runs with pictures, so make them good. If an editor accepts a feature idea and asks that it be written, this also means photos. Fact is, it is not unusual for photos to carry the story.

There also are many mechanical tasks involved with publicity, such as getting the right clearances, protecting your trademarks, and dealing with errors (yours and the editor's).

And, finally, good writing sets the professional off from the amateur. Be sure that any news material of yours that crosses an editor's desk provides answers to the right questions, contains news and information for the readers, and is written in a way that necessitates little rewrite.

8
Attracting Attention with the Right Photos

People like to look at pictures. That simple statement of fact has paid off for a client of Jeff Blumenfeld and Associates, a New York public relations agency. The client, a Colorado ski resort, made a sizable investment in getting excellent action and family skiing photos by John Russell. Because the client was willing to spend money to get the very best, the pictures have been used extensively in several outdoor and ski publications, newspapers, airline in-flight, and consumer magazines.

Good photos can help a company that has no staff publicist or agency get media attention. Kay and Jim Henry, who own Mad River Canoe Company in Waitsfield, Vermont, are both excellent photographers. When they were building their business a few years ago, they realized that the outdoor press was very important. Today, outdoor writers and publications know they have a wide selection of photos of just about every canoeing situation, and the Henrys get lots of calls for photos. While not the largest canoe company, Mad River has positioned itself as the leader, in part because the effort has been made to work closely with the outdoor press.

Good photography is just as essential in product publicity as good writing. If a photo is appealing, an editor will find it hard to resist, and it may very well determine whether the story is used. If an editor is tight for space or is laying out a page that needs visual interest to break up the news columns, a good photo may be just the solution.

A photo provides something straight copy can't—a visual concept or illustration of the story. It's a tossup whether a reader looks at the headline or the photo first, but the odds are that if the photo is outstanding, it will attract reader attention to the story. So the publicist who makes it an objective to get creative and imaginative photos to illustrate a story has increased the chances of the story being used.

What Makes a Good Photo?

If you have the "three basics for good publicity photos," your success rate will be higher:

1. It should tell a story.
2. It should show a product benefit.
3. It should show, or at least imply, action.

There are perhaps a few instances when none of the three would apply. But a photo of someone using a product, which suggests action, is far better than just a photo of the equipment, whether it's a toaster or heavy industrial machinery. The equipment operator shown in a photo will indicate the size. The photo should somehow show that the new equipment makes the operator's job easier, and provides a benefit to the employer. There are places where the static photo of the equipment or package will be used, such as in some new product columns in the trade press, but in general, showing someone eating a new food product is a far better photo than just the container. Always try to show an implied benefit: The person eating the food is obviously enjoying it, the skier is getting a good workout, the family paddling a canoe is having fun being together.

Many times the photo and what it depicts will be remembered longer than the story.

There are a few situations where photos aren't needed with releases, such as those announcing a distributor, some backgrounders, some personnel releases. When in doubt, however, spend the time and money and get the pictures. It's rare that the absence of photos can be justified because it would be too expensive or not appropriate, or "I didn't think it would fit." In every case, an exclusive *must* have photos.

An editor assigning a story to a freelancer or reporter will always ask for photos or send a photographer. It's automatic. And so it should be with publicists.

Nick Hancock, editor of *Canadian Machinery & Metalworking,* tells of receiving a news release describing a half-million-dollar machine tool that had no photo with it. The story was not used—there was no way to illustrate the points made in the printed release. Unlike Hancock, most of us know little about machine tools. But what we should know is that a person familiar with the industry can look at one and tell you what it does and how good it is. Including the photo would have added to the validity and supported the facts presented in the news release.

Most editors agree that a good photo does make a difference, either in deciding whether to run the story, or how much prominence to give it. They most certainly don't like to run just columns of type with no visual interest.

Thinking Like an Editor

Common sense dictates that publicists should not submit "Polaroid" prints, but that is exactly what more than one editor has complained about. Another gripe is receiving photos where nothing is identified.

If you ask editors what they like, the answers are quite general: The photo should be 8×10 size, tell a story, have good resolution, and show the product from an interesting angle. What these general comments really are saying is "I know a good photo when I see one." This means a publicist should know one too. The editors also suggest that if there is any question about the size of the product, a person or readily identifiable object should be placed in the picture. It often is a matter of the publicist's creativity and imagination.

Editors seem to glow when they get good pictures. Unfortunately, they get them about as often as they get well-written releases. But poorly written releases can be rewritten. Nothing can be done with poor photos.

Strong photos that can tell a story by themselves can be sent as a "photo release," meaning just a photo and caption. Several photos may also be submitted as a sequence, showing a step-by-step occurrence or stages of growth or building. A story may not have the news value to merit much consideration, but a photo or photo sequence that's visually interesting and appealing will frequently be used. Look for dramatic, creative photos that have an immediate attraction and then hold the viewer's eye. Figure 11-1 in Chapter 11 is an example of a photo release.

Shots with high visual interest are sometimes picked up and used on newspaper business pages. But the photo must be *good*. It is not uncommon at the wire services or newspapers that envelopes containing photos are not even opened, particularly if the editors have received unusable photos from the source in the past. Bob Goldberg, a former AP photographer who is currently with Wagner International Photos, offers this advice: "Get in close, then closer, to see things others don't see or what may not be apparent at first glance."

Another way of saying this is to take an unconventional look at the product. Shoot from a different angle. Get the photographer in the middle of the product, on a ladder, or on her knees. One misconception in product photography is the belief that it is essential to show the whole product—the machine, the medical instrument, the vehicle. It is not. Many more creative photos can be made if this idea is discarded. Look at the product as if you never saw it before and were challenged to make a photo that could hang in a gallery—or be acceptable to a wire service.

Good composition is the key to a good photo. A product photo often fails

Attracting Attention with the Right Photos 153

because the photographer is thinking about what the client wants instead of thinking about what might stop the readers and make them want to read the caption and the adjoining story. Focus on the benefit, not the product. (Compare the effects of Figures 8-1 and 8-2.)

Some Technical Tips

- You must show the outline of the product or its use. If you think black and white even when you are shooting color, you can avoid having background tones blending with the tones in your product or product feature.

Figure 8-1. A very dull photo is a product sitting there doing nothing. This is not a can opener, but a "pneumatic positioner," which won a design award. It could have profited not only from cropping, but also from showing how it is used. How many readers will even have a clue from looking at the photo?

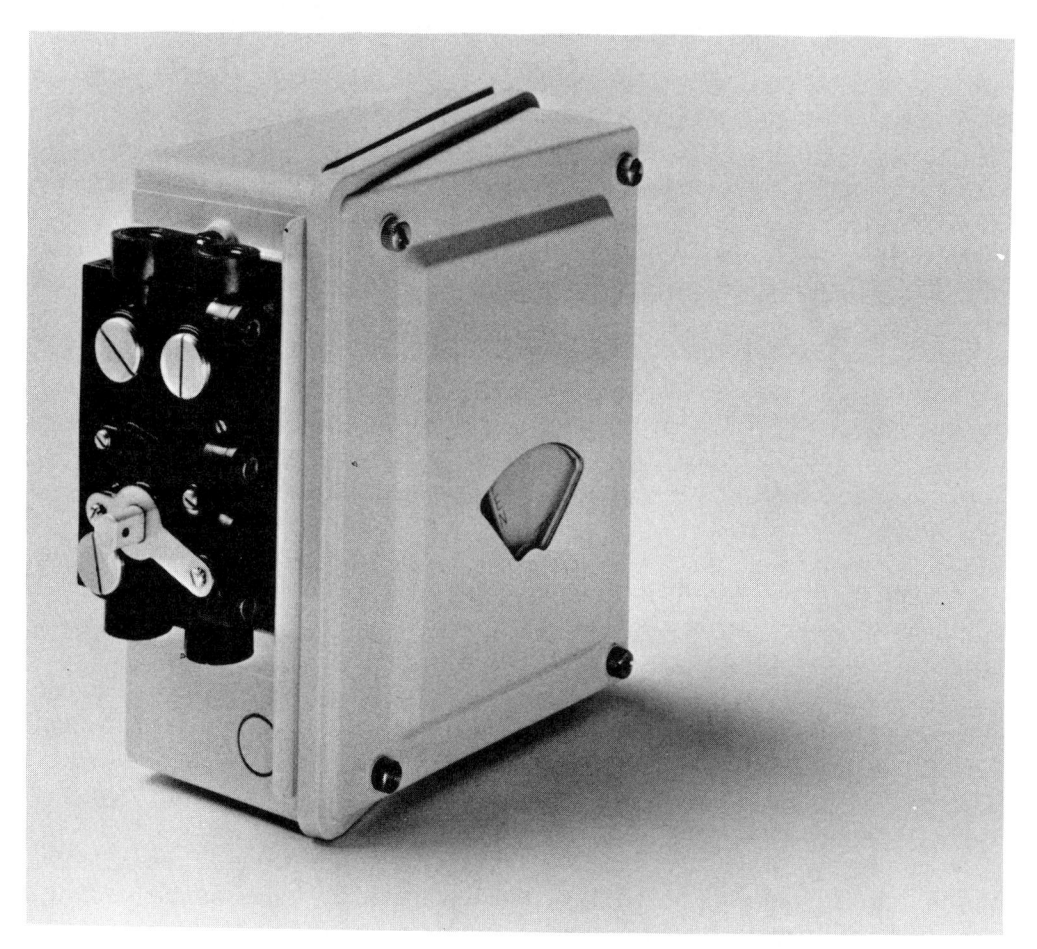

Figure 8-2. Here is an example of a photo that is a real eye-catcher. Called "Getting a Handle on Shock Absorption," this photo illustrates the use of a polyester elastomer to create a built-in spring steel shock absorber for the hammer handle.

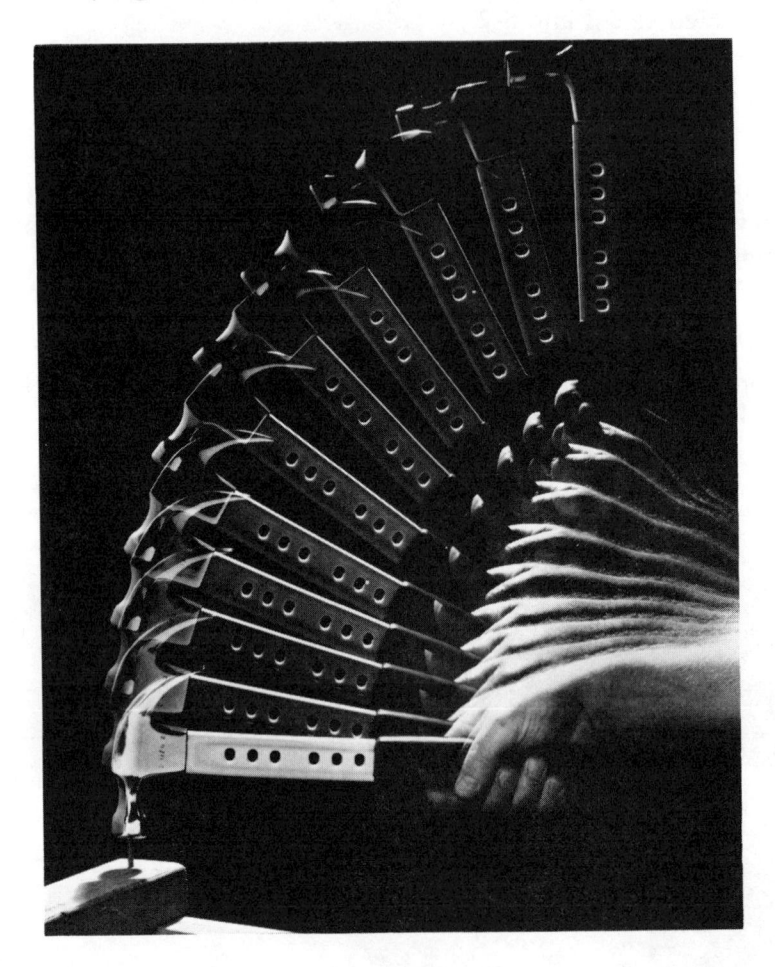

• Crop tightly and creatively. The publicist should crop extraneous areas of the photo, not leave it to the editor. Cropping will most always improve the photo, because it will bring the subject and action into better focus.

• When you are shooting color transparencies, you must always crop in the camera. Check the full frame before shooting. Look at how the photo is framed and how the subject fits in the frame.

• In setting up a photo of people, stay away from the "spread-out" look. Get them in close together, with your products arranged in a tight area.

• Think column width rather than depth. The editor has to fit the photo in column format. Unless it's a head shot, which will fit in half a newspaper column, your photo will likely be used in one column as a vertical, or two or more as a horizontal.

Attracting Attention with the Right Photos 155

- Try your best to avoid having to use callouts, arrows, boxes, and other devices to make a point. Your unretouched photo should tell the story. If a component using your product is part of a large assembly, it may need to be identified with an arrow. But also take a closeup of the component, and show its size. An alternative is line art with an "exploded" area to illustrate how something works or where it fits.
- It's essential to show size. I once reviewed a photo of an object that looked like a child's Mickey Mouse hat. Fortunately there was another photo showing a hand and a spare tire; the object was identified as the lug nut that holds a spare tire in place in a car trunk (see Figures 8-3 and 8-4). Be creative: placing paper clips or pencils near the product is overdone. The use of hands, people, tools, or known objects is much preferred.
- Always keep in mind that an 8×10 photo, unless it will be used on a cover, will be greatly reduced in print. In one instance, an 8 × 10 photo was supposed to demonstrate that an electric drill could survive a fall from a three-story building. The photo showed the entire building, with the drill passing by the second story; an insert on the 8×10 revealed that the drill had subsequently landed intact. The trouble with this photo was that the falling drill appeared as little more than a blur. If the photo were reduced, the drill in flight would have disappeared entirely! A simple shot of the drill being used after it was dropped would have been much more effective. The caption line could have described the perfect operation of the drill, despite the three-story drop onto concrete. In an even better approach, an individual could have been shown bashing the drill with a hammer, followed by a shot of the same individual using the undamaged, and still functional, drill.

Why send 8 × 10s if they are going to be reduced anyway? Aside from the fact that it is standard practice, and the way photos are sent over the news wires, the best reason is that an 8 × 10 is far easier to see and evaluate than a smaller size. Details are clearer. And it is easier to crop, if cropping is needed. It must be sharp and in focus because if it's sharp to begin with, it will be sharp when reduced. But a fuzzy photo won't be any less fuzzy when it is reduced; in fact, it will be fuzzier.

- For color photos, most publications prefer 35 mm. slides or, better still, 3½ × 3½ or 4 × 5 transparencies. (A few will still want to see 8 × 10 color prints. I suspect this is so the editor can see the photo better and doesn't have to hold it up to the light as with a transparency.)

Working Well with People

Before you photograph people, whether they are in a supermarket, at a factory, at the office, or on a farm, make sure they are in complete agreement that their likenesses may be used for publicity purposes. Even if they are your own employees, ask each to sign a photo release (see Figure 8-5). Some lawyers recommend this permission be in exchange for "good and valuable consideration," which can be $1 to each person photographed.

Figure 8-3. This is a spare tire wing nut, but you'd never know it from this "Mickey Mouse" hat photo. There is no indication of size, and the product is just sitting there.

Figure 8-4. This is a much better photo of the wing nut because it shows how and where the product is used. The caption for this photo concisely explained the item's benefits.

Figure 8-5. Sample photo release.

DATE _____

For good and valuable consideration received, I,

_____
(please print)

hereby grant my full and irrevocable consent to the use and publication by (name of company) or its assigns for commercial and/or art purposes, the photograph or photographs described below.

Story or subject: _____

_____

Signed: _____
(parent or guardian of minor subject)

Address _____

_____

_____

Giving a dollar can seem like an insult if the person believes he or she is being paid as a model. You must make it perfectly clear the photos are for publicity (a brief explanation of that may be appropriate) and, while you appreciate their taking the time to work with you, you need a photo release and the dollar just makes it legal. "It certainly can't compensate you for the time you spent." This practice *is never followed* in Europe because it might create highly disagreeable and embarrassing situations — the token amount is deemed insulting. Be careful in the United States too. Explain very carefully that it is not a payment for services. Also, agreement for publicity does not automatically cover advertising use.

You don't need prior agreement or releases if you are photographing a horde of shoppers in a store, or a crowd around your booth at a trade show. You also don't need to get clearance from a public figure such as a mayor or governor, if that person is visiting your company or attending a company event. But celebrities such as film, stage, and sports stars are not considered public figures and their photos cannot be used for commercial purposes, even for product publicity.

Give people advance notice of your plans. Most people when they learn they will be photographed will, despite their protestations, be flattered. Women will want to fix their hair and wear a clean smock or blouse, and the men wear a pressed suit or clean coveralls. If you get to the site and find you can't use the photos, take them anyway and send copies to all the people who got ready for you. Even if the photos are never sent to a publication, send prints to the subjects. It's good customer relations.

If you're doing a story on a customer, send a set of photos along with the story for review. When shooting a head and shoulder shot to accompany a release on a promotion, transfer, award, or the like, show a number of proofs to the subject and let him or her make the selection. Also get a nice 8 × 10 as a surprise gift. (The photo sent out with the news release can be a 4 × 5.)

Adding people to a photo of otherwise inanimate objects can add interest, but try to avoid the posed look. The key is to use the person to help explain how the equipment works. If it's medical, a technician can be checking or running a sample. If it is industrial equipment, a worker should be seen using it. If it's a consumer product, the photo should relate to the consumer benefit. The photo does not have to show the entire product, particularly if it's equipment. It's better to photograph part of it from an interesting angle, and focus on the benefit.

It is a rare publicist who releases photos of scantily clad women to attract attention to a product, but editors still receive them. Granted there are some publications that will run these, but this is no excuse to consider them. There is nothing inherently wrong with showing an attractive woman in a photo. It is not exploitive if she is doing something she logically would be doing as part of her job. The focus must remain on the product and she must not detract from the actual product or its use.

Taking Good Product Shots

A sure way to get a photo rejected is to show the nameplate or product name as the key focal point of the shot. If you go on an assignment with a sales representative, you nearly always will be asked to take a photo with the product name displayed prominently. There seems to be a strong desire by many salespeople to move a drum or can into the picture, as if the editor or the readers will fail to get the point until they see the product's name and company logo. Logic seldom prevails in these situations. Rather than try to explain why editors won't use these kinds of photos, take the "product" picture, then take the pictures that have a chance of being used. The nameplate on machinery or a vehicle can be shown if it fits and is an integral part of the equipment. But even here, don't emphasize.

A classic example of turning the mundane into the magnificent was a photo suggested by a Du Pont publicist for reverse osmosis. In brief, this is a technology widely used to turn brackish or sea water into potable water. A tube contains the membranes that do all the work. The ends of these look like fluorescent lamp units. By themselves they are of very little visual interest. The creative publicist removed the membranes from the tube, coiled them, lit them creatively, and created a striking photo that was used on three covers and in innumerable stories (see Figure 8-6). This was a case where the photo literally carried the story. This goes somewhat against the advice to stay away from arty shots. The exception is: unless you can get something great. And if you can, go for a cover shot.

Think "cover" on any photo shoot and always try to find a cover shot in any situation, whether on location or in a studio. Be sure to shoot a vertical format. But shoot a cover photo with a particular publication in mind. It is probably not going to cost any more to set up for it. For a given publication, you must know where the publication title and logo appear on the cover, and leave enough room on the transparency. You also must compose your photo in such a way that there is room for type "billboarding" the inside features. In other words, leave "white space" for type. And give the photo lots of depth with good backlighting and color contrast.

Shooting on Location

The rule for location shooting is "Shoot everything in sight." But first scout the location to understand what will be in sight and what may be restricted, so the photographer won't be yelled at or sirens set off. If you're shooting in a plant, ask the superintendent to send you some pictures of the plant. These may be unusable for publicity, but will give you some idea of what to expect when you get there, what you will need for your story, and what kind of equipment to take (such as

Figure 8-6. These membranes were removed from a reverse osmosis unit. Skillfully lit, they are far more effective than a photo of the tube or unit that holds them would have been.

lights) and to borrow on site (such as a ladder). Review your assignment sheet (see Figure 6-4) and try to determine what kind of photos you will need to support the story. Then discuss these with your business or plant contact to review what will be available to you.

Check the shift changes and breaks, particularly if you're working in a union plant. Union or not, it's good practice not to ask anyone to work one minute longer than necessary or interfere with anyone's break. Work around their schedules. When the 5:00 whistle blows, it's quitting time for the photographer too.

Check in advance with a company's public relations office or the employee publication editor, because many times these people can help you get your story

Attracting Attention with the Right Photos 161

and photos. The plant newspaper or the PR people may also have file photos that can help your story, and they may be able to suggest some photo ideas. Some plants do not have a public relations person on site. In this case, make sure corporate PR people or the agency folks know where you are and what you are doing *in advance.*

Setting Up

If the area you are shooting in is dirty or cluttered with rags, cans, and so on, clean it up. It may look that way all the time, and return that way when you leave, but a sloppy or dirty environment can only reflect poorly on the company, fail to show the product or action properly, and may cause the photo to be rejected. And clean up the film boxes and containers and other trash you create when you leave.

Follow good safety practices. Not only should you and the photographer observe to the letter the safety rules in force where you are shooting, you should make sure that the people you are shooting are wearing proper safety attire too. If it calls for hardhats, wear hardhats and take photos of people in hardhats. Ditto for safety glasses, masks, and special apparel.

Check power sources. Know your power requirements and make them known to your host. Strobes won't pull enough power to blow the area's fuses and circuit breakers. If you are using other types of lights, you may need help from the company electrician to help you tap into additional power. Don't shut the plant down by overloading the circuits.

Finally, let the photographer do her job. If you have briefed her well, she will know how to proceed. Let her set up and direct the shot; that is, show people where to stand or how they should relate themselves to the product or action. If you have any comment or criticism, ask the photographer to step away from the action for a moment. Consult on the shot quietly and in private. Chances are, the photographer will be working to please you and showing you the Polaroids, or ask you to look through the eyepiece before tripping the shutter. (Many photographers shoot Polaroid prints first to check lighting.)

If you cannot go on location, you should provide thorough directions on what you expect, but also fill the photographer in on some of the people she might meet, especially if you expect the sales rep to "direct" as well. The understanding should be that the photographer gets your photos first. Then, if there is time, she can accommodate the sales rep. Make this clear.

Shooting in the Studio

Many product photos are shot in a studio. The product can be a new machine small enough for a tabletop, new garments on professional models, all the way to a full room setting. Where a photo must be well lit, where lights need to be reset for different angles, where a photographer needs ample room to move around, and where changing and dressing rooms for models are needed, it is essential to use a studio. It may even be worthwhile to arrange for a full room setting in a studio where you can light the subject well, rather than go on location and have to set up lights and worry about power. A number of photographers are equipped to do this. Many food photographers, for example, have permanent kitchen sets and home economists as consultants. Armstrong Co. is a major supplier of kitchen setting photography to the major women's interest magazines, and has full studio facilities at its Lancaster, Pennsylvania, site.

Writing Captions

A photo may be worth a thousand words, but it still needs a written explanation. This caption, or underline, is attached to every photo sent. It is in two parts. One section, which stays with the photo, has the name, address, and telephone number of the person and company or agency sending the photo. The second section, which is sent folded up over the face of the photo and then torn off by the photo editor, edited, and sent for typesetting, describes the photo — no more, no less. It should not repeat verbatim copy that is in the text, and it should not include any additional points not covered in the release.

The caption identifies by name any person or persons shown in the photo and what they are doing. A caption describes, in the present tense, any action taking place in the photo, or any products shown. That's normally all that is needed.

Copy that is unrelated to what is in the photo belongs in the accompanying news material. I have edited copy on photo captions that was not in the story, and also photo captions that were so detailed the editor could ignore the story and just use the caption.

A "kicker line" or brief headline (in all caps) of four or five words can be used, but is not necessary. Consider that most captions run in publications are only two or three lines at most, so keep them brief.

The exception is a photo release, where no release or feature is sent with the photo, just a caption. You must provide interesting material in the caption, so it will be longer than usual. The *Associated Press Stylebook* has some good suggestions for photo releases.

The *AP Stylebook* sets out some basic rules for captions for photos it sends out on the wire to member newspapers: "The caption's job is to describe and explain the picture to the reader. The challenge is to do it interestingly, accurately, always in good taste. A further challenge is to write the caption, whenever appropriate, in a sprightly, lively vein."

Attracting Attention with the Right Photos

The book cites the Ten Tests of a Good Caption:

1. Is it complete?
2. Does it identify, fully and clearly?
3. Does it tell when?
4. Does it tell where?
5. Does it tell what is in the picture?
6. Does it have the names spelled correctly, with the proper name on the right person?
7. Is it specific?
8. Is it easy to read?
9. Have as many adjectives as possible been removed?
10. Does it suggest another picture?

And Rule No. 11, the Cardinal Rule, never, never to be violated: *"Never write a caption without seeing the picture."*

Rule No. 11 should be observed by publicists distributing copy for clearances and review before they have received the prints from the photographer. Not only does it make little sense to write captions describing photos you *think* you will see, but the company people reviewing (including legal) must see the photos along with the copy. Clear them with customers too, where called for.

Distributing the Photos to Media

Send only clear, sharp prints, with good contrast. As one editor said, "I want to see the pores in the person's skin." Don't try to cut costs by making prints on machines or by other automated devices. Make custom prints. If the photo is good, why spoil it by sending just a *fair* print?

If a publication uses color photos, don't send black and white. Send color transparencies or slides. Conversely, don't send color to publications that run only black and white.

Some company and agency mailing lists are keyed to show those publications that use photos and those that seldom do. The latter group can be dropped from the photo release file, but before you do, you might wish to send a brief note to the editor asking if he wants to continue to receive photos.

My colleagues in Europe do not send photos to publications that may not end up using them but instead attach an order form with a phone number an editor can call to order photos. The editors know which photos are available because they are reproduced on the news release. This system seems to work quite well in Europe and can have a decided cost benefit. Considering the large group of countries to which releases are distributed, the number of releases and photos needed can go into the hundreds. However, because the media lists used by most U.S. publicists to reach their markets generally consist of less than a hundred names, the system is not as cost effective in this country and is used to a lesser extent. Keep in mind also that not many editors have the time to call for the photo and then hold the story until it arrives. To summarize, the possible return on investment in getting good photos out promptly to editors outweighs the costs of printing, handling, and mailing.

What about a massive mailing to newspapers? Even newspaper lists need to be set up so that the most important ones in terms of circulation, demographics, or ADIs are selected. So there probably will be far less than the 1,500 or so dailies involved. The best approach, however, is to try to place a wire story or a wire photo. If the subject has high visual interest and is photographed by someone who understands the needs of the wire services, it will have a good chance.

But no matter what media or how many, never ask that a photo you have sent for consideration be returned. It may be proper at times to ask that a color transparency be returned if the editor requests a photo from you. It's good practice to have an ample supply of transparencies (and black and white prints) of particularly good product photos for just such instances.

Finding a Good Photographer

You can't go second class, and you need to select your photographer most carefully.

The product publicist, unlike her associate in advertising, seldom has the luxury of having an art director when determining what photos will be needed to illustrate a story, or selecting and directing the photographer who will take them. She's on her own, so she's got to find the best photographer to do the job—and then supervise the work.

Because much of the work is news-related, it would seem that the logical place to look would be at a newspaper. If a newspaper photographer is freelancing, he or she will have a portfolio and references. There is an advantage to using photographers with news experience. They will see news value far better than a photographer whose specialty is advertising. Many newspaper photographers are talented and will take the photo you want. Bob Goldberg claims virtually any subject can be made interesting if photographed by a good news photographer. And many will be acceptable to the wire services. On the other hand, I've found that some good news photographers are just not suited for publicity work.

Make sure the photographer will use some creativity, not just take the mundane. While you can't afford to be too arty when you take photos for newspapers, the photographs that win the regional and national photojournalism awards are dramatic and eye-catching.

Attracting Attention with the Right Photos

Before you hire any photographer, check the portfolio, keeping in mind you are seeing only the best work. If you spot some work you particularly like, ask for a reference. Check the reference. Find out if the photographer completed the assignment satisfactorily, if the photos were delivered on time, and what was charged.

The Yellow Pages is not a good source. Many photographers listed specialize in family and wedding photography and can be quite expensive. They are usually adamant about who owns the negatives, because selling prints is a big part of their business. And many do not think journalistically.

A good solution may be to work with a photo service; see Chapter 11 for more on this.

The Contract

Before any agreement is reached with a photographer, the buyer should be familiar with copyright laws and "work for hire" guidelines. The person for whom the photos are being taken should own all the negatives. This is "work for hire" and must be spelled out in writing before anything else. If the photographer will not agree, or wants to limit the agreement, find somebody else.

The provisions of international copyright laws on the protection of creative works makes this a must. Unless agreed to beforehand, these provisions state that the photographer is the owner of the copyright to any photos he or she has taken. In very practical terms, this means that such photo cannot be reproduced without the photographer's permission and a fee can be extracted every time a photo is published. It also means the photographer can hold the negatives and originals and insist on being the sole supplier of any prints or duplicates. This can get sticky, and can place the publicist in a difficult spot if photos are needed quickly or there's not enough in the budget to pay for excessive print costs.

It is essential to be clear on who will own what when the job is completed. The *owner* should be the company hiring the photographer. Owning worldwide rights to photographs means you don't have to renegotiate every time you want to use the photos. One way to accomplish this is to insert the following paragraph in your assignment sheet to the photographer with the request that a copy be signed and returned before the job is undertaken. This should be adequate to protect your interests, but I suggest you check with your legal department.

> All right, title and interest in the photographs, including negatives, under this order shall pass to the purchasor without territorial or other restrictions on its ownership and use upon payment of the supplier's invoice.

Signature of photographer/date   Client signature/date

Figure 8-7. This photo is a good, tight product shot showing new outdoor garments. Note the models are professionals and that they have not been stiffly posed.

Attracting Attention with the Right Photos   167

Figure 8-8. This product photo, which illustrates sleeping bags, has numerous problems. The photo is too busy, has only fair contrast, and does not emphasize the campers enough. The photographer could have improved the photo by moving in closer and showing the people getting out of the bags in the morning, thus suggesting that the campers stayed warm and slept well.

If the photographer's print costs are reasonable, I normally leave the negatives with the photographer and order prints when I need them. A photographer is likely to be responsive to deadlines, provide good prints, and generally do a good job for you because he wants to keep your business.

If there is the slightest chance that publicity photos might be used in advertising, I believe it is fair that the contract spell out that an additional fee will be paid for advertising use. You also can include in the contract that the photographer has a right to exhibit "your" photos (as his own work, of course) and use them for gallery showings and promotional purposes. But the photographer cannot sell prints, because he no longer holds the rights to them.

The Costs

There is no rule to follow on costs. They can run a few hundred dollars a day for publicity, and several hundred more if the photos are going to be used for advertising. High-fashion and architectural photographers cost more than those that take factory shots. Big-city photographers cost more than small-town ones. Add to the cost the model's fee and studio time (if any). You also pay travel and film/developing costs. Make sure all the details are understood up front.

Many of the better photographers have assistants. They perform a valuable service, and can help move the work along quickly by loading film, moving lights, carrying gear, as the photographer concentrates on what he or she is supposed to do — take pictures. Usually the photographer's fee includes the assistant.

If you cancel an assignment at the last minute, expect to pay a half-day or day rate. This is included in most contracts. However, many photographers work without contracts, so be fair.

If the photographer did not get all the photos you requested, he or she should have a good reason for the failure or agree to reshoot. If an "act of God" was involved in the failure, there should be an understanding of what this entails before the shoot. If you failed to give clear directions to the photographer, and need additional photos, you are obligated to pay for them.

Because photography sessions can be expensive, there is often a temptation to try to recycle advertising photos. Resist. The rule is, don't use photos that have appeared in space advertising for publicity. This is similar to the rule that if a product has been introduced through advertising, it has lost its editorial value. However, it may be possible that a photo used in a brochure, and only for this purpose, can be sent to illustrate a feature. In submitting some background information to *Fortune* for a story it was doing on one of our products, we sent along a brochure. The editors, in addition to using the photographs they had made for the story, selected one of the brochure photos. This is unusual, but since the picture had not been published in the media, it was a bona fide candidate for publicity. Figure 6-5 shows the photo that was used.

Figure 8-9. Photographer's assignment sheet.

Date _____

To: (name of photographer)

Assignment

    Place: _____

    Date: _____

    Time: _____
    Site contact: (name, title, and phone number — not needed if studio)

Photos Needed

    Describe each shot. *Be very specific and detailed.*
    Indicate whether black and white or color; also camera type and format.

If possible, provide sketches or other illustrations.

    List *must* photos.
    List restrictions such as proprietary equipment or processes, areas to avoid, etc.

Delivery

    Date material must be submitted:

        Contact sheets _____

        Slides or transparencies ____

        Prints (if any) needed _____

On the other hand, many good publicity photos will work with ads. Photography costs can be reduced if advertising that will follow publicity is considered when the publicity is photographed. My own experience has not been good, however. I find that whether I get good pictures or not, the ad agency art director will want to use his favorite photographer and get his own pictures. Be adamant. Discuss his needs and invite him to provide an assignment sheet and even come along. If both publicity and advertising photos can be made at the same time, the cost saving can be significant.

Working with Models

Work only with legitimate model agencies, who should be known by your photographer. Let the photographer book the models, subject to your approval, of course. Many photographers have preferences in models because they have found some they can work with easier than others. The photographer should also be responsible for paying them and obtaining photo releases. Most models will carry books showing hours spent, hourly rates, and their own photo release forms. Models' time on the set and costs should be clearly understood in advance.

The model should suit the situation. You don't need a high-fashion model for a photo of a woman pushing a shopping cart or using a computer. And resist any offers from amateurs.

It is far better to use professional models even if you know any attractive young men or women in the company who have "modeled," or their co-workers rave about how "they could be models." Perhaps so, but the chances of them being able to relax and move properly is small. Being attractive, even beautiful, does not mean that a person is photogenic. Use professionals and you won't be putting anyone in an embarrassing position if the photos turn out to be unusable. An exception is when an employee is actually involved in the situation you are photographing. Then the employee will probably feel comfortable. Figure 8-7 shows how models can be effectively portrayed; Figure 8-8 is a photo in which models have not been used to their best advantage.

Giving Good Directions

One last word: Check and double check all directions and have everything in writing, including an assignment sheet such as the one shown in Figure 8-9.

In summary, the person responsible for publicity not only has to be a good judge of photography to meet editorial standards, but also must frequently spend considerable time contracting for and directing photography. Even when the publicity person works with a public relations agency, much attention to detail and direction are needed.

9
Strategies for Using Broadcast Media

Today, newspapers are no longer the prime source of news for most Americans. It is television. Thus, broadcast—what *Broadcasting Magazine* calls "the fifth estate"—is growing more critical as a publicity outlet, especially with the proliferation of cable television and satellite program transmission. And radio has also certainly held its own, in spite of competition from television, as a viable publicity outlet.

The Nature of Broadcast

The importance of broadcast is that it is increasing its influence as *the* way most people get their news and as the source they find most credible. A 1984 report by the Roper Organization for the Television Information Office shows that 64 percent of the public gets most of its news from television, 40 percent from newspapers, 14 percent from radio, 4 percent from magazines, and 4 percent from other people. (This totals more than 100 percent because of multiple responses.)

Share of audience breaks out to 51 percent for television, 31 percent for newspapers, and 18 percent for all others. Even more interesting, 46 percent of the respondents said that television is the single most relied-upon medium; newspapers got a low 22 percent share. Small wonder then that publicists are concentrating more on television than ever before! And just think of the number of outlets:

According to *Broadcasting Magazine,* in early 1986, there were 4,888 commercial AM radio stations, 4,293 commercial FM radio stations, and 1,404 educational radio stations. Among commercial TV stations there were 563 VHF and 623 UHF; among noncommercial TV stations there were 117 VHF and 211 UHF. Interna-

171

tional Communications Research figures show 6,668 U.S. cable systems as of December 1985, most of which offer an outlet for local programming.

Exactly how many radio and television stations have talk shows is hard to determine, but a look at local program schedules shows that a lot of them do. And many of these are looking for guests—opportunities for the smart publicist who can match the stations' needs with his or her client's.

The public's increasing appetite for visually exciting news is reflected in the growth of local news shows. Many that used to be on for a half hour at dinnertime and again at 11:00 P.M. are now broadcasting in the morning, midday, an hour or more at pre-prime time, and again at 11:00 P.M. The audience is there not only for the local shows, but for cable as well. Interviews and talk shows, as well as business news, are also popular cable offerings.

Although many experienced public relations people are print-oriented and do not use broadcast as often as print, the newer breed of practitioners grew up with television and appreciate it as a powerful way to reach large audiences.

Why It's Not Like Print

It need not be difficult to work with the broadcast media, but it does require some special skills and approaches. Publicists must understand the requirements of news directors or program producers, just as they understand the requirements of print editors. They must also be familiar with how these media work. The "news" that interests broadcast is often different from the news directed to print.

Unlike print, broadcast is not "targeted media." There are some very broad considerations to be aware of, but in general, the difference is that television reaches vast numbers of people. Thus any publicity material released should be of fairly wide interest.

Unlike print, broadcast gives you far less time to tell your story. Broadcast stories are here and gone in just a few seconds. So you must be aware when recommending or creating publicity material for broadcast that the best you can expect is increased awareness and a favorable impression. Because audiences are "bombarded with stimulae, that's about all television can do," says Marvin Friedman, vice president of Hill and Knowlton.

There are other things to consider. Unlike print, broadcast is a costly medium. Because it is highly visual, the cost of a video news release can run to several thousand dollars, compared with only a few hundred for a print release, including photos.

Furthermore, broadcast's effects are difficult to measure. And the results of the publicity efforts are harder and more expensive to merchandise than print. Unless it is transcribed, there is no permanent record—as there is with print—for publicists to show their efforts.

Strategies for Using Broadcast Media

Television and radio publicity work best when they're part of a well-organized program, but they should not be the focal point. So develop a well-planned, strategic approach using all the appropriate media. Unless you understand how broadcast works and use it wisely, your effort and investment will be wasted.

Which Experts to Call

To understand the broadcast media, publicists and agencies have had to learn how to work with them. And just as public relations firms once recruited from the newspaper field, today's publicists now hire broadcast producers and news directors for their special talents and knowledge of the medium.

If you have a communications program for a product with national interest and you need broadcast coverage, get some outside help. Many public relations agencies are skilled in the special techniques and approaches needed to work effectively with broadcast.

There is also a growing number of firms specializing in producing and distributing video news releases. Some are headed by former broadcasters; Jerry Gordon, who runs Gordon Newsfilms in San Francisco, has been a news director and producer on all three networks.

In fact, most of this chapter is based on knowledge gained from agency broadcast specialists, notably George Glazer and Marvin Friedman of Hill and Knowlton in New York, Joanna Hanes of Hanes and Associates in Washington, D.C., and Jerry and John Gordon of Gordon Newsfilms in San Francisco and Washington.

When to Think Broadcast

There are three basic areas where product publicity directed to TV and radio can be effective: introducing a new product, reinforcing the product value, or tying in to news opportunities.

Introducing a New Product

If the product can be made visually interesting for television—and there is a new and novel lead to it—the same possibilities for coverage exist that do for print. The needs of the audience must be considered, however. The story material should be of interest to the viewer; but it should not be bogged down with data or statistics—a sure way to have it rejected by a news director or producer. Remember, think visual for TV, sound for radio, and brevity for both.

Reinforcing the Product

Unless the product is new, of broad interest, and has a good news angle, opportunities for coverage are rare. However, the message can be delivered in a more subtle way on network morning news or local offerings that tie-in with these shows. A publicist can also easily find a variety of outlets to approach in nearly every market: local television feature shows, which may be termed "pop news" programs (for example, "PM Magazine"), and the many local talk shows that cover entertainment, trends, styles, and community activities. Add the plethora of local news programming plus the growing number of hours devoted to news, and publicists can find increasing opportunities to develop and place publicity.

Tieing-in with News Events

The publicist can often take advantage of an event that is in the news, if the product or service can relate directly to it. Look for trends, fads, and seasonal events (Christmas shopping, Easter fashions, and the like); good tie-ins are products or services with health and safety benefits. The Carl Byoir agency (now a part of Hill and Knowlton), for example, worked with the Consumer Product Safety Commission on a television news clip that recommended nonallergenic makeup rather than masks for youngsters at Halloween. There was no product mention, just a visual of the container and footage of mothers helping their children put it on. This low-key but effective use of television paid off with increased product sales in the cities where the spot ran.

Television

Developing Television Interest

There are two basic ways to get television coverage. One is to get the station to come to you, with an attention-getting media event or a press conference offering significant news. The second is to take the story to them by way of a video news release. More on this technique later.

Television has some additional needs. As Joanna Hanes points out, "You must understand how the broadcast media works before you can use it." For publicity to work, it must meet these criteria: It must be *news*. It must tie in with breaking news or a newsworthy subject of current interest, or demonstrate why *this* product makes a difference to the audience. Not just a part of the audience — but a *big* chunk of the audience.

Making a Good TV Story

The ingredients necessary for television are very clear.
- *Is there human interest?* Can the viewer relate to the product, or empathize with the person on the screen? Will the viewer feel good, be happier, healthier, make a job easier, have more free time, be loved or admired as a result of using the product?
- *Is it timely?* Is it *news*? The subject may be a new miracle drug, a quick-rising yeast, a service to business, or a new way to prepare or store food. What do consumers think about it? How does the person pushing the shopping cart in the supermarket feel about it? Is there an expert to attest to its safety? The subject may also be a new way to reduce highway accidents, or the danger of fire. It may sound ghoulish to use disaster to promote a product, but the fact is, a safety-related product will be far more newsworthy if you show how it could have saved lives or reduced injuries.
- *Is there a pocketbook interest?* Will it help people make money or save money? Many new products claim they "save" money for those who use them. Often, product publicists develop a television angle for a wholesale product with an indirect consumer benefit — with its use, a manufacturer can cut his product's cost and this will ultimately benefit the consumer. If a button manufacturer discovers a product that can be sewn onto a garment once and never fall off, then you not only have a print news story but also a visually interesting one.
- *Is there a health angle?* Will you live longer, stay thinner, prevent flu, reduce your chance of a heart attack, stop getting migraine headaches? Even an industrial process that reduces the amount of sulphur dioxide in the air is health-related, and can be visually dramatized. Losing weight is a perennial issue, but so are jogging, walking, quitting smoking, eating more fruit and less red meat (or eating *more* meat, if you listen to the cattle-growers), eating more of the right carbohydrates — all are health angles that lend themselves to broadcast publicity. And if anyone can come up with a way to cure the common cold, the media will be beating down the doors.
- *Is it trendy?* If the product or service can ride the crest of a trend or, even better, be at the forefront of one, there is television interest. It could be lifestyles, cars, vacations, or clothing inspired by a hot TV series. It could be health-related trends (jogging, physical fitness classes and cassettes), which are now a multibillion-dollar industry. It could even be toys. (Remember mothers battling other mothers over Cabbage Patch dolls?) They're so trendy these days that the annual New York toy show is very well-covered by media every year. No question that media coverage can create a demand for toy robots, talking bears, and even "ugly" dolls.
- *Is it visually interesting?* Avoid the "talking head." This is fine for a public television station interview program or a Sunday morning "meet the mayor"

hour, but it is not suitable for a good product feature. If all you have is a spokesperson, there is very little chance of coverage.

Marvin Friedman sums up what to look for to get television attention: The product must be shown in an interesting way, and the message must be newsworthy, not commercial. The message should have an angle and should affect the audience in some way.

Getting Attention

It is becoming more and more difficult to get the attention of news directors and program producers. And because there are few second chances with broadcast, publicists must be well-prepared before they make an approach for coverage.

Step 1: Make a Phone Call

The first contact is the most important one. There is little time to get the idea across. If it isn't sold after the phone is answered, it's dead.

Make sure you're calling the right person and the right station. And before you pick up the phone, write down in front of you every point you want to make. Whether it's an invitation to a press conference or for a guest appearance, the way the product is positioned and the reasons why have to be clearly presented.

Call the person responsible for *that show and that show only.* Then, quickly and succinctly, explain what is going on. Eric Seidel, an experienced broadcast news executive and media consultant, points out that the publicity person should begin with, "This is what we have and here is why you should be interested." No pressure is applied; the decision is entirely that of the media person. Get to the point quickly. Broadcast people, just like print editors, welcome good ideas and listen to people they can trust. But they are likely to be turned off by someone who comes to them with ideas that don't relate to their audiences, even if this person finally suggests one that is workable.

Joanna Hanes also stresses the importance of reaching the person who will make the decision. She points out that because the event takes place "now," only the person responsible for the targeted show should be contacted. (There are day staffs and evening staffs for Monday through Friday; there are weekend staffs, and even different people for holidays.) She also says that because the station switchboards open at 8:00 A.M. and close at 5:00 P.M., it helps to know the direct telephone numbers of those people who can't be reached during business hours.

Consider also the great deal of movement in the broadcast area—shows are born and shows die; their schedules change frequently too. So try to stay on top of changes that may be important to your business.

A list of companies that publish guides and directories of TV contacts, shows, and stations follows:

Strategies for Using Broadcast Media 177

- Bacon's, 332 S. Michigan Avenue, Chicago, Ill. 60604. Publishers of *Bacon's Radio/TV Directory.*
- TV Publicity Outlets, 33 Whittlesey Avenue, New Bedford, Conn. Special guides, including those that list cable TV networks, are available from this firm.
- Television Digest Inc., 1836 Jefferson Plaza, N.W., Washington, D.C. 20036. Publishers of the *Television & Cable Factbook.*
- Larimi Communications, 5 West 37th Street, New York, N.Y. 10018. Publishers of "TV News."
- Broadcast Publications Inc., 1735 DeSales Street, N.W., Washington, D.C. 20036. This company publishes *Broadcasting Magazine,* which will help keep you up to date on activities in the broadcast industry. In late 1986 a one-year subscription cost $65.
- Public Relations Publishing Company, 888 Seventh Avenue, New York, N.Y. 10106. This company annually publishes *The Professional's Guide to Public Relations Services,* an excellent handbook that provides a worthwhile list of sources for information about broadcasting media and also offers suggestions on where to look for help for just about any public relations activity.

Step 2: Provide Full Information

At this point, I am assuming the idea has been sold over the phone. By now you should also have B roll footage—that is, short takes of scenes that relate to your story. TV stations use these clips to help develop their own stories and to cut away from a commentator or an interview subject, thus avoiding the talking head. All the other elements—spokespeople, for example—should also be in place. The next step is to send the news director or producer a brief outline or media alert. An example of a media alert is shown in Figure 9-1. I have achieved good results from media alerts like this one, and the format can be adapted to suit your own situation.

At the time you submit the outline or media alert, you should also send along a press kit or a brief backgrounder so that more detailed information will be available. The idea is to make it easy for the directors and producers. They may take the time to prepare a show based on your ideas and press information and will appreciate your help.

Gary Hill of KSTP-TV in St. Paul, Minnesota says his station prefers to do its own shows. And he would use good product publicity ideas that have local or regional interest. He gives an intriguing example: What if 3M invented a glue that enabled people to walk up walls? He would prefer to shoot production footage himself, but if the area where the glue was made were off limits, he would accept footage made and cleared by 3M. And he might also feed it to other member

Figure 9-1. Example of a media alert.

FROM:	John Smith Zenith Public Relations 100 Main Street Somewhere, New York 10000 216-555-1212
WHO:	EZ-KLENE Corporation, manufacturers of commercial dry cleaning equipment
WHAT:	Introduction of first safe compact home dry cleaning system
WHEN:	10 A.M., Monday, July 2, 1987
WHERE:	Plaza Suite, Hotel Ritz
WHY:	Reduce household dry cleaning costs by less than a quarter, using nonvolatile, nontoxic chemicals.
NOTES:	• Unit will be demonstrated by leading home economist. • Researchers and company president available for on-camera interviews, over phone for radio. • B roll showing manufacturing, testing, before-and-after results.

stations of a satellite network called CONUS, to which KSTP and about 50 other regional stations belong.

Hill says he never uses any of the dozen or so video news releases he receives daily, but his reporters do listen to PR people, and the station uses guests suggested by publicists on its feature programs. But what he finds most annoying (and this is true for print editors too) is getting detailed information and then finding out that his assistant, who might develop the idea into a show segment, also has all the information. So don't waste anyone's time (including your own) marketing news or features to more than one broadcaster in one place.

Keep in mind that it's a good idea to contact the TV station again, either the afternoon before your news takes place, or that morning. It's fine for you to send along the media alert in advance—just be sure to follow up.

Placing a Prepared Story

Earlier we said that one way to get TV coverage is to entice the media people to come to you. The other is to provide them with the finished story, ready for use in their medium. The basic way to do that is with our old friend and editors' nemesis, the news release—not a news release on paper, with still photos, but on videotape. These are known as video news releases or VNRs or, as Hill and Knowlton prefers, video news clips.

This video news clip is often sent together with a major announcement about a new product. Although such a clip is expensive to produce, if it fits with the objectives, it can be money well spent. But it better be interesting. If it has limited news value, doesn't tell the story visually, doesn't relate to the audience, and doesn't create interest in an issue, a person, or a trend—stick to print.

Another type of video news release is called "evergreen" because it is not *hard* news and does not have to be used at a given time. However, news directors aren't likely to put it aside and save it for next month—even an evergreen clip should have some current interest. For example, a publicist I know sends video news releases on fashion trends to a select group of stations. These are usually filmed in an exotic location, and depict fashions the audience may see in the coming season. The product is mentioned and is subtly related to the fabrics worn by the models.

A Question of Ethics

An article in *Public Relations Journal* says news directors continue to question the ethics—from their point of view—of using material from public relations firms. In the article Ernie Shultz, executive vice president of the Radio and Television News Directors Association, says that it's a gray area and that there's a wide range of opinions among TV news directors. Shultz considers as his guidelines whether the release has news value, and if the source has been properly represented.

Many stations, particularly in the larger markets, have policies against using clips provided by publicists. Others make sure they don't give the impression that the station filmed footage publicists provided by superimposing the name of the company on the screen, such as "tape provided by Acme Widget Company."

As more and more publicists use video news releases, news directors are under more pressure trying to decide which ones to use—if any. It would appear that the agency or distribution company that gains the trust of the TV stations by sending good newsworthy material will be the ones whose releases will get first consideration, just as it is with print. And while responsible agencies and distributors will send only material with news interest, news directors, like print editors, will continue to receive material of no value.

Producer Jerry Gordon says, "You must have a good reputation in the newsroom. I don't want to send anything out that is a bummer." He says he will turn down a company or agency if he feels the material has no news value and is not suitable for television. If this policy were followed by all agencies and producers, it would surely ease news directors' suspicions about "free" material.

Sending News Clips

There are two basic ways to send video news clips. One is through the mail or by overnight air; the other is by satellite. Those sent by mail are on ¾-inch videotape, usually no more than 90 seconds long. (As this is written, the industry is considering changing to the ½-inch tape.) Because of high duplication costs, they are normally not "broadsided," but sent to selected stations in selected markets—for instance, the markets in which a new product is being tested or the top 20 ADI (areas of dominant influence) markets.

A news clip is sent with a brief "press kit." This is not a *print* press kit. You can send the name of a local authority or expert for an interview, and perhaps a copy of the print press release, but you cannot ask the news director or a news writer to sit down and write the story, as you would a print editor. Rather, this press kit tells the news director briefly what is on the tape, plus the background, significance, and local interest of the story it is presenting, and why he should want to use it. It includes a script, a brief description of the video sequences, and other footage or outtakes called B roll. (These last elements are in the tip sheet in Appendix B.) This saves the news director the time of screening the cassette. And if he becomes interested on the basis of the written information, he most likely will decide to look at the tape.

Another way to send a video news clip is by satellite transmission, which most television stations can receive. This is done when the timing is critical, when the news release has to get to the stations as the story is breaking—an important announcement at a press conference, for example.

A press package is generally sent in advance to reach key markets. However, Marvin Friedman suggests that because there are about 600 stations that can receive satellite transmissions, "Why not tell everyone that it's up there?" The usual technique is to follow the press kit with a mailgram a day before transmission to reiterate the elements and the context, and to give the stations the technical information needed to receive the clip. Character generation information is sent with the alert.

The transmission opens with information that it is free, then describes the elements it contains, the participants, and any other additional footage. Repeat the sound and video more than once, in case a station doesn't get all of it the first time.

Friedman advises sending additional footage (and this should be of good quality) because some stations may use it to develop their own story. A part of this B roll could be computer-generated animation — this can be quite expensive, but it's a good way to show something that is difficult to tape. Illustrations and charts, while not nearly as good, can also be taped and used as cutaways.

Always send sound — the sound of a car being driven, bottles clinking as they are filled on a line, manufacturing noises, and the like. The audience expects to hear the sound.

As I mentioned previously, if you have a local expert on the subject, let the station know that this person is available for an interview. Make it easy for the station to do its own story — it may turn out to be better than the one on the news clip. This advice applies to both the mailed and the satellite VNR.

The advantage of sending the news clip by mail or air is that the voice track can be kept separate from the visuals. This way, the station has the option of using a local commentator, or just a voice-over narration, as long as the natural sound is on another track. Thus, the station can take the B roll footage, tape its own, interview a local expert, and come out with its own version of the story.

Filming a Quality Production

Filming should be done by professionals — not just someone who can point a camera. It is far better to hire a professional camera crew to cover your event and make your B roll than to rely on footage someone else may have shot.

Production costs vary. It was often said that a good estimate for a film was $1,000 a finished minute. This was and *is* a myth because it does not take into account the variables of travel, talent, crew, studio, film and film processing, editing, and all the other elements that affect the final cost. In general, tape is less expensive than film. It is possible to transfer from one to the other, but as of now, the end-result quality is far better from film to tape than from tape to film. And if it is to be shown before a large audience, film is preferable. Before the material is distributed to the media, however, tapes must be made in the professional format, not the home video size. A video news release can be made for as little as a few thousand dollars, far less than the cost of a television commercial. While production values count, they are not as important as for a commercial. What is important is how the subject relates to the audience interest, and whether it is news.

Multi-media presentations have their place for big events, and are impressive when well done. But they are intended for live audiences only, aren't very portable, and are hard to use for television. If you are planning one for a sales meeting, a major product launch, or some other event that requires a spectacular approach, think the elements through first to see if there is a way the show can be converted into a news clip. Don't wait until it's finished. Plan it along with the spectacular.

The point is that a station, even a major network affiliate, may accept footage it can't get easily by itself *if* it is well done and noncommercial. So make sure yours is.

Eric Seidel says he prefers to get his own footage, but will take it from a publicist if it is inconvenient to cover. This cutaway footage is essential in smaller markets because of limited budgets, so be sure to produce it and provide it.

Planning for TV

If you will be introducing a new product that has visual elements, then plan for television along with the other media. You will need an articulate spokesperson who is trained to appear on camera. You may have to bring in an outside authority—someone who will support and perhaps expand on your presentation. Be sure this person is fully briefed and has had training in TV techniques. Storyboard the visuals that you feel a TV station might be interested in. Don't limit yourself to one or two scenes. Try to think of as many different scenes as possible to give the news director a wide choice. Place yourself in his or her position, as if you were going to do a short news story on the product. In many of these areas, agencies can be helpful in identifying your needs and in structuring the presentation so that you will be covered not only by the TV (and radio) stations but also by remote pick-up, either with a VNR or via satellite feed.

A Du Pont example illustrates planning and proper timing: The company manufactures an oral flu vaccine, amentadine. It has an arrangement through its agency, Burson-Marsteller, and with a number of doctors in various cities who are willing to appear on television and discuss the serious and life-threatening aspects of flu whenever an epidemic is imminent. B roll footage on flu is given the stations to help the audience relate to the illness. The doctors do not sell the Du Pont product—that would be unethical and no respectable medical authority would do it. The agency also provides video news clips showing other doctors delivering the same message. This approach works because it alerts the community to the seriousness of flu, and urges viewers to see their doctors so that the right vaccine may be prescribed. This is a legitimate use of television and of film clips.

Just like any program, the flu message took long and careful planning. If your communications program has been well planned, its tactical elements will have been identified along with the justification for each of the media used in the program. A video news clip is just another tactic and must contribute to achieve the program's objectives.

It all boils down to: *What do you really want to achieve?* Again, remember, the best you can expect is increased awareness and a favorable impression.

Radio

Much of the focus in broadcast publicity is on television. Yet radio is also a good outlet for both hard news and features. Radio is effective because it is so widespread. (After all, it is difficult to watch television or read a newspaper while plowing a field or driving a car.) It is also a word-of-mouth medium: "I heard on the radio today . . ." News programming on radio runs the gamut from the five-minute break every hour to all-news stations.

An article in the November 4, 1985 issue of *Time* magazine noted that there are at least 23 national radio networks today compared with just 4 in 1968 and 9 in 1974—another reason why radio must be taken seriously by publicists.

Radio is more audience-directed than television. So it is important that you target your message to the right audiences. For example, it is highly unlikely that a rock station, with its young audience, would be very interested in a story about a yeast that allows bread to be made in half the time it used to take, or a story about an innovative courier service. But if the story is about a new technology in stereo reception, then the rock station might be interested.

Radio's Needs

Radio editors, like their counterparts in print and television, get frequent calls and press kits from publicists who haven't thought through the needs of the audiences they want to reach. Print press kits are of no value to a radio station.

Radio stations need information as the event takes place. They must get the information before the newspapers have used it. Once it appears in print, the news value is gone.

Because news anchors or commentators at some stations may do their own editing and make decisions on what goes on the air, try to determine who they are and when they are on the air. Don't call during air time, or an hour or so before. If they are on in the afternoon, they will be in the station in the morning. Some radio people get in as early as 7:00 A.M. If you have an important event coming up, remember that radio stations require lead time, and give your contact some advance notice, such as a few days for a press conference.

Don't waste time when calling. Get right to the point: why the story is important, why the audience will be interested in it, and what you have to offer—perhaps a phone feed and a local expert the station can follow up with for a supporting opinion.

Another option is to use a taped actuality, which can be sent over the phone line if the station agrees, or through the mail or via overnight air service. An actuality has a voice-over intro opening and closing and in between a statement from a company spokesperson or expert discussing the subject. The station may use the intro as is, or use its own staff anchor or announcer for the intro and close. The station also has an option to call the expert(s) for more information.

Jerry Gordon of Gordon Newsfilms sends 60-second actualities over the telephone, after he has alerted the radio news directors and determined their interest. (Calls from his West Coast office begin at 6:00 A.M. to catch the East Coast stations at 9:00 A.M. Then the caller works slowly west.)

To avoid sending a "commercial," Gary Hill says the product can be mentioned once and the company "maybe one or two times."

If you are writing the radio station in advance, you should develop a radio "press kit." This can be as simple as a media alert (see Figure 9-1) and a copy of the short news release. You may also wish to include a cover letter explaining the news value and angle of the story, an actuality on tape, a fact sheet with additional information, the names and phone numbers of your experts, and a brief backgrounder on each to support their expertise. Or, as Joanna Hanes suggests, "You could include all the necessary information in a letter." If you don't know the news director's name, just address it to "news director." It will be reviewed. If you believe the event is very important, you can send a mailgram or overnight air package.

Once you've sent this material along, follow up on it—contact the stations 24 hours in advance to see if they will take a feed or an actuality on the day of the event and confirm the time. If you're calling about a press conference, arrange for the feed to take place shortly after the conference ends. As I mentioned earlier, I recommend the same type of followup with regard to television.

Media Tours

If you're promoting a consumer product, the media tour is a good way to get your message on television and radio (and on print, too). Here the "message" is delivered by an expert or a dynamic spokesperson, via television, radio talk shows, and newspaper interviews. The commercial part of the message must be quite subtle, seldom the prime subject of the interview. Find a way to show how the product fits into the lives of the people in the audience. And make sure that whoever is being interviewed is an interesting guest who can talk about more than just the product.

A good example is a media tour by an author to promote a new book. If the book's topic is of high interest to the audience, such as what our society may be like 20 years from now, the book itself may very well be the subject of the interviews. But if it is a new novel, the author might talk about his vegetable garden, why he lives in New Hampshire, or how writers make a living when they are not writing. Of course, the book *will* be discussed; the show producer, the host, the author, and the publicist who set up the tour all understand that. But media tours do not work if all the guest can talk about is the product.

Strategies for Using Broadcast Media

Planning in Advance

There is a myriad of details to cover. *First,* early on, your costs must be budgeted carefully. These include:

- The celebrity or expert's fee.
- Advertising and promotion to merchandise the tour.
- Airline, hotel, and food expenses.
- Car or limousine rentals.
- Agency fees.
- Out-of-pocket costs to the agency, not the least of which are long-distance phone calls selling, lining up, and confirming the appearances.
- Receptions for distributors, customers, and their spouses. ("Meet Celebrity Jones at the local sales manager's home.") Be sure to include the local salespeople.

Make certain that there is a full understanding up front of all the costs involved. After you have gone through the exercise of costing out the project, realistically determining whether your investment will meet your marketing objectives, you may decide to abandon the idea.

Whatever the decision, a media tour must not be undertaken lightly. It should be scheduled as one part of the communications plan, not the heart of it. Some media tours are just "smoke and mirrors," executed to impress a lot of people but with no effect on product marketing. Don't fall into that trap.

Second, media tours must be carefully scheduled for each locality. When drawing up a schedule, the person planning the media tour must select cities that cover the market and be totally up to date on programs in these cities. He or she must also consider logistics such as the most efficient and cost-effective way to reach each city. Time of year is a factor: Snow Belt areas should be avoided in the winter because there is always the danger of airport closings and highway blockages.

Third, the approach to television, where much of your effort will be directed, must be thought through. Creative publicists must consider what they can offer visually—this can affect whether or not the event will get air time. B rolls are also very useful for television interview programs to use as cutaways. They can be an actual demonstration of how a product works or some other interesting facet of its properties or qualities.

Fourth, the planner must know—or make every effort to find out—the name of the person to contact: the news director, if booking a guest onto a news show; or the producer, if an entertainment or feature talk show. That individual is the prime contact with the show. Exceptions are radio stations, particularly those with small staffs; often the host of a talk show also schedules its guests. The planner must also know how the program is structured and what subjects can and cannot be covered.

Selecting the Media Targets

National Television

The early-morning network shows are highly prized plums for publicity practitioners. There is a lot of prestige and high recognition when a client appears on one of these shows. Although the audience reach is small compared with the network evening news shows, "Today" and "Good Morning America" attract about 5 million viewers each, depending on who is leading in the ratings at a given time. That is still a significant number of people, and they represent every demographic category from the chief executive to the blue-collar worker in the plant, both watching as they get dressed, eat breakfast, and get ready for work.

The morning shows *do* use ideas developed by publicity people, but be warned that they are tough to crack. They are deluged by calls from publicists seeking to get their clients exposure. Jerry Liddell, a producer for "Good Morning America," says his office receives "hundreds of phone calls a day" from publicists. Watch the show and you'll see how few of these callers are successful. Nevertheless, if you feel you have an interesting story with a good angle, write a brief note outlining your idea and suggesting a visual way it might be presented. You may not hear from them right away, but don't get discouraged. Follow up with a phone call to the person you wrote to.

Local Television

You will seldom have any success with network news outlets, but there may be a number of opportunities with local news programs. And there are many of them—in the morning, at noon, at the dinner hour, and during late evening. Cable news programs (primarily "Cable News Network") are as interested in "news" as the networks or locals are, and may give a good story a more extensive treatment.

There are also locally produced shows tied in with the network morning shows. They may go on before the network show, or follow it. They use the same format and will do guest interviews on a variety of subjects.

And then there are some regional "entertainment shows" that run highly visual short features, with commentary by one of the hosts. Other opportunities exist on TV talk and interview shows, which nearly every station has, and specialty shows on homemaking, gardening, home improvement, car repair, cooking —all appealing to special but limited audiences.

Radio and Newspapers

Radio can be effective on a media tour. There are all-news stations in many cities that are continually seeking interesting guests. Many of these stations have call-in shows, which use guests who can speak with some authority on a subject of current interest.

Another viable outlet in a media tour is interviews with the print media. The book reviewer for the local newspaper may welcome the opportunity to interview the author; the "home" or features editor may find an interesting story in the celebrity's life, or a fire safety angle in a demonstration of fire-resistant fibers.

Choosing the Spokesperson

The success of the tour will depend a great deal on the credibility, charm, and talent of the spokesperson. He or she must be skilled in talking about the product in noncommercial, inoffensive ways and, as we've said before, must also be able to discuss other topics. From the show's point of view, the product is not the primary subject. Thus, the publicity planner must position the story to have very broad audience appeal, and the spokesperson must be able to carry through this positioning.

An example is a media tour a few years ago set up by the Burson-Marsteller agency to promote a product that helped make carpets stain-resistant. The spokesperson was Julia Meade, best known as the hostess on "The Ed Sullivan Show."

She appeared on a number of television and radio shows and was interviewed by many newspapers in various cities. But her reason for the appearances was not just to talk about protecting a carpet from spills. She was also able to talk about preparing for a dinner party so that it could come off smoothly, and cleaning up wouldn't be the chore it usually is. The message about the carpet protector fitted in very well when she skillfully directed the conversation to what happens if guests spill food on the carpet. She had film clips showing food preparation and a guest dropping food on the carpet. His embarrassment turned to a smile when he saw how easy it was for the hostess to wipe up.

The tour was a success because the spokesperson was believable and had something of value that appealed to the audiences. She was well known to many of the news directors, producers, and anchors, and was able to warm up the interviewer with some anecdotes about the Sullivan show.

Celebrities or Not?

Be careful in using celebrities. Several agency people told me of some who were very demanding—and very expensive. A good agency, like Burson-Marsteller, which has broad experience and success with television and media tours, can be of inestimable value in picking the right person. Be wary of using sports celebrities—either active or retired—to promote your product. They may be difficult to schedule except, perhaps, for a sports interview, and if there is no natural tie-in to the product, you will attract attention away from it and *to* the athlete.

Your spokesperson need not be a celebrity. It can be an articulate person from your company, or someone from the outside who is an expert on the topic. Joanna Hanes worked with a college dormitory manager concerned about the flammability of the dorm mattresses. He had done his own testing, and was articulate and expert enough to talk on this subject on both television and radio and for newspaper interviews. The manufacturer of the flame-resistant material paid his expenses. (He believed in the product enough that he did not ask for a fee.)

In this case, the visuals were very helpful. The dormitory director had film showing what happened to conventional mattresses after they were ignited, compared to fire-resistant mattresses under the same conditions. One station built its own story and used footage from a major hotel fire to drive home its point.

Training the Participants

Your experts and company spokespersons should exude authority, speak clearly, get to the point—and understand how the media work. For television, they must be attractive, suitably dressed, and well groomed. Suitably dressed for men generally means a light, solid-colored suit, a pastel shirt, and an appropriate tie; for women, a simple dress with a minimum of jewelry to avoid shine and glitter on camera. Many viewers are suspicious of people in casual attire speaking as authorities on a subject.

Your spokesperson must come across as being mature, sensible, and believable—self-assured without being egotistical. He or she represents an ideal, and must meet an audience's expectations of that ideal.

A spokesperson must be able to answer questions directly without hemming and hawing, without "ums" and "you knows." The answers must be short and to the point. There are just a few seconds on radio or television to make a point, and make it so that it is understood. Some programs and interviews are cut. If the spokesperson rambles in his or her answers or statements, the cut may delete the important points.

Spokespersons must be able to reply to "trap" questions or questions about proprietary information without seeming to be ducking an answer. They must always be aware they are on camera, and remain cool and collected—whatever the question, or the questioner's attitude, may be. Unless the person is caught in a hostile situation (a plant disaster, for example), he or she will normally be treated well. But no matter how friendly the interviewer may be, there may still be questions that the interviewee feels are "nobody's damn business." Mishandling these questions can blow an entire show, no matter how well the person does otherwise.

Everyone who will be or may be interviewed on television or radio should receive media training. This can take a couple of days, several hours at the very least, but the time is well spent. Speaking habits and patterns can be analyzed and, if necessary, changed. Eye contact and the ability to relate to both inquisitor and camera can be learned. So can tone of voice, grammar, posture, and emotional control.

Training sessions are taped in a studio setting with a "host" or "hostess," to help the trainee understand broadcast media in a "real" situation. By viewing the tapes, the students can clearly see what the TV audience will see. The students will learn how to answer questions in a positive manner, even if these are phrased to provoke a negative response. They will also learn how to keep their answers simple, skillfully ignore hostile questions without appearing to do so, and rephrase a vague question, turning it around so that the answer is positive.

A number of public relations agencies and other organizations offer this kind of training. But be sure to check references before enrolling in any training course. The main objective is to have unflappable, articulate spokespersons for your company—not glib spielers.

Getting Ready

When interview time is approaching, the publicist must swing into action on two fronts: He or she must make sure both the spokesperson *and* the show's host are well prepared.

For the host, the publicity person must provide the producer with enough material so the interviewer can appear knowledgeable and ask the appropriate questions. Since the *idea* for the appearance was originally discussed with the producer, the show host knows little about it.

For the company executive or spokesperson, the publicist must provide a thorough briefing on the products and services to be discussed so the spokesperson can cover all the points the company wants to make, beginning with the most important. Prepare a short 30-second statement (about 60 words) outlining points in their order of importance. (See Appendix C for a sample "briefing manual" prepared for the flame-resistant mattress interviews.)

Then, prepare a list of every possible question that might be asked, and rehearse the agreed-upon answers. This is similar to the standby statement for a press conference or briefing; for broadcast, however, the answers must be memorized, not read from a prepared statement. Think of all the possible embarrassing questions and develop answers in advance. If a tough question is asked and the spokesperson does not know the answer, there is nothing wrong with saying, "I don't have that information or enough knowledge to answer the question, but I will be glad to get it for you." This response is proper as long as most of the other questions have been answered in a positive way. It's only when the spokesperson fails to respond adequately to most of the questions that the person or the company is in trouble.

There may be other participants at your interviews. In fact, if the third-party participant is on your side, he or she may do more for your product than the company spokesperson. If you can find an independent authority who can speak for you and your product, or support you on the same show, all the better.

But prepare also for the unknown expert who has been invited by the producer to provide another point of view. Find out as much as you can about this person. If he or she might dominate a discussion, practice with your media adviser how to make your points without appearing to demean the other person.

If the interview will take place in a studio, the spokesperson is on unfamiliar territory. Anyone who has had media training will be prepared for this; those who have not may be dazzled by the lights, cameras, and cables. So it's wise to get to the station early and become familiar with the layout, the producer, the interviewer, and the possible "mystery guest."

If the interview will take place on location, such as at a press event or a trade show, it will probably start quickly with little time for niceties. Thus, the expert or spokesperson must be prepared to have a microphone stuck in his face. Minicams have made location coverage a breeze, so there are few places television can't cover.

Using Newsclips in Other Markets

You could extend the reach of your tour without having to travel to the cities not on the schedule. Simply film or tape a two- or three-minute segment with the expert or celebrity and distribute it to the stations you won't visit personally. But before you go to this expense, make a careful determination of potential success. Approach the question as you would any video news release:

- Are there cable or local stations with the type of programming that might use the material?
- Is the producer or program manager known to you or your agency?
- Have you had previous success with these stations?
- Is there a good chance that the station will program it at a time when someone is listening or watching? (Using it as a filler for a 2:00 A.M. break after the horror movie will get you only insomniacs, hardly the audience you wish to reach.)

Merchandising the Tour

If the tour is undertaken, as it often is, to impress distributors and customers, it must be merchandised to ensure that they understand your objectives and how the publicity will support *them*.

Schedule direct mail or space advertising telling these important people that Expert Smith or Celebrity Jones will be appearing in their city on the Molly McGuire Show to talk about everyone's favorite wall paint. (She'll really be an expert on home decorating.)

Print special brochures or flyers on using the product so that the station or the guest can offer something the audience can write for. This is one more promotional tool, as well as a way of measuring how well you did on a given show. The stations will invite the viewers or listeners to write the station, or the company itself, for the literature. In either case, be prepared to respond. Alert the person in your company handling requests for literature or information. Stations don't like to antagonize their audiences by offering something that isn't sent or sent promptly. Except for this indication of audience interest, you may not see immediate results from a media tour.

For your own merchandising and reporting of the tour, have a tape made of each appearance. Frequently, the station will provide one, either for free or at cost, if you take a blank video cassette with you or send one in advance.

Summing Up

I have placed emphasis on getting help with your broadcast programs. If you are planning a national roll-out of a new product, it is the only way to go. I work for a major corporation with people skilled in just about every area of publicity. But we still need extra hands to help us structure a presentation, develop the proper format, shoot the film clips and B roll, prepare the news material, and distribute it for us. We need help making the initial contacts and the necessary follow up. Still there is a lot we must do ourselves—decide on the timing, get customers, distributors, and sometimes retailers involved, and *manage* the entire operation. It's by no means a turn-key operation.

If the publicity program is limited, with only a few broadcast outlets involved, someone who understands media can handle it without having to bring in an agency. But again, the keys to success are preparation, attention to detail, and planning so that the program results in a pay-off to marketing.

10
Successful Press Conferences

Your company has an important announcement—a new product or a new service, one you're going to invest a considerable sum of money in—and you want to make sure your customers hear about it. How can you get the press to cover it? One of the first things that comes to mind is a press conference.

Planning and organizing a press conference will take all your publicity skills, experiences, and talents—including some you didn't know you had. You'll need to be part orchestra leader, part logistics officer, part drama coach, and part magician.

What if you schedule a press conference and nobody shows up? It has happened, of course, but we will explore ways to help make your press event a success. And I'll offer some suggestions on alternatives, which are often just as effective (in some cases better) and on ways to increase the odds that the media reaching your markets will cover your announcement. Costs are high, the atmosphere is nervewracking, and there are no guarantees, but the ordeal is worth it, for nothing is more satisfying than getting your new development off to a good start with good coverage.

Just what is a press conference? Nearly any time media is brought together by a company to make some kind of statement, it's referred to as a "press conference." Most marketing people and publicists think of press conferences as the formal podium, speakers' table, media seated classroom style, with an opening statement, speeches, and presentations by technical and marketing people, followed by questions and answers. It could also be a press "event," a special occasion created to induce the editors to spend some of their valuable time hearing what a company has to say.

But whether it is called a press conference, a technical briefing, or a press update, it requires an enormous amount of preparation and attention to detail. With the growing importance of electronic media, creativity in presenting a visual treatment, in addition to a verbal one, places even more demands on the publicist.

Turning the press out to listen to you and your marketing or research people requires creative planning, even if the company is as well-known as IBM, General Electric, or Du Pont. Serving breakfast, lunch, or cocktails may not be enough. And in this chapter you'll discover ways to organize and plan original and worthwhile press conferences.

Is a Press Conference Warranted?

The main objective for holding a major press conference is to get all interested media, both print and broadcast, together in the same place to present important news to everyone at the same time. There must be a compelling reason to hold a press event; it must offer something that an editor can't get any other way.

You normally use a formal press conference to make a major announcement—when you have *hard* news to present, such as a significant new medical discovery, a major investment in research that relates to an important product, or a major new product development. Be advised that the superlatives in the statement "our lab has achieved a breakthrough that will revolutionize the industry" are not likely to impress many editors and should not be allowed to creep into your press materials and speeches.

The most important concern of the media is the effect of your new development on the markets you serve, be they consumer, specialized, or industrial. For example, the introduction of a new salt substitute can be tied in quite nicely with current health concerns about the need to reduce salt intake.

For a formal press conference, you don't necessarily need to create an event around the announcement because the news has enough significance to carry the day. Even so, the turnout is often disappointing, and the expected results never materialize. For this reason, holding a press conference should be considered carefully even when there is a major development in your company that rates press attention. It must be important enough to *other audiences*—not just important to your company—to merit serious consideration from the key media covering your markets. You must be very hard-nosed about the significance of your news announcement.

A less formal press conference format is appropriate for bringing editors up to date on a particular product development or technology, announcing new and significant markets, discussing improved products, or discussing the results of an important survey or test. Target audiences for these activities should be selected as carefully as for major events.

The Editor's Viewpoint

If you are planning any type of event, particularly a major announcement, consider it from an editor's point of view. In fact, before you begin planning, you might wish to check with one or two key editors to see if it is something they would cover. However, be sure you know these editors quite well. If you don't have a previously established relationship, you may get an evasive reply. Someone who doesn't know you is not likely to offer advice or to help you make a decision that might imply a commitment on his part. When you do sound out an editor, you need not reveal what you are going to announce, but you must provide enough information to get a good reading on whether he will attend. You can also check possible dates you are considering to see if there's a conflict.

Then ask yourself: Is it a truly new development that by its news value alone will get editorial attention? Or must you create an event around it to draw press attention? Is it a "breakthrough" in a specific technology? Will it affect your company's earnings? Is it important to your customers or consumers? Are there visual elements suitable for television? If you can honestly answer "yes" to these questions, then consider holding a news conference.

No special event should be considered if your chances of reaching your target market audiences through the media are few. Be realistic. A leading trade editor says there are too many press conferences about "insignificant things, such as plant tours, new facilities, new marketing plans." They will probably not pay off with any news coverage. Worse, dragging editors out for a non-news event can hurt your chances when you really have something to say. These topics may be of high interest to your company's marketing or corporate staffs, but they are not news and should not be presented at a press event. Be prepared to say no to management.

Unless you can attract the key media and offer them hard news you can't deliver any other way, and unless you are dead certain you have made a good news judgment, don't even try a press conference. Consider some of these very good alternatives:

- Meet consumer or trade editors one on one in their offices, if only a few publications are involved.
- Set up conference calls among editors, you, and your experts.
- Get together with editors at a trade show, industry conference, or exhibition.
- And the obvious: Perhaps the announcement can best be presented in a news release.

The Project Preview

One very useful device to help you analyze the need for a press conference is the project preview. With the preview, everyone involved, including prospective participants and those who must approve the budget, will see exactly what is included in the proposed event. A preview is also a good tool to help guide you through the planning. Previews become even more important when more than one product area is involved. This would include multiproduct events or major trade shows, such as the Society of Automotive Engineers Show in Detroit as well as regional and national electronics, hardware, sporting goods, and housewares shows.

Once it's all written down, you may decide that a press event is not the best way to reach your audiences, especially since staging a press event can take as much time and eat up almost as much money as holding a national sales meeting.

The first step is to pick a tentative date and give the project a working title. This is how the project will be identified from start to finish. Then identify the products or services involved. Next, identify the activity: Is it going to be a full-fledged press conference, a briefing luncheon, an editorial seminar? Review the proposed project in light of the marketing communications objective. What specifically do you hope to accomplish? Will it meet marketing objectives? Why this approach? Has another approach been considered?

Do you need a press kit? What will be included: releases, speeches, backgrounders, biographies, photos, product samples, special remembrances such as pens or briefcases?

Take a hard look at the story itself. What is the news angle? What is the product's most compelling feature? What are the other copy points? List benefits, properties, in order of importance.

Then, consider the logistics. When and where will the event take place? What resources are needed—talent, product, outside speakers, scriptwriting, slides, displays, photos, film, video?

Identify the individuals who will be involved from marketing, management, and the lab. Keep them to a minimum or they may outnumber the editors. This selection is very important. Try your best to pick speakers who are articulate, who have both knowledge of the products and some charisma. It may even be worthwhile to schedule beforehand some media training, to help them better structure the presentations for the media and answer questions succinctly.

Identify the audience—not the editors at the event, but the people to whom the message is directed. Now list the press people who are to be invited. Identify the primary target media, those publications essential to reach the target audience. If the number turns out to be small, a press conference may not be the best approach. Personal visits to the publications with one or two company experts may be preferable.

Figure 10-1. Project preview.

PRESS EVENT

(This is to provide management and marketing with the rationale for a press event. The information provided below is the basis for a "go/no go" decision.)

Date of Planned Event _____

Working Title _____

Products/Services _____

Type of Activity _____

Marketing Communications Objectives _____

Press Kit _____

News Angle _____

Key Copy Points _____

Timing/Suggested Location _____

Resources Needed _____

Company Participants (management, marketing, technical) _____

_____

Audience _____

Target Media _____

Rehearsal Dates/Sites _____

Deadlines _____

Restrictions _____

Budget _____

Evaluation _____

Agency Participation _____

Assuming you can predict a good turnout of quality media, start your scheduling. Set the date for invitation mailing. When and where are you going to rehearse your presentations? Establish all needed deadlines. When must all copy approvals be received, for example? Set a critical path.

Consider restrictions. Are there any topics to be avoided?

Work up an approximate budget. Briefly detail the various elements, and estimate costs; add in a contingency.

Preplan an evaluation process. How will you determine whether the event was a success and whether you reached the target audiences? Finally, specify the role of your public relations agency; briefly outline the tasks the agency will be responsible for, if any.

As a summary of sorts, all these steps are outlined in checklist form in Figure 10-1.

Planning the Big Event

Once the decision is made to go ahead, including all the necessary budget approvals, you are ready to begin planning the press conference. The project preview has helped you sketch out the big picture, of course; now you are ready to fill in the details. The press event countdown (see Figure 10-2) will help you visualize the sequence and the relative time requirements of the steps described here.

The Environment

In the consumer product area, most press events are highly creative. The events themselves may create news, or be a very strong platform upon which to base a news story. Industrial publicists, taking their cues from consumer publicists, are becoming more creative in developing a "news peg" and making the event one editors will attend because the setting is as much a draw as the subject. (Just be sure the event doesn't overshadow the news.)

Try an unusual setting, something other than a hotel suite. Product demonstrations are sometimes most impressive at the company's plant, where the product can be seen in action. A home product could be shown in a kitchen, and the editors can be given a chance to try some creative cooking. At the beginning of a program for, say, Fleischmann's, letting the editors bake bread will get them involved quickly.

Or suppose you're an agricultural publicist. What better place for an agricultural chemical demonstration than a farm? A creative farm publicist dug a giant

198 *The Complete Book of Product Publicity*

Figure 10-2. Press event countdown.

Actions	Week 6	Week 5	Week 4	Week 3	Week 2	Event Day ↓ M T W Th F
Query editors	⊢—⊣					
Project preview*	⊢——⊣					
Writing of needed press material	⊢———⊣					
Shooting of needed photos	⊢———⊣					
TV tape		⊢———⊣				
Audiovisual needs and equipment	⊢—⊣					
Site and format selection	⊢—⊣					
Go/no go date		⊢—⊣				
Invitation list		⊢—⊣				
Design invitations, reply cards		⊢———⊣				
Presentations (start)		⊢———⊣				
Visuals (slides)			⊢———⊣			
Clearances (start)			⊢———⊣			
Mail invitations			⊢—⊣			
Edit speeches			⊢—⊣			
Rehearsal				⊢—⊣		
Follow up with editors					⊢——⊣	
Print press materials					⊢———⊣	
Make arrangements (editors and staff)					⊢—⊣	
Guest badges					⊢—⊣	
Assemble kits						⊢⊣
Confirm food and setup					⊢—⊣	
Send reminder mailgrams						⊢⊣

* If major event such as laser show, teleconference (satellite), or musical, allow 6 months if possible; longer if trade show.

Actions	Week 6	Week 5	Week 4	Week 3	Week 2	M T W Th F (Event Day)
Review full checklist					⊢―――――――⊣	
Site rehearsal						⊢⊣
Audiovisual rehearsal						⊢⊣
Security						⊢⊣
Directional signs						⊢⊣
Staff, participants' briefing						⊢⊣
Press conference day						⊢⊣

hole, covered it with a tent, furnished generated lighting, and invited farm editors in to see the root growth produced by his particular farm chemical.

Show roofing material from the roof, if you can get editors up there! And do take into account that it might rain.

A major press meeting was held on a boat on Lake Michigan in connection with a major industry show. The host company had a captive audience, and everyone enjoyed the boat ride. Another example: Some colleagues of mine, who wanted to get better acquainted with editors and wanted editors to become better acquainted with their products, had the Second City troupe in Chicago develop a show based on those products. The editors gathered in Chicago for a trade show, were transported from their hotels to the theater by bus, and a continental breakfast was served before the show. Every one of them was enthusiastic.

Press briefings have also been held at such places as the Rockefeller Center skating rink, where winter garments were introduced by having professional figure skaters model them. A promotion on a new, faster-rising yeast was held at the Waldorf ballroom with satellite transmission to six other cities, and, as mentioned in case study number 2 later in this chapter, part of a log home was built at New York's Tavern on the Green.

But try to match the location to the subject. Significant developments in automotive technology were announced at the posh "21" restaurant. While "21" is certainly a prestigious location, the automobile company may have been better served with an outdoor event where demonstrations with visual interest for television could be staged.

Finally, some locations are appropriate and traditional to certain industries. Fashion introductions, for example, are almost always staged in New York City (or other fashion centers). And the most important publication in fashion—*Women's Wear Daily*—is in New York.

The Media

You have made a careful decision to proceed. Now you must identify the media you wish to reach. Separate them into two or more groups: the very media that reach your markets, and secondary media that will help deliver your message but are not vital. Every effort should be expended to turn out the first group. You may not get them all—80 percent is considered a good average turnout—but make every effort. If you are not sure who they all are, there are a number of ways to check. Review *Standard Rate and Data*; this will give you an idea of markets and demographics. *Bacon's Publicity Checker* and *The Working Press of the Nation* are other good sources. If you are working with PR Aids or PR Data Systems, consult them too. (See Chapter 11 for access information on all these sources.)

If you want to get your message across, include television. You have a wider selection than ever before, now that cable is becoming an important source of news. And if the story is good enough for television, invite radio too.

If the news situation involves a major capital investment, the *Wall Street Journal* and other financial publications may be interested, even if they are not the key media reaching your markets. (Incidentally, the *Wall Street Journal* has a $10 million rule of thumb on whether it will *consider* capital investment announcements, but many times it will not run a story even if this guideline is met. There may be other more important stories that day.) Even if your story meets the criteria for the *Wall Street Journal* or *The New York Times*, you shouldn't hold a press conference when a release over the PR Newswire or business wire will do. However, announcing significant new capital expenditures that relate to the product introduction will strengthen your story. Dollar amounts must be used and, if pertinent, include facts on the number of new jobs to be created, anticipated effect on earnings, and the effect on the plant or headquarters community. When a major announcement is made, you also may expect the press to query consumers, your customers, and your competitors.

Of course if you can't discuss corporate issues such as effect on earnings, markets, or costs, don't invite the business and financial press. They won't attend, and you won't disappoint your marketing associates who might expect them to cover.

Don't overlook the national news weeklies. And don't forget the columnists and business writers for your local media: newspapers, state and city business publications, city magazines, Chamber of Commerce newsletters. Put a name with the publication and ask that person.

Find the Right Person

Newspapers, wire services, and syndicate editors are most important when announcing consumer products. But you must invite the proper person. Media

Successful Press Conferences

directories will have this information, but it may not be current. If there is the least doubt, phone the publication. (If you have a consumer product but are more at home with industrial products, consider hiring an agency to help develop the planning, staging, and turning out the media.)

When making initial contact, it is important to reach the editor or managing editor. They may not attend personally, but they make the assignments. For radio and television, it's usually the news director. On smaller publications, one or two people might be the entire staff so you won't go wrong inviting the editor. If you're still in doubt, call the particular medium and ask for the name of the person by title. If you identify yourself properly, you should have no trouble getting the information from whomever answers the phone. Of course if you are actively handling publicity and have kept your contacts up to date, you can avoid a lot of the research.

The Budget: Special Costs

Most of the costs for the press conference can be estimated fairly closely, once you have made some basic decisions; the budget checklist in this chapter (Figure 10-3) can help you work up the numbers. One item may be worrisome, in the sense that it can be controversial. The question of whether to pay travel costs for editors to attend out-of-town conferences is not easy to answer.

I personally believe it is proper to pay for meals and, sometimes, lodging, but not travel expenses in most cases. Some trade publications do not have travel budgets, and perhaps the only way you can get them to turn out is by paying. I don't believe the others will be offended if you don't pay for them as well. On the other hand, some publications have a set policy of paying all their expenses. In general, these are trade publications that are part of a publications group such as McGraw-Hill or Chilton. In addition, most consumer publications and nearly all daily newspapers follow a policy of not accepting expense payments from companies or agencies. It's best not even to ask any of these if you can pick up the tab.

You may decide to charter a bus to take editors to an event or a customer's plant. Or you may provide limousine service as did a colleague of mine for a breakfast event at a hotel. In this instance the editors who were covering the conference were staying at a number of different hotels, so it was quite proper to pick them up and take them to the breakfast. Another of my colleagues held a press briefing on an oil rig in the Gulf of Mexico. The editors were taken to the rig on a company helicopter, and this novelty contributed to a large degree to the success of the conference.

Don Dreger, an editor at *Machine Design,* located in Cleveland, points out that even a short press conference, if held in another city, can eat up a day and a half of his time. So whether you are paying expenses or not, you must keep in mind that asking a publication's people to travel from one location to another costs them

Figure 10-3. Press event budget checklist.

Press kits
    Design (if necessary)
    Writing
        Releases
        Backgrounders
        Q&A
        Technical data information
        Presentations
        Biographies
    Printing
    Assembly and collating
    Shipping to site

Invitation and reply card
    Design
    Printing
    Mailing

Photography and art
    Product photography
    Duplicate prints
    B roll
    Other film, tape
    Artwork
    Graphics
    Posters
    Signage

Production
    AV material (B roll, slide shows, tapes, films)

Staff travel
    Hotel
    Airline, train, auto
    Food

Talent, outside speakers
    Fees
    Transportation
    Hotel, meals

Editors
    Transportation
    Hotel, meals

Food service (at event)
    Breakfast, luncheon, refreshments

Site costs
    Rentals
    Storage
    Setup
    Security
    Labor
        Porters
        Projectionists
        Electricians

Equipment
    Lighting
    AV rentals
    Sound system

Product for demonstrations
    Shipping, setup

Miscellaneous
    Name tags
    Mailgrams
    Phones
    Giveaways
    Tips

Agency fees
    (Estimate of total hours)

time—something editors do not have enough of, and is a factor in a publication's operating costs. Dreger feels it is proper for a company to pay meals and lodging and that travel expenses can be offered to *all* publications; their acceptance will depend on individual magazine policy. Even so, he very carefully weighs the decision to go to any press conference on its potential news value and on the amount of time he will spend away from his office.

The Date, the Time

Even though you may already have an indication of a good date from one editor, phone the other key publications and check their editorial closing dates. If you don't, it will be just your luck that some will be busy the day of your conference. Don't schedule the day before closing, either.

The question of time of year deserves some thought. While news outlets work year-round, scheduling an event in the summer might not be easy for your company's staff. Scheduling it in the spring is better, but that means any stories in monthly magazines will appear a couple of months later—in the summer, when readership may be down.

Many newcomers to publicity are reluctant to speak to editors on the phone. Be assured, however, that journalists do a lot of their business over the phone and are usually quite helpful. If you fail to check your key media in advance, you may be disappointed later.

Of course, in one sense the date is out of your control. Be prepared to get shut out of mass media if a major story breaks; it will get attention in the daily press and television, often at the expense of other events. However, if your major audience is trade editors, you don't have to worry about being preempted by breaking news.

To get daily press and television coverage, hold the conference late morning so they have time to get back to their newsrooms to prepare the story. Don't plan lunch for them; because they must meet tight deadlines and may have other stories to cover and write the same day, they won't come. Most trade writers will remain for lunch because they are not on as tight a deadline, and it will give them additional time to ask questions.

The Site, the Facilities

Now that you have a better idea of when editors should and should not be invited, and have sounded out a few on whether or not they will attend, it's time to firm up the site selection. The prime consideration is that it be convenient for the media. If possible it should be in the city where most of the media are located, and it should be recognizable and easy to reach. If it is unfamiliar, be sure to provide a map and instructions on public transportation and parking. If you have a product or service that is best demonstrated on-site, such as a plant or lab, pick the appropriate place. Don't try to set up elaborate demonstrations in a hotel suite.

If your conference is scheduled away from your home base, the local convention center or chamber of commerce can suggest possible sites and can tell you if another event is planned in their town at the same time that would limit your coverage. It's hard to compete if a major political figure is in town for a speech, particularly if you are hoping for TV coverage. Check, too, for local community celebrations or special holidays that would work against you. If you plan a satellite news conference, you'll need to make some special arrangement for this too.

If the best site turns out to be a hotel, check facilities carefully (use the facilities checklist, Figure 10-4). Look for a place with adequate lighting, a good sound system, ample air conditioning, plenty of electrical outlets, and most of all, a cooperative staff. I like having a window in the meeting room, but make sure it looks out on the street and not across an alley at another building. Don't forget to check whether the site is on the approach path to an airport. And you may need extra power if you are demonstrating equipment.

Some locations have special facilities for press conferences. The Essex House in New York, for example, has a special press auditorium, with TV platforms and lighting. All major hotels have good convention facilities, which means they should have meeting rooms to suit your needs. Don't accept, however, assurances

Figure 10-4. Facilities checklist.

Size of room
Location (check street noises, lighting)
Seating arrangements (theater style or classroom)
Power outlets
Dimmer switches
Thermostats to control temperature
Sound equipment (system built in or brought in)
TV platform
Projection tables
Screens
Lectern
Room for product demonstration, exhibits
Fire exits
Near to restrooms, phones, elevators
Coat room
Area for coffee service, refreshments
Room for luncheon, cocktails (same or different)

Successful Press Conferences

that they will give you everything you want but can't let you know the exact location until a few days ahead of the meeting. Make sure you have a contract in writing, with all the items spelled out. Treat a press conference the same way you would a sales meeting—get everything written down in detail.

How do you estimate how much space you will need? First off, if you are serving food and beverages, use a separate room. Use your meeting room for demonstrations, displays, presentations. (See Figure 10-5 for suggested room

Figure 10-5. Room layout.

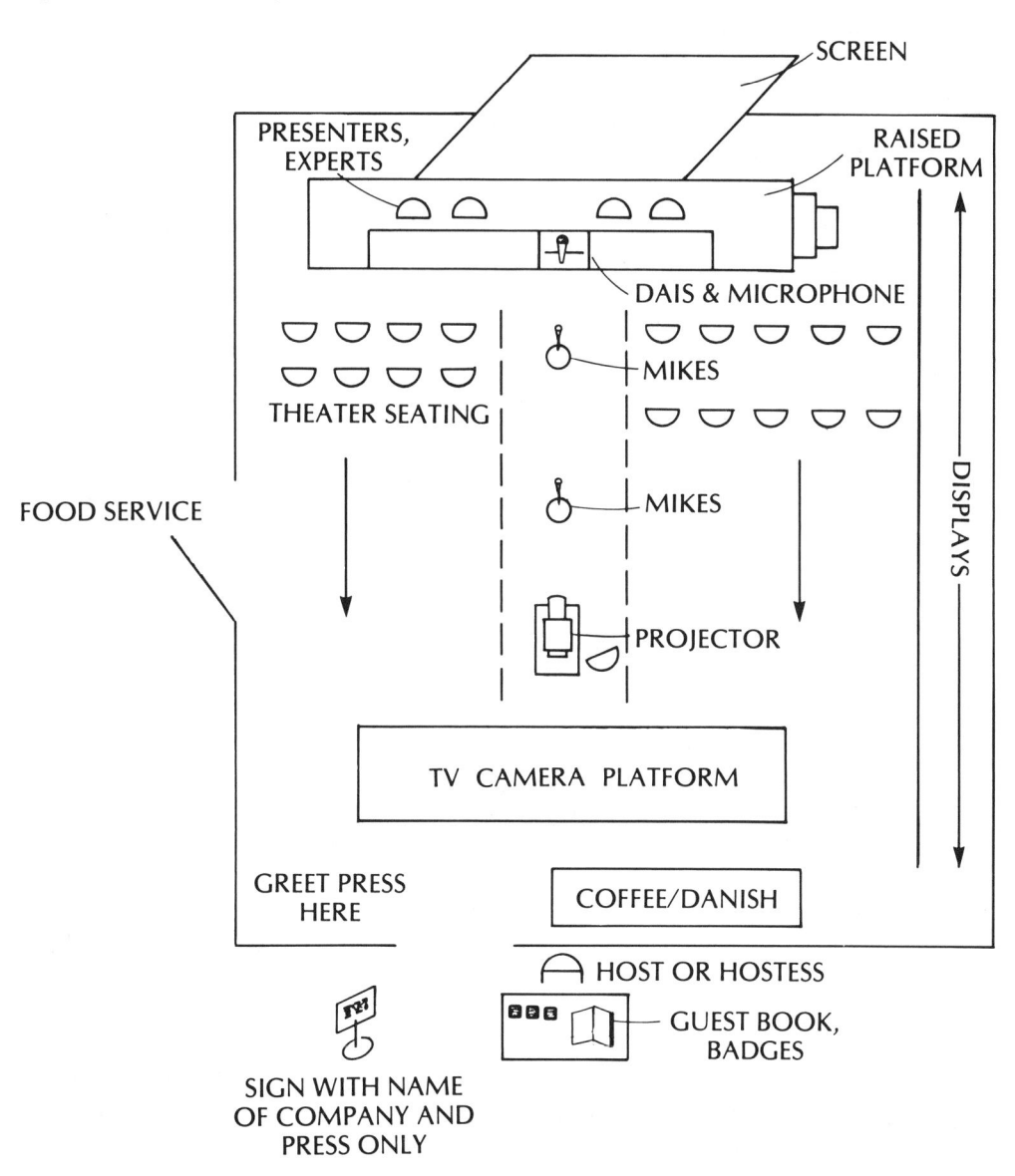

layout.) Before you look, be sure you know how much space you'll need for displays and demos and how many people you expect, including your company representatives. Consider space for TV camera platforms in the back, if you anticipate coverage, although this is not nearly as important now with the use of the mini-cam.

If you're serving lunch, I recommend a buffet rather than a "sit-down, every-person-gets-the-same-thing." A buffet offers far more flexibility if you don't have an exact advance count of the attendees. Most guests seem to prefer it, too.

A tip: If your conference will be held in or near a hotel, book a suite for yourself. It's handy as a place to make last-minute calls to editors, brief participants, check visuals, leave briefcases and coats, and possibly meet an editor after the conference. Of course, if you are at a trade show, chances are the marketing staff already has booked a suite in which to meet and entertain customers.

The Invitations

Once you've identified the media and picked the place, date, and time, the easy part is over. You must devise an invitation that encourages editors to come and arouses their curiosity, but doesn't give away too much information.

A colleague of mine held a press briefing in Philadelphia in connection with a trade show. One of the products involved was used in the headphones of a stereo tape player. She very creatively used both the site and the product in her invitation. All editors received a stereo set and a cassette recording of "Ben Franklin" inviting them to the event, which was being held in a historic tavern. She didn't have to wait long for replies. The editors began calling her with acceptances.

Joanna Hanes, of Hanes and Associates, suggests a novel approach. Combine the invitation with a spiral stenographer-style notebook. Many reporters use these to make notes, and aren't likely to throw them away; they certainly won't be forgotten when you call to check an editor's plans.

Mail the invitation a minimum of three to four weeks before the event, and include a postage-paid reply card. It should not offer a choice of not attending; the only alternative is sending someone else in the editor's place. (See Figure 10-6 for a sample, showing both sides of the card.)

You should call those editors who haven't responded within ten days to two weeks of your mailing. Editors get a large volume of mail daily so your invitation may not even have been noticed. Or, perhaps the editor was unable to make a decision when the invitation was first received; you are calling now to ask for that decision. Make sure that everyone has been contacted by phone at least once and often twice: the laggards to determine what their plans are, and the affirmatives for confirmation. After all this is done, send mailgrams to everyone, timed to arrive the day before the event, as one more reminder.

To help you keep track of all these details, create a media contact log specifically for the event. A sample format is included in this chapter; see Figure 10-7.

Figure 10-6. Invitation reply card.

```
BUSINESS REPLY CARD
FIRST CLASS   PERMIT NO. 9   WILMINGTON, DE
```

NO POSTAGE NECESSARY IF MAILED IN THE UNITED STATES

POSTAGE WILL BE PAID BY ADDRESSEE

James D. Barhydt
Marketing Communications Department
Room 2466-A Nemours Building
Du Pont Company
Wilmington, Delaware 19801

☐ Yes, I plan to attend your Editorial Seminar on Pollution Control, Wednesday, September 16, 1981.

☐ No, I am unable to attend but I am sending:

_____

Name:_____

Publication:_____

The Rehearsals

Your objective should be stumble-free presentations that are visually interesting, factual, and to the point. An important element is rehearsals. The first

Figure 10-7. Press event media contact log.

EVENT: **DATE:**

1. Name/Publication	2. Invitation Sent	3. Returned	4. Attending	5. Sending	6. Mailgram	7. Phone	8. Response	9. Comments

Key:
1. Names and publications of editors invited
2. Date invitation sent
3. Date reply card returned
4,5. Remarks on reply card
6. Date reminder mailgram sent
7. Date phone call made
8. Response to call (even the reply card "no's")
9. Response, attending, not attending, send press kit, etc.

Successful Press Conferences

should be at company headquarters with all the participants and all the visuals. Look for ways to cut; your total presentation should run no more than a half hour.

Plan to run over your program one more time in the environment in which you will hold your news conference, even if you work far into the night. Remember that rehearsing your event is no less important than rehearsing a presentation to a company president or chairman of the board! Every one of your participants must come across in a businesslike, professional manner. That means not just rehearsals but rewrites (you might even be able to trim) and reviews. Slides must be right side up and drop into place at the right time. (Incidentally, use glass-mounted slides; cardboard ones will not focus properly in automatic-focus projectors.)

No one should stumble going to the dais, and everyone in the audience should be able to see the screen and speaker. If you are planning a product demonstration, make sure the product works. Don't take anyone's word for it. Ask for a demonstration when you are planning the conference and again at the meeting site. Many press conferences have been disasters because the demonstration—the one thing that couldn't go wrong—did.

Rehearse not only the people, but the equipment. And when you are finished rehearsing, make sure the area is secure. Hire your own security guard to watch over your equipment and material when you are not present.

It's a small investment compared with what it would cost if you opened the meeting room the next morning and found it had been robbed.

The Press Kit

Press kits are an essential at any press event. Contents should include:

- News release on the product(s) or service(s) being presented
- Backgrounder(s) on same
- Technical data
- Copies of speeches and presentations
- Releases on speeches
- Biographies of speakers
- Background literature (but don't load with sales promotion literature)

You will recognize that this is basically a print media kit. You can adapt it for the broadcast media, but you will need some additional items if you expect television coverage.

Radio should be notified, too. You may not get on-the-spot coverage, but you may be able to set up a telephone interview. See Chapter 9 for details on working with television and radio.

Plain or Fancy?

Some — agencies particularly — like fancy press kit folders and release letterhead designed especially for the event. These seem to impress the company holding the event more than the editors attending it. It's what is inside the kit that counts. Resist the temptation for a four-color press kit carrier. Don't design special news release letterheads for a press conference. In my opinion, it's a total waste of money. Editors in general agree that what the story says is far more important than its physical format. So make a good impression at little expense by providing information and news useful to an editor rather than puffery dressed up in a fancy jacket. It's also true that editors seldom keep much of the material after a press event, anyway, no matter how fancy it is — another good reason to cut your printing costs.

Tips on Kit Design

If you have never used press kit folders, here are some tips to remember.

Keep the folder simple. Work with your printer or graphics designer to find a good solid-colored heavy stock. I prefer a matte or semigloss finish. Print or silkscreen the name of your company in a contrasting color across the top and, in the same color, PRESS INFORMATION in bold letters across the bottom. Don't print the date or the event on it. You will be using these over and over.

When opened, the kit should have sturdy and ample pockets on each side. On the right pocket, die cut four slits to insert your business card. Place the releases and backgrounders on the right side and the photos, presentations, biographies, and literature on the left.

If you need to identify a particular product or an event for your standard folder, print a decal with the product name and stick to the cover. Some of my associates print a cover card, insert it in front of the material, and enclose everything in a plastic bag. It keeps the material clean and dry, which is important if the conference will be held outdoors or on location. Figure 10-8 shows a drawing of a sample press kit.

The Teleconference

If you want to reach media in several cities at the same time, one good way is to hold a teleconference. Your press conference, in a primary or "host" city, is transmitted to other cities by satellite.

Here's how it works. Editors are invited to a press event just as they are for a regular press event, and those who are not in the host city (most often New York) watch the event on television as it is transmitted via satellite from the host city to wherever they are. The picture transmission is one-way, but the audio goes both

Figure 10-8. Sample cover and contents of a press kit.

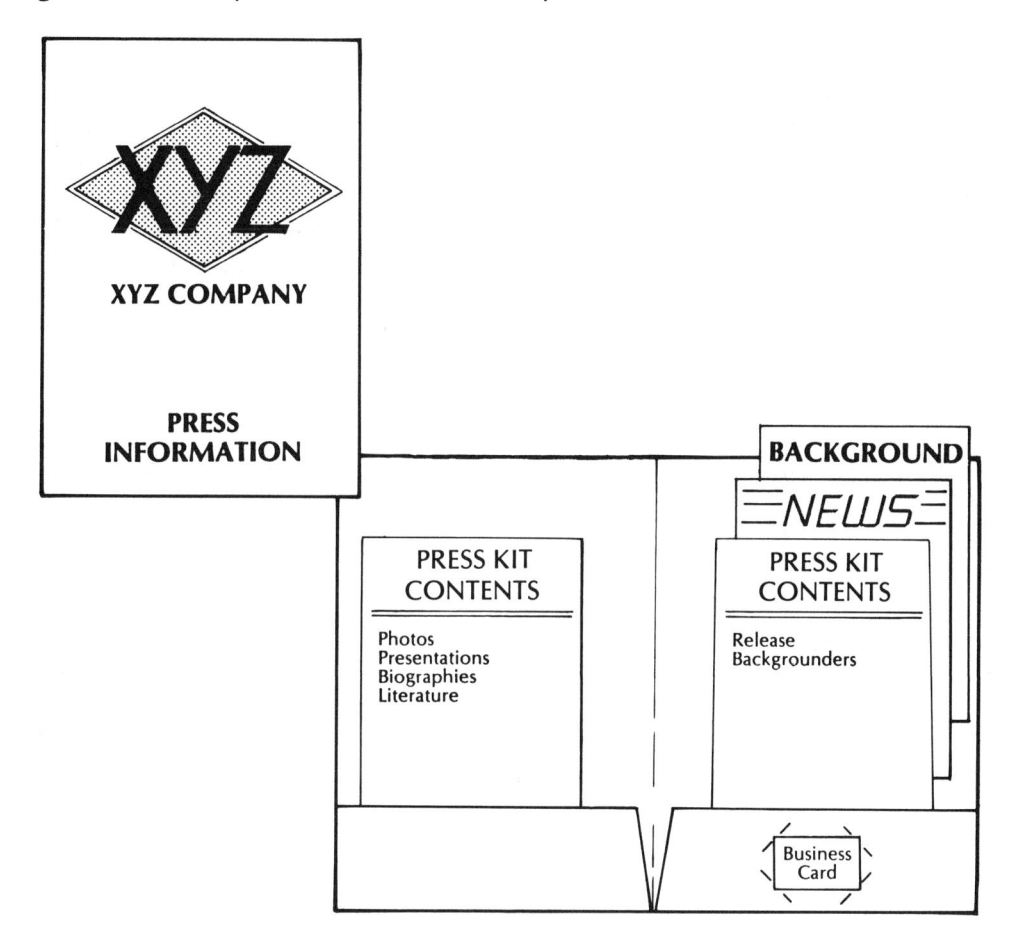

ways, so editors in the receiving cities can question people in the host city and see and hear the answers. It is not quite as good as face-to-face, but it is an excellent way to reach media where they are located. In some cases, it's not only editors. Distributors, retailers—anyone who is or may be involved with a product introduction—can participate.

All this is not easy. It takes much preparation and accurate timing, because you must rent satellite time (usually an hour) and may have to schedule your event in several different time zones.

Your expenses also will include receiving equipment in each city, either a studio that has satellite capabilities or rental equipment set up at a site such as a hotel. You also must hire technicians to operate the equipment and have your own staff in the various cities to take care of all the many arrangements that go with any press conference.

A way to reduce satellite costs is to rent a television studio in each of the cities, because most have satellite facilities. For example, PBS stations can send and receive by satellite. On the other hand, most television studios aren't very fancy, and not good places if food will be served. You will have to have it catered, and even then there may not be enough room in the studio to serve it. In addition, many television studios are not in midtown locations. So the size and nature of the audience often will dictate the setting, just as it does for the print press event.

Another alternative to a video conference is to take the show on the road, but you have to consider staff time. If your spokesman is the chief executive officer, other top company executive, or an outside expert, they have to be out of their offices for an extended period of time, even several days.

The real issue to consider, says Marvin Friedman, vice president in the broadcast division of Hill and Knowlton and a former network news director, is not cost-effectiveness. The real issue is time. Using a satellite, your company representatives can spend an hour or so talking to media and other guests, answer all their questions, no matter where they are located, then return to their respective desks, doing what the stockholders expect them to be doing, not on the road meeting editors. If you don't need your CEO to be the spokesperson, a road trip may be worth considering.

What you are really doing with a satellite conference, as Friedman so aptly points out, is creating your own live TV program on your own network. It isn't easy, but it is often quite effective.

The Day of the Event

Be sure to get your event on the facility's daily calendar, and post your own directional signs at the facility door and in strategic places. Should you distribute the press kit before the presentations, or after? There are arguments on both sides. If you pass it out ahead of time, you may have editors checking one thing and making notes while trying to listen to the speaker. However, if you do pass it out in advance, you give the editors the opportunity to check the information for questions they may want to ask later. Many editors prefer advance distribution; most publicists prefer not to. If there is time for editors to review the material before things get underway, by all means pass it out in advance.

Registration

Set up a table outside the presentation area and greet the editors as they arrive. Register everyone in a guest book and then hand letter a name tag. Don't print name tags in advance, except for your company staff; a reception table with unused name tags gives the appearance that your event was less than a success.

No matter how many editors tell you they will most assuredly be there, there will still be no-shows. Bring mailing labels and envelopes so you can send kits by air service overnight to all out-of-town media and by messenger the same day to local media. Make prior arrangements with a messenger service for a pickup following the conference.

The Presentation

The presentation should not be styled like a sales meeting, with long introductions and even longer speeches. The product may be important and be expected to have a significant effect on its markets, but if the presentations are dull and cast in corporate gobbledegook, the message will suffer. This may seem obvious, but I have heard of editors being so bored at press conferences they walked out.

What can we offer our visitors that they will find so interesting that they will *have* to pass it on to their readers? If we can answer this question, we are on the way to having a successful press event.

Bill Tortolano, an editor at *Design News*, reflecting the views of most editors, suggests this basic presentation format.

- A brief introduction telling the audience what will be presented.
- A film or tape showing the product in use with its advantages and potential clearly demonstrated, or an actual demonstration.
- A brief presentation from company experts and authorities.
- Question-and-answer session.
- Opportunity for editors to meet one on one for further questions.
- Press kits with company and speaker information.

Get the right people saying the right things. You should introduce the speakers, and later direct followup questions. One of your top executives should give a general overall view of the new development. The heart of the development and what it means to the markets, industries, publics, and consumers can be presented by one of your more articulate scientists. Spend no more than a half hour *total* on speeches; 20 minutes is even better. If your presentations are brief and to the point, and if high interest was expressed in your product display and demonstration, you did your job.

Tip off your management that they should not expect many questions right after the presentations. Because editors prefer to meet your experts personally to develop their own story angles, they may not wish to ask questions in front of their competition.

A tip from Don Cannon, contributing editor to *Chemical Week:* Your key people must be at the conference. "We journalists want answers then and there. And we want a chance at the executives alone—away from the shrimp cocktail and other reporters." Bill Tortolano of *Design News* says he does not want to ask questions in front of other reporters. He wants a format that permits him to develop his own story, and that means he must have time to speak to individuals.

Even after you have presented your story, editors will frequently query the end users of your product or service. This is particularly true of consumer products and developments that may affect a particular segment of society. For example, if the product is directed to the health field, most TV reporters will ask for comments from doctors, because their audiences are consumers whose health may be affected by your health-care product. In this case, you should have your medical consultants or outside doctors available. For any event, of course, it is wise to have experts (including noncompany ones) present to respond to questions. Always consider the step beyond the immediate audience and plan how best to make your point with the ultimate user.

If the editors can make your product "work" or in some other way get involved, this is very much in your favor. One of my colleagues was involved in a trade show with little to offer in the way of publicity. But at the show he found a solar-powered bicycle that used one of his products. Guess what? He stole the show. He got great coverage in the local newspapers and television news shows with shots of editors riding around on the bicycle in the parking lot. The moral: involvement. Product demonstrations are musts for television consideration (as you recall, news directors shun talking heads and look instead for action and human interest). If you are inviting TV reporters to your conference, plan to produce videotape showing how your product works and send it to the stations in advance, or make sure the person you spoke to at the station (news director) knows you have this footage.

And don't forget the simple courtesies. A group of editors complained to me that they often get to a press conference and there is no one to greet them and introduce them to the company people. They said they stand around talking to themselves until the program is ready to start.

Also, check your invitation list against the guest book. Send those who did not attend press kits by mail or, if in town, by messenger. And here's a tip: Make up labels with the name and address of every editor you invited. Weigh the press kit and envelope to see how much postage is needed, estimate how many editors won't make it to the event, and take enough stamps with you so you can drop the press kit in the mail to them right after the conference. If you want it to reach an out-of-town editor in a hurry, send the kit via Federal Express. Federal has drop boxes in many major cities, or it will make arrangements to pick up the material.

Press Event Checklist

General

- ☐ Direction sheet filled out and cleared.
- ☐ Budget cleared.
- ☐ Site booked and confirmed.
- ☐ Location convenient for editors.
- ☐ Date and time does not conflict with other events, or with publication deadlines or closings.
- ☐ Food and beverage arrangements agreed upon by company and facility.

Invitations

- ☐ Press list developed.
- ☐ Dates set for design, clearance, printing, and delivery.
- ☐ Mailing date set and met.
- ☐ Invitations by title only or by name. If name, was proper editor invited? Is editor still at publication?
- ☐ Topic clearly stated.
- ☐ Time, date, and locale included.
- ☐ Map of site/location.
- ☐ Food or refreshments.
- ☐ Name and telephone of company contact.
- ☐ Deadline for response.
- ☐ Reply card included, with space for alternate; "Can't come but send kit." "Can't come but will send . . ."
- ☐ Parking or transportation facilities.
- ☐ Date set for followup with nonrespondents.
- ☐ Confirmation letter or mailgram.
- ☐ Reminder phone calls.

Participants

- ☐ Speakers confirmed.
- ☐ Time allowed for presentation preparation.
- ☐ Time allowed for clearances.
- ☐ High-quality visuals with consistent style.
- ☐ Visuals prepared and cleared.
- ☐ Speeches in speech type.
- ☐ Agenda for participants (copy for guests).

- ☐ Rehearsal dates set.
- ☐ Backup speakers designated.
- ☐ Speakers briefed on makeup of press, possible questions.
- ☐ Q&A list prepared and cleared.
- ☐ Projectors and other audiovisuals set.
- ☐ Name cards on speakers platform.
- ☐ Name tags for company personnel, editors.
- ☐ Person assigned to introduce speakers, direct questions.
- ☐ Photographer.
- ☐ Dimmer switches to brighten and darken room; operator assigned.
- ☐ Electrician available.
- ☐ Thermostat in room to control temperature.
- ☐ Sound equipment, mikes, speakers. Person assigned to check.
- ☐ Mikes for audience.
- ☐ TV camera area or platform.
- ☐ Special lighting.
- ☐ Displays, photos, products.
- ☐ Security.
- ☐ Disturbing sounds: next room, street, airplanes.
- ☐ Projection screen, clear visibility from all seats.
- ☐ Front or rear projection decided.
- ☐ Projection equipment monitors, backup projectors, bulbs.
- ☐ Remote extensions.
- ☐ Person to test AV equipment, sound, focus.
- ☐ Slides in trays in proper order; tapes and films wound correctly.
- ☐ Operator for projectors. Cues marked in speech copies.
- ☐ Location of wall outlets. Extension cords. (Will anyone trip over them?)
- ☐ Overheads clear. Overhead projectors will not block view of slides or films.
- ☐ Charts, chart pads viewable, markers on stand.
- ☐ Lectern: pointer, water, glasses, lighting.
- ☐ Room available in advance for setup, rehearsal.
- ☐ Fire exits clearly marked. Escape routes understood.
- ☐ Coat room and restrooms nearby.
- ☐ Registration table at door. Guest register book.
- ☐ Person to welcome, write out name tags.
- ☐ Telephone nearby. Arrangements for messages.
- ☐ Place where editors can meet privately with participants.
- ☐ Room for lunch refreshments.
- ☐ Meal: sit-down, buffet, catered.
- ☐ Coffee, rolls on arrival.
- ☐ Coffee break.
- ☐ Date set for number guarantee on food, beverage service.
- ☐ Arrangements clearly spelled out. Contracts and guarantees signed.
- ☐ Person to inform captain of number for lunch, to avoid empty tables.

Successful Press Conferences

Press Kit

- ☐ Carrier.
- ☐ Assembly checkoff.
- ☐ Releases.
- ☐ Backgrounders.
- ☐ Speech copies.
- ☐ Releases based on speeches.
- ☐ Photos, illustrations, captions, transparencies.
- ☐ Technical data reprints.
- ☐ Bios of speakers.
- ☐ Timetable and checklist for clearances—management, marketing, legal, customer.
- ☐ Mail, messenger arrangements for nonattendees, secondary media.
- ☐ Person assigned to distribute kits at the beginning or at end.
- ☐ Personal business cards.
- ☐ Followup with editors.
- ☐ Copies of non–press kit visuals available.

Budget

- ☐ Design, printing, mailing invitations.
- ☐ Printing assembly press kits.
- ☐ Hotel expenses, suite, rooms.
- ☐ Electrician.
- ☐ Projectionist.
- ☐ Porters.
- ☐ Storage, checking.
- ☐ Trucking, transportation.
- ☐ Equipment rentals.
- ☐ Security.
- ☐ Luncheon, refreshments.
- ☐ Sign printing.
- ☐ Display and setup.
- ☐ Press kit production.
- ☐ Photography and prints.
- ☐ Releases and kit mailing.
- ☐ Messengers.
- ☐ Special fees: agencies, freelance assistance.
- ☐ Cash for gratuities.
- ☐ Followup photos or slide production (from presentations).

A Few Examples

Press conferences are usually developed as a leadoff of a planned publicity program. The case histories used here are good examples not only of innovative and effective use of press events, but of sound planning.

Case History No. 1

Client: United Vintners

Agency: Hanes & Associates

Competition for attention in the wine industry has always been intense, and wine writers are inundated by requests to sample new wines, offers of trips to wineries and invitations to posh tastings.

Joanna Hanes, a Washington public relations executive, had previously directed several new product launchings for a company called United Vintners by creating and implementing appropriate events to position the wines before target markets. Then, in 1978, Inglenook, one of the wineries owned by United Vintners, introduced a dessert wine called Muscat Blanc, expensive and severely limited in quantity. Its introduction was designed to offset harm to Inglenook's reputation for quality following its introduction of a line of mass-produced, low-priced wines. And Hanes was called in again.

To achieve this strategic positioning, Muscat Blanc was introduced at an intimate dinner with the winemaker, which was held on an eighteenth century sailing ship anchored in the historic seaport of Savannah, Georgia. The choice of the ship was designed to emphasize the centennial of the founding of Inglenook by a sea captain. Several of Savannah's most respected community leaders known to appreciate fine food and wine were invited to participate in all stages of the event, from planning the historic menu and writing menu notes on the cuisine to a reception in a seaport museum at which the mayor was host.

Ten key wine writers were invited to the dinner, along with Inglenook's winemaker and Savannah gourmets. The writers represented national gourmet publications or wrote nationally syndicated wine columns. Each received a bottle of the new wine, hand-delivered by local wine distributors, with a special label providing the invitation ("Permission is granted to come aboard Wednesday").

While elegant, the dinner also emphasized the fun of entertaining, as can be seen from the slogan: "A new twist on launching a boat with wine: This wine will be launched with a boat." At the end of the dinner all the guests were given after-dinner clay pipes as souvenirs.

Despite lack of advertising, wine newsletters, daily papers, and gourmet publications carried highly favorable reports of the wine. The first vintage of the wine sold out immediately, although it was the most expensive wine ever sold by Inglenook at the time.

Case History No. 2

Client: Lincoln Logs Ltd.

Agency: The Alexander Company

Lincoln Logs is a manufacturer of do-it-yourself log home kits in 22 different plans. The kits include wall logs, caulking, insulation, doors, windows, roof, nails, and blueprints.

The company's accomplishments have been impressive. During the four-year period from 1981 to 1985, annual sales rose from $2.9 million to $7.2 million. Richard Considine, Lincoln Log's founder and CEO, gives major credit for this increase to the company's publicity effort conducted by The Alexander Company.

Roy Alexander, the president of the PR firm, explains his agency's approach: "Every action in the program was designed to accomplish one vital objective — industry leadership. We decided early on we wanted to create a 'knee jerk' reaction among American consumers: Hear log homes and think Lincoln Logs." He succeeded. Lincoln Logs is the best known company of its kind today.

At one point The Alexander Company decided to hold a building demonstration for the media in order to gain quick acceptance by national magazines and newspaper feature syndicates. Tavern on the Green, a New York restaurant, was chosen as the site. Because the restaurant was situated in Central Park, the actual demonstration could be held outdoors.

Connie Jason, executive vice president for the firm, recalls that the morning of the event New York had a severe rainstorm that flooded the restaurant and soaked the logs that were to be used for the construction. The company was very lucky, however, because before noon — in time for the event and prior to the arrival of about 70 media people — the weather cleared and the logs dried out. On with the show!

To demonstrate the ease of construction, two women helped "Fast Eddie," a local ABC-TV television personality and pitchman, put the house together for the cameras. The demonstration included installation of one of each element of a log home: a door, a window, and so on.

The "Good Morning New York" show on WABC-TV carried a four-minute segment on the demonstration, with Fast Eddie saying, "What we found out is that log homes can be a very viable alternative source of housing." He gave the company's name and location. The segment ran on two different dates.

Barbara Mayer, an Associated Press columnist, interviewed the Lincoln Logs founder. This produced scores of clippings. *Science and Mechanics* ran an article on how to build a log home.

Country Living worked with the agency on what turned out to be a seven-page story with color photos, titled "Luxury in a Log Home." Another home was decorated in Chestertown, New York, company headquarters. Each room featured a different decor from rustic to modern, to show potential customers the versatility of log homes. A color page appeared in *Woman's World* magazine.

Broadcast coverage included two-and-a-half-minute features on constructing a log home circulated by Newsweek Broadcasting to about 40 stations. A syndicated radio interview was released to 100 stations. United Press International in Atlanta distributed color slides to cable TV stations.

In retrospect, the press event was regarded as a key element in Lincoln Log's overall promotional program—a program characterized by well-planned strategies and clearly defined, measurable objectives.

Case History No. 3

Client: MCI Mail

Agency: Hanes and Associates

MCI Mail is a product and concept of the computer age. The objectives of its introduction were both to explain what it was and to find the special market that could use instantaneous messaging.

General media, business reporters, and reporters who covered the telecommunications industry were invited to a news conference in a manner designed to pique their interest without giving away the news. Two weeks before the event, reporters were sent a letter saying that letters would soon be obsolete and inviting them to a news conference to find out why. The next communication was a Western Union Mailgram, which said that Mailgrams would also soon be obsolete. Neither the letter nor the Mailgram indicated who was giving the news conference.

The conference originated from Washington, D.C., and was sent by closed-circuit TV satellite hookup to New York, Chicago, and Los Angeles. In all, more than 200 reporters attended.

One MCI Mail service is a four-hour hand-delivered letter. This was demonstrated at the news conference by MCI's chairman, William McGowen, who dictated a letter that arrived at each site before the conference was over, in less than 60 minutes.

Following the launch, a spokesperson for MCI Mail toured all 15 cities where MCI had its postal centers and positioned MCI as the leader with this technology in TV, radio, and newspaper interviews. Businesspeople were targeted in this effort.

In addition, professional groups working in fields where deadlines and time limitations are extremely important were identified. Included were lawyers, advertising executives, and public relations people. These groups were targeted for special emphasis through trade media interviews, MCI-conducted workshops, and exhibits at their national conventions.

Now, two years later, MCI Mail is recognized by the business world as a separate and distinct product and is used by more than 250,000 subscribers. Press coverage contributed not only to making consumers aware of the product but also to alerting potential customers to its specific market applications. For example, a story in *The New York Times* led a *Fortune* 10 company to utilize MCI Mail to solve *internal* communication problems caused by incompatible computers.

Case History No. 4

Client: Fleischmann's

Agency: Hill and Knowlton

An excellent example of a teleconference was one held to introduce Fleischmann's Rapid Rise Yeast, a new strain of yeast that would allow home bakers to make bread in half the time. The problem confronting Hill and Knowlton was that the competition had already introduced a similar product. The introduction of the Fleischmann product had to be spectacular and effective to assure that the company would maintain its leadership position in the yeast business.

A seven-city satellite teleconference was beamed from the Waldorf Hotel in New York to Dallas, Atlanta, Denver, Chicago, Seattle, and Los Angeles. It was timed so that the first few editors to arrive in New York were whisked off behind a curtain to knead some dough. During the cocktail hour, the bread rose and was baked in the hotel kitchen. When the conference opened to other cities, the bread had just been baked.

Not only were the trade press, food editors, and broadcasters invited in the various cities, but cooking school teachers, consumer specialists with various food chains, extension and other home economics professionals, teachers, trade representatives, the sales force, and food brokers. The teleconferencing enabled the participants to see what was taking place in the host city, and ask questions and get answers to their questions from the company executives. The video went one way; audio both ways.

The events of the conference were shared with media in other cities. A 45-second video news clip including tape made at the event was sent by satellite to 400 stations immediately following the event. A radio actuality was sent to 2,000 radio stations the day of the event. And press kits were sent to 500 newspaper food editors, 300 consumer specialists, and 3,000 extension home economists. A follow-up media tour to other major markets was also held.

The press results were excellent, but equally important, 80 percent distribution of the product was achieved within a month.

- The New York *Daily News* ran a full page that was widely syndicated. Other newspapers with extensive lineage and photos included the *Chicago Tribune, Atlanta Journal and Constitution, Denver Empire Magazine, Seattle Times, Los Angeles News*.
- There were major stories in 125 newspapers with a combined circulation of 8.5 million.
- *Good Housekeeping, Family Circle, McCalls, Better Homes and Gardens, Woman's Day*, and *Bon Appetit* ran stories and photos.
- Spokespersons made appearances on television in nine major cities.
- United Press International ran a major article.
- A feature article appeared in *Advertising Age*.

The key was careful planning, attention to detail, and involving not only the press but the other decision makers who would have an effect on the product's future.

Case History No. 5

Client: Norcliff Thayer

Agency: Hill and Knowlton

The introduction of NoSalt by Norcliff Thayer, the proprietary drug division of Revlon's Health Care Group, is a perfect example of the need to incorporate press conferences into a total promotional package in order to achieve successful results all-around.

NoSalt is a salt substitute developed in 1981, a year after the U.S. Department of Agriculture and the Department of Health, Education and Welfare issued joint dietary guidelines urging *all* Americans to reduce their sodium intake. Media surveys showed that although consumers were aware of the dangers of eating too much salt, they were hesitant to eliminate it from their diets.

Because the taste of salt is acquired in infancy, curbing the salt habit would, without extensive consumer education, be difficult. The introduction of NoSalt demanded a sustained public information campaign to teach consumers that it was possible to enjoy a healthy, salt-free diet.

The Hill and Knowlton people utilized two key marketing strategies to introduce the product. One, they emphasized taste by positioning the product as the first salt alternative with flavor enhancers to eliminate the bitter aftertaste found in most salt substitutes. Two, they concentrated on the product's universality by

Successful Press Conferences

having it marketed to all consumers, not just to those who were told by their physicians to reduce salt intake.

The foundation of the agency's campaign was a consumer education program alerting the public to the dangers associated with too much salt. The agency put together backgrounders, leaflets, and fact sheets as well as a recipe booklet explaining how to replace cooking salt with NoSalt.

After these materials were circulated, it was time to contact the media. Here are just a few of the many activities undertaken:

- A news release was prepared to reflect the overwhelmingly positive response to the product.
- A second release was sent to 100 regional and national trade editors to inform them that sales of the product for the first four months had *doubled* Norcliff Thayer's projections.
- Cornelius O'Donnel of Corning Glass conducted a nationwide media tour in which he held cooking demonstrations using NoSalt.
- A press kit containing samples of NoSalt and brownies made with it was sent to food and consumer newspaper editors.
- *Time* magazine ran a cover story in its March 1982 issue entitled "Salt: A New Villain?" in which spokespeople for NoSalt were interviewed.

And, in conjunction with all these efforts, a luncheon was held for the press. It featured a three-course meal with 19 dishes prepared with NoSalt. More than 30 magazine, syndicate, wire service, and television editors attended this luncheon, and it also resulted in two UPI stories distributed nationally.

Tips for Success

1. Don't ask reporters and editors to take time out of their day to hear your story unless it's very important.
2. Be sure to use a project review.
3. Don't schedule anything on the day of the publication closing, or even the day before.
4. Check the local convention and visitors bureau.
5. If you are planning a press event at a trade show, check show management for conflicts. If you schedule something at the same time as an important industry meeting, the entire industry association will be angry—and your customers may be members.
6. Be sure your budget considers union labor.
7. There is no such thing as too much rehearsal. If possible, the final rehearsal should be in the room in which you are holding the event.
8. If the hotel or meeting place tells you it won't assign the suite until the day before, take your business someplace else. You need to be sure your needs are met more than adequately.

9. Get a room in a good location: away from street noise and with windows, enough power, and easy access to facilities.

10. Don't expect the daily press to stay for lunch. If you want them to cover, hold the event late morning. The trade editors will stay for drinks and lunch. Television crews, if they cover at all, are in and out fast. Be sure you have good visuals (B rolls) for them; talking heads seldom appear on the evening news.

11. Coordinate the "look" of your visuals.

12. Have a messenger standing by to deliver press kits to no-shows. Air express to out-of-towners.

13. Take backup audiovisual equipment and bulbs.

14. Take a guest book and ask everyone, including your own people, to sign in.

15. Set up a product display, and make sure the product works.

16. Hire your own security guard, if you plan to leave anything in the presentation room overnight. Don't rely on hotel security.

17. Check and double check all arrangements.

18. If you don't have media contacts, hire an agency that knows the industry.

19. If you use an agency, work closely with it. Don't leave everything up to the account executive. It's your company that is holding the event and hoping for coverage, not the agency.

20. Pray for good weather.

21. Make sure all the speakers arrive the night before, and encourage rest, not recreation.

Press Events at Trade Shows

Press events are often held at trade shows. Most editors in the industry will be at the show, so in a sense you have a captive audience. On the negative side, editors are very busy at trade shows and must make decisions about how many publicity people they can meet and which of the many press conferences they can attend. Consider the competition: press events are held by the exhibitors at breakfast, lunch, midafternoon, and dinner; from early morning until sunset and then some.

It's risky, but if you decide to hold a press meeting, check show management or its public relations agency and block out the time and space for the press conference when your company contracts for the exhibit booth. Show staff can help by recommending locations and can alert you to any other scheduled meetings, including their own. You won't be able to schedule your conference at the same time show management (or the sponsoring organization) is running one of its own events. Don't try to compete even off the show site; it will only antagonize the sponsors if you attempt to take press away from their show.

Try to book a trade show press event at least a year in advance. If you can't and find show sites filled, book your event at the headquarters hotel or a nearby

Successful Press Conferences

location. If this can't be done, charter a bus and transport editors to your special event.

Costs at trade shows may run higher than at other locations. Budgets should take into consideration the high cost of working with trade unions—carpenters, electricians, food service employees, maintenance people, guard services, and projectionists, among others.

Meet Me at the Booth

An unusual approach, but one that has worked when a new product will be shown for the first time or something newsworthy has happened since the last show, is to hold a press conference at your exhibit on a morning before the show opens to visitors. This works best when you have a good exhibit. If it tells a story, has eye-catching visuals, and you can effectively demonstrate the product there, then a booth is an excellent site.

If you are showing more than one product, get your executives and experts together and schedule them well in advance for interviews with appropriate editors. Pick the top publication in each product area and set up one-on-one meetings with your experts. You can assure each publication that it will be able to develop its own approach or angle, and your costs will be kept relatively low.

If there is only one product, but you have some news to offer, set it up the same way as a mini press conference, inviting the key editors covering your markets at the show. In any case, follow the guidelines for a conventional press conference.

Be sure to alert show security so that your guests can get into the hall and exhibit area. Better still, meet them at a given time at the information booth or some other convenient place and escort them to your booth.

Holding your press meeting this way can help avoid most conflicts with other show events, can assure that each publication will get its own story or be able to develop its own approach or angle, and can keep your costs relatively low. You will still need to prepare press kits, but no elaborate presentations and visuals. Releases, photos, backgrounders, fact sheets, and bios of your experts will make up the package. You'll also need to provide some refreshments; coffee and danish are fine.

This approach does take careful, detailed, and time-consuming advance planning and selling. You must phone to set up appointments, convince the editors to cover the new developments or technology, determine their specific areas of interest, line up the best experts for each interview, and then check and double-check to ensure that the editors show up. But the payoff for your efforts is often excellent coverage of your new show introductions.

The Suite as a Site

If only a very few publications cover a particular product or service area, your presentations and interviews can be made in the company hospitality suite. If this is the alternative selected, be sure you have a clear understanding that the suite is yours for the agreed-upon time so there are no salespeople bringing their favorite customers in for a drink when you or one of your executives are making a presentation. Follow the guidelines on invitations to assure attendance. Press kits, of course, and perhaps a sample or two and a simple foam board display are all you need.

The Trade Show Press Room

If you want to dominate the show, offer show management your staff and services to run the press room, if no professional organization is running it. You obviously have to present the suggestion in such a way that you can assure all exhibitors and participants equal access to the editors. You may get some takers, particularly at smaller, regional shows. Grumman Aircraft, for example, runs the press room for the National Business Aircraft Association Show, by no means a small show. If the offer is declined, the show management may be amenable to your offer to help staff the press room.

Whether you are planning a press event or not, press kits should be prepared for the press room and for the company exhibit when the editors drop around. (But *only* editors. If you permit the people at the booth to give your press kits to prospects, you will soon run out.)

Be there the first day when the press room opens. Place your press material in a prominent spot. Stop back a couple hours later to check to see which editors have registered. Check your press kits. If more are needed, replenish them. If someone else has covered yours up, move the others aside.

Other publicity people will pick up your press kits in the press room. If it appears you are running short, keep enough for your booth, and drop kits off to the editors at their publications' exhibits. The publication exhibit will be staffed by advertising salespeople, so write a short note to the editor by name, leaving your business card and information on where you can be located if there are questions.

Press Updates

Press updates are usually not major newsmaking occasions, but events to bring editors together for other reasons, such as introducing a greatly improved product and discussing its effect on the market. These updates should all be backed up with hard facts—for example, results of market tests, research, and customer experience.

Most of these events will involve business-to-business or trade publications and will concern industrial products. There are exceptions, of course, for such industries as transportation, sports, electronics, where other special interest or consumer groups would be interested. (It's still a car; but what is new about it *this* year?) And the nonindustrial press updates have far more razzle-dazzle and are more like full-blown press conferences.

Most industrial press updates are held in a meeting room and lunch is generally served afterward. Other meetings are often held at major trade shows. Still others take place at locations where a product can be demonstrated in its best environment. A good example is from a colleague who scheduled a press event on building roofs in three cities to dramatize the energy savings of her company's roofing material.

Industrial press updates take the same careful planning as press conferences, but the invitations can be less formal, and the meeting not as high-powered. But any time the press is involved, the stakes are just as high, and there must be a news reason for the event.

The Role of the Agency

A public relations agency can be most helpful in assuring the success of a press event and making editorial contacts—one of the main reasons you retain an agency. If your experience with press conferences is limited, an agency can recommend some highly creative ways to turn out the press. It may offer some unusual and creative story angles and make the product presentation more appealing editorially.

An agency will work with you and your staff to make sure all the details are taken care of, such as press kit assembly and delivery of kits and other materials to the conference site. An agency will want to impress you and your company. That can work very much in your favor, but also means it is important to have a clear understanding of objectives and budgets.

Using an agency does not relieve the company publicist of any responsibility. The agency and company should work on the project as a team or special task force. The publicist must be the inside contact; the agency can handle much of the outside work. But the final authority for decisions rests with the company, not the agency. Stay very close to everything the agency is doing for you. If anything goes wrong, it is the company, not the agency, that gets the bad marks from management and media.

Alternatives to Press Conferences

Remember, there is no law that says you *have* to have a press conference. In fact, the law says the opposite: do *not* have one unless you have genuine news. If you have been working to develop a news conference, if you have planned well, done everything right, and are still getting a lukewarm reception from editors to attending your press event, cancel it. It won't make you feel very good, but it is far better than scheduling a press conference and having no one show up.

All is not lost. There are some very good alternatives.

The One-on-One Interviews

Identify the publications that are most important, and take the message to them on a one-to-one basis. Many consumer and industrial products are covered by only a few publications in a given area. This technique also helps the editors develop the story angle from their publication's point of view.

The person closest to the new development or one who can speak about it with the most authority should be the interviewee. The publicist's job is to provide the releases, backgrounders, and photos. Call the editors first, suggest an angle for their magazine, determine interest, then follow up with a letter asking the editors to call you. If you haven't heard in a couple of weeks, phone again.

Be sure to brief your expert on each of the publications you plan to visit, its policy on sending copy for checking, and the general area the questions will cover. You can't ask for a list of questions in advance, but if you know the publications, how they treat company stories or profiles, and the editors, you should know the kind of questions that will be asked, including embarrassing ones.

Take notes during the interview because someone in your company will want a report on the meetings, and it will help you recount the meeting if anything appears in print that someone takes issue with. It's okay for the editor to use a tape recorder; it's not okay for you.

If the interview begins getting into sensitive areas, be prepared to interject yourself. Rather than have your expert say "no comment," you can point out that the information is proprietary and can't be discussed. (See Chapter 6 for more on how to handle an interview.)

The Press Briefing Tour

One of my associates is a strong believer in alternatives to a press conference, whenever possible. Cathleen Branciaroli, who is responsible for barrier packaging resins, wanted to announce the availability of a new one, and at the same time position her company as an expert in barrier packaging.

Instead of trying to get 15 different plastics, packaging, food, and cosmetic industry publications together in one place, she embarked on a whirlwind tour with two of her experts, to all 15. In just four days, she met with all of them in New York, Boston, and Chicago.

The interest was extremely high, more than she had expected. While she had planned two hours with each publication, some of her interviews lasted far longer. She and her team met with one editor at nine of the publications, two at a leading plastics publication, three at a food processing journal, four at another plastics periodical, five at a plastics and a packaging magazine, and a surprising eight editors at a leading packaging magazine.

Because she took the trouble to prepare her presentations well, including a morning of media training with Joanna Hanes of Hanes & Associates, she developed a number of in-depth articles—far more than expected. Her bonus was making some very valuable editorial contacts and promise of future coverage.

The Direct Mail Press Conference

Another approach to developing stories with key publications is called a direct mail press conference. The editor stays at the publication, the publicist and the person being interviewed stay in their office. This takes some preparation, but is worth the effort.

Begin by assembling a press kit, just as you would for a full-fledged, out-of-the-office affair. Call the editors. Explain some of the important aspects of your product or development to arouse interest.

Follow by mailing the press kit with a cover note, recalling the conversation, and offering to put the editor together on the phone with one of your experts. Note that you will phone for comments on a specified date.

The phone call has set the editor up for the kit, and the cover note on the kit for another call. If you have news and have done a good selling job, your next call should meet with some success—an appointment for an in-person or phone interview with your expert. Select your media carefully; work with the ones you believe will reach your target audiences. There may only be a couple, but the results will mean more than if you spent a lot of money on an off-site meeting and reach only secondary media.

The Focused Interview

In nearly every industry, only a few publications are considered tops—maybe only one. When you want to reach one publication with your special story, you can make the editor an offer that is seldom refused. The technique, which was mentioned in Chapter 6, is called a focused-group interview or roundtable. The focuser is the editor; the group is your experts, anyone who can provide answers in the area of interest: scientists, researchers, or marketing, product, or technical people. The subject has to be of high interest, and the experts must be prepared to sit down for two hours or more and answer a lot of questions. This approach can pay off handsomely, but it needs the same intense preparation as a press conference, without all the fancy presentation material.

If possible, it should be held away from the editor's and the company's offices. A relaxing hotel suite at which a nice lunch is served is an excellent place.

Advertising

The other alternative is, don't do any publicity—advertise instead. But don't forget that once it's advertised, it's no longer news. You will lose all that valuable exposure of your product in the editorial columns and waste all the resources available in a marketing communications program. Set objectives for when you want the publicity to run and don't schedule advertising on the same subject at the same time.

In Summary

The press event can be an effective way to get important news out quickly through the media to a company's target audiences. And there also are other reasons for bringing the press together. The point of any press event is to provide news that editors can pass along to their readers or viewers, without wasting their valuable time.

As a review, these are the primary types of press events:

Press conferences are for major news events. They must offer editors solid news and they must be planned carefully. Use a checklist, and double check every item on it.

Press updates are just that. Again, they must be planned carefully, but the atmosphere is less charged, because they usually are held for business-to-business publications. Editors must leave with story material.

Trade shows are good places for press events because most publications covering that particular industry will attend. The competition is fierce for attention, however, so offer good news value at a time that does not compete with show events. A booth meeting before the show opens can work well.

Alternatives to press events should get equal consideration when a conference is suggested. They give editors an opportunity for one-on-one, in-depth interviews. The result is often better coverage and longer, more detailed stories.

Take the messages directly to the editors, especially if there are only a few important publications covering your industry. Go well prepared.

Use a video news conference as an alternative to taking the show on the road. This is recommended when your top executives can't be away from their offices for more than a few hours.

Use a direct mail interview. Arrange it through the mail and carry it out over the telephone.

Support services and agencies can be extremely helpful for any press activity. Just make sure the agency understands that the way to get the best results may not be with expensive press kits and razzle-dazzle events.

11

Support Services and How They Fit

Support services (we might also call them peripheral services) are independent businesses that help publicists with the mechanics of reaching the media and recording and analyzing the results. There are many such companies, and taken together they provide a staggering scope of services, from the esoteric to the mundane.

One way to find these firms is through a good directory. One I have used often is *The Professional Guide to Public Relations Services* by Richard Weiner (Professional Publishing Company, Inc., 888 Seventh Avenue, New York, NY 10106). This extensive and detailed directory covers a wide range of public relations services, from broadcast monitoring to VIP services, to such exotic items as skywriting.

In this chapter I won't attempt to duplicate what has already been done, and done well, in such directories. My purpose is to explain the procedures and the benefits of some of the basic services that can support a product publicity program. I have found that using these services has helped extend the scope of my programs and also permitted me more time for program management, planning, and editorial contacts. Some of them are creative, others perform mechanical services; some are needed all the time, others part of the time, and some rarely.

The most important services for any agency or corporate publicity department, no matter how large or small, are (1) those that handle mailing and list maintenance, and (2) clipping services that tell you whether your publicity was used in the media it was sent to, and provide a "clip" or broadcast report to verify this. There are no options with photographers; you must have good ones. You may use agency writers or have an in-house staff. Even so, there are times when you will need to use outside writers. You may or may not use a mat and syndication service in your program. If you are doing extensive broadcast publicity, you will be working with outside producers and distributors. Very few PR agencies have in-house production capabilities.

Specific companies noted in this book are those I have had personal experience with; most of them would also, I think, be considered the "standards" in the business. As an aid to those who have not worked with these kinds of services, addresses and phone numbers appear at the end of this chapter. However, it is not my intent to endorse any particular company. As a publicist, it is up to you to determine which of the competitive services you wish to use. Review their presentations and materials, ask for references, and make your own judgment of whether the services fit your needs.

Distribution Services

Assuming you have identified the media important to your markets, the most important services are those that distribute news material to the media on a day-to-day basis.

Of course it is possible to do this yourself, maintaining mailing lists in-house. It is probably easier to do this now than it was a few years ago, thanks to the computer. But the list must be kept up to date, and with the high turnover in media, list maintenance is still very time-consuming. The outside services have excellent resources and, considering your company time and personnel costs, are reasonably inexpensive. In my opinion, it makes little sense to keep extensive media lists yourself and physically do your own distribution. A publicist should maintain just a list of *key editorial contacts*.

Essentially, distribution services take your original materials (releases and photo negatives), duplicate them, and mail them to preselected media. All will retype copy if you request it, but I recommend sending only camera-ready materials; this way, you can make sure the copy is error-free.

You may find it handy to use a computer linkup or some form of electronic mail to send release copy or detailed instructions to the distribution service. Of course you will still have to send your photo negatives, transparencies, literature, and other enclosure material separately.

A distribution service will work with you to develop lists keyed to your company's needs and based on its own data bank. Generally, it makes no difference whether a news release is sent to a particular editor by name. If for some reason you prefer that your releases be addressed by name, then you have the option of maintaining your own lists, or using a service that keeps up with editorial changes (PR Aids is one that does).

PR Aids

This firm basically does media mailings, but is far, far more than a printing, inserting, addressing, stamping, and mailing service.

PR Aids has an extensive and very sophisticated computer-based system of media selection. Users of PR Aids have access to its MediaBase, which includes 26,000 media with some 106,000 contacts by name. The system permits clients to search through the media base by publication name, editor's name, or editorial category and obtain information such as addresses, contact name, title, editorial content, and more. This can be helpful in developing lists for special one-time mailings or press events.

Lists can be tailored to client needs, and used either on a one-time basis or stored for later mailings. Release text can be sent direct to PR Aids for transmission and feedback of costs and media count. Personalized notes to editors can be added to releases.

PR Aids also offers a service called MediaTrack, which it claims makes followup easier. It gives a name-by-name summary of mailings, with editors' names and telephone numbers. PR Aids also offers data on release use, shows circulation reach, and gives space-equivalent advertising dollar costs.

Bacon's Clipping Bureau

One of the advantages of using Bacon's for release distribution is that it also is one of the nation's leading clipping services. Bacon's media bank lists some 5,500 magazines (trade, farm, and consumer), 1,800 daily newspapers, 7,500 weekly newspapers, 1,100 television stations, and 7,000 radio stations. The names are available individually or grouped by market classification, circulation, city, state, network, ADI (areas of dominant influence), or SMSA (standard metropolitan statistical areas) breakdowns.

Bacon's will provide pressure-sensitive labels for general or customized media lists. It also will handle complete mailings, including photo reproduction, captioning, collating, folding, and press kit compilation and distribution. Clients of Bacon's have access to the company's media bank through their computer terminals.

Bacon's is capable of handling any size job, any frequency. The company is efficient and responsive.

PR Data Systems Inc.

PR Data Systems not only distributes news material, it also analyzes the results. Its services are valuable to companies of any size. While it can work for an agency, the system is set up on a company-by-company basis, and its mailing philosophy, which reflects that of most editors (and my own, incidentally), may not mesh with the thinking of some agencies. Mailings are made to publications by editorial title, not a person's name. Most of the time it's "editor," but could also be garden editor, financial editor, farm editor, or fashion editor.

Jack Schoonover, president of PR Data Systems, calls his company a "total communications service." The system consists of five independent but related services "to better target external corporate communications." All are predicated on the use of the company's interactive computer program. You don't buy just a mailing service. If you use PR Data Systems, you use all five services.

1. Media List Development. From the file of 35,000 media addresses, users can build their own customized and proprietary lists to focus on their key target audiences. Lists can be "built" right on a client's own computer, and then printed out.

But you have to do the thinking. Let's walk through the process, using an imaginary product.

Your company makes "The Little Red Machine," an appliance that will, among other things, prepare tomatoes for canning, freezing, and for making pasta sauce and tomato soup. A recipe book is included. The market for this small appliance is primarily amateur gardeners.

You must think both consumer and trade media. Consult the *Standard Rate & Data Media Catalogs, Bacon's Publicity Checker,* and the *Working Press of the Nation* for complete, up-to-date listings.

Probably the first audience for any household or kitchen product is the housewares trade. Included for this list are two very important publications: *Housewares Magazine* and *Home Furnishings Daily*. You also may include publications that reach retailers, such as *Appliance Merchandising, Midwest Retailer, NARDA News, Retail Report,* and *Retailer and Marketer News*. Also *Hardware Age* and *Hardware Merchandising*. If the product is sold in Canada, include such publications as *Hardware & Housewares Merchandising*.

Also include *Chain Store, Mass Market Retailers, Chain Store Age/Merchandising Editor*. If it will be sold in supermarkets, as some appliances are, include these trades as well.

The consumer lists are not too difficult to develop, but the product must be available nationally before any consumer publicity is done. There is no point in creating broad consumer interest if the product can't be purchased. It may be necessary to develop regional communications plans, rather than go national, if either your production is limited or your distributors or jobbers do not sell into all parts of the country. Always be certain that your product is available in the areas where you are releasing publicity.

Begin with the publications that run food and food-related news. Some of these are *Lady's Circle, McCalls, Ladies Home Journal, Redbook, Woman's Day, Woman's Day Best Ideas for Christmas, Women's Circle, Family Circle, Good House-*

keeping, and the bridal publications such as *Modern Bride, Brides Magazine,* and *New England Bride.* In Canada include such publications as *Chatelaine* and *Today's Bride.*

There also are a number of publications devoted to the gardener. These include *Better Homes & Gardens, Better Homes & Gardens Christmas Ideas, Country Living, House & Garden, National Gardening Magazine, Rodale's Organic Gardening,* and *Sunset Magazine.* There are many more, including a large number of regional ones.

Don't overlook newspaper publicity, from Pierre Franey's column in *The New York Times* to the many gardening and cooking columns in daily and weekly newspapers. Start with *Standard Rate and Data* if you wish to develop special lists according to ADIs.

If the product is expensive, you will want to develop lists of media that reach higher income families.

Special stories can be developed for the senior citizen magazines such as *50 Plus* and *Modern Maturity.* There are more than 20 such magazines. Also include cooking magazines. You may not get coverage in *Gourmet,* for example, but may in *Cooking Magazine.*

Metro Associated Services (see later in this chapter) runs special promotions for Christmas and Bridal Giving. This is a good way to reach smaller daily and weekly newspapers. Other mat services provide similar services.

There are excellent opportunities for exposure on local television or radio talk shows if the product can be demonstrated easily. Check the media directories cited to develop broadcast lists. Tips on broadcast publicity are in Chapter 9.

Exclusive lists can be developed for every media category by selecting those publications targeted from the general lists that are stored in the PR Data computer. Special lists can be made up on screen for a company's exclusive use and can be securely stored under a unique code.

2. *Distribution.* Using indicated media codes based on your target media (either from the master list on the computer or a custom code), release mailings are ordered. PR Data also has the capability of localizing media distribution by state, county, or zip code levels.

3. *Clipping Analysis.* This is the heart of the service, an actual diagnosis of and report on precisely what was used, how it was used, and where. Basically, here's how it works: The client company identifies the primary media, product, product group, or service *copy points* to be checked in the clippings. The company's clipping service forwards the clippings to PR Data, which issues quarterly reports telling the client whether important copy points in the publicity plan are being delivered through the media and the number of times such points are transmitted. The same reports also provide data on circulation, photo use, and lineage in a number of media categories. By reviewing the reports, the publicist can determine if the program is succeeding or if its emphasis needs to be changed. For more on this valuable service, see Chapter 12 and Appendix D.

4. *Media Diagnostic System.* Data are developed for each news release or for a program based on clippings and stored on the computer. The release or event can be called up on the computer so that one can see at a glance which publications used the story, which did not, and where photos were used. The computer will also identify publications that did not receive the release, but that used the story. (This, by the way, is not uncommon. The story may have been sent to a sister publication, picked up from a daily or weekly or some other source, such as a customer. It may even have resulted from a phone query.)

5. *Mailing.* Finally, PR Data Systems has complete mail capability, including photo reproduction. It can handle everything from a one-page release to assembly and mailing of a press kit.

Clients can get on line with the PR Data System computer 24 hours a day, seven days a week.

I like this system because it provides data on use—target media, reach, circulation, copy point delivery—that can be very valuable in seeing where a program is and how well it is doing, and in planning future activities and programs. It won't tell you if anyone *learned* anything from the publicity; marketing research can do that. But it can tell you quite effectively whether you are reaching your objectives in your target media and exposing the audience to your messages. It requires a commitment on the part of the publicist or agency to spend some time with it: developing customized mailing lists, setting it up so that it reports data that are wholly applicable to a particular market, monitoring, and reviewing reports and results.

PR Newswire

PR Newswire describes itself as the nation's press relations wire service, which "flashes your news release—simultaneously, in full, the way you want it—to high speed teleprinters in newsrooms or directly into computers via our own private network. PR Newswire is the electronic link between you and the news media."

News is sent via the Associated Press satellite system to nearly 600 news media, including newspapers, wire services, magazines, radio, TV, trade publications, and financial institutions. The publicist selects the media and can tailor distribution to city, state, regional, national, and international. The copy is handled by a staff of experienced news professionals who will style it to conform to wire service standards and computer format.

PR Newswire has a number of newslines. The basic one serves 350 media including the major dailies, wires, magazines, radio, and TV in the East, Southeast, Southwest, and Midwest. There also is a Western wire, and several others covering other media areas in the country.

Two services are of most interest to publicists: the general newswire and the feature news service. General news stories are "slugged" to the attention of appropriate news departments and editors to reach city rooms and leading business media as a back-up in case wire services for these media do not attend the event. Topics relating to product publicity include science and medicine, sporting events, and new-product introductions of high national interest.

The feature newswire sends copy to media over five basic newslines— Western, Florida, New England, New Jersey, New York State—and all major Chicago media. Subjects include lifestyle, food and nutrition, science and medicine, sports, entertainment, travel and leisure, health, and publishing and the arts.

Audio and video transmission can be made to more than 2,400 stations on the AP, UPI, NPR, and other radio networks.

The service can provide a listing of trade and technical publications on its newsline. As of 1986, these are somewhat limited to categories of general news, advertising and marketing, aerospace/aviation/travel, building and construction, chemicals/plastics, computers/electronics, energy, finance, international business and foreign trade, merchandising and retailing, mining and metals, plus a number of trades in other markets.

The service is highly versatile and efficient. Because it is staffed with wire service and newspaper veterans, it can help you evaluate the success of your effort and will be straightforward about the chances of pickup. It is not, however, a counseling service, and you must use good judgment in deciding whether a product story or feature has any chance of success with PR Newswire. Remember that *any* story that goes out on the newswire must still pass the receiving editor's scrutiny.

For straight product publicity, you may find that you use PR Newswire infrequently, but if you also handle corporate public relations, PR Newswire is a good service for your company.

Clip Services

Aside from subscribing to all the publications identified as media targets, there is only one way to find out whether media are running news of your products and services, and that is to retain a clipping service. There are three main services that cover the national media: Bacon's, Burrelle's, and Luce. (There are also a number of state and regional services, and they can be helpful if your publicity campaign is concentrated in a given area.)

At best, they will clip only about 30 to 40 percent of the items and stories about your product. This estimate is not mine, it comes from one of the more

Support Services and How They Fit

efficient services. Most who hear this for the first time react with surprise. They can't understand why the services don't get better results. But considering the amount of material pumped out every day, the services aren't doing a bad job.

To raise efficiency, the publicist must provide the services with information that can make their search easier. This entails more than just sending a list of product or brand names and asking them to clip anything they find that is listed. To work efficiently with a clipping service, you must provide the name of the product, including trademarks, brand names, and generics, and a very brief description of each. And make sure the service is kept up to date on any changes.

Don't make the instructions too complicated and with too many exceptions. Provide the service with the generic of the brand name, but you may wish to exclude clipping any stories that just mention generic, unless it is used with the company name. If you are interested only in product publicity, you may wish to exclude pricing changes, earnings reports, etc. Keep your product lists up to date.

Send a list of the media to which a release was sent along with a copy of the release. It's very important too that a clip service be notified of any direct contacts with editors who may be running stories about your products. If it is a story someone else said was placed on your behalf, then ask the clip service to check for it. Try to give the service an idea of the issue in which it might appear, if it will be soon. If it's only a possibility, and may run six months from now, wait until you can be more definite before notifying the clip service.

If it appears that you may have some stories picked up by the wire services, you should instruct the clipping service to clip wire stories appearing only in major cities, and name the cities. Otherwise, you may get piles of clips from one wire story. (You pay for each one.) If the major newspapers carried the story, you can assume that it also was used by most of the medium- and smaller-sized papers.

If your company has an extensive publicity program, consider using two clipping services. Bacon's would be my first choice for magazines, and either Burrelle's or Luce a second choice for both magazines and newspapers. To make sure I truly needed two services, and wasn't paying for two when I might be able to get the results I needed from just one, I surveyed the clippings from both Bacon's and Luce for one month (with the kind cooperation of Luce), and found that there was about a 15 percent overlap in magazine clippings. Luce produced far more newspaper clippings than Bacon's. Bacon's found more trade product mentions and stories. It was clear that I needed both to get the best evidence of story use. This might not apply to some limited-product companies, but is recommended for large, multiproduct corporations that may receive thousands of clips a year.

The key to getting the most from a clipping service is communications. Inform the services of every action taken. If there is a possibility a TV crew will be covering a trade show, for instance, and the station has shown some interest in your product, let the service know in advance.

Discuss your needs with the clipping services to be sure they can meet all of them. Bacon's, for example, does not provide the full scope of video coverage, but does extremely well clipping magazines.

How They Operate

Clipping services charge a monthly fee, plus a charge for each clipping. If some of the clippings sent do not jibe with your clipping instructions, they can be returned for credit.

Most clipping services read the daily and Sunday newspapers, plus the major Canadian ones. They read more than 8,000 weeklies and most of the ethnic and religious publications, including black, diocesan, Jewish, and Spanish-American. They also read two AP wires, three UPI wires, Dow Jones, and Reuters Wire. And they cover some 6,500 trade and consumer magazines.

Broadcast news and public information programming is monitored for the networks—including, ABC, CBS, NBC, and PBS—and cable news shows: CNN and CNN Headline News, Financial News Network, ESPN, and USA Network. Local TV stations are monitored in major cities and major market areas.

Specific program coverage includes "CBS Nightwatch," "The Phil Donahue Show," "Good Morning America" (ABC), "Hour Magazine," "The MacNeil/Lehrer News Hour" (PBS), "ABC 11 O'Clock Report," "Today" (NBC), and "CBS Morning News." Weekly shows include "20/20" (ABC), "Washington Week in Review," and "Wall Street Week" (PBS). They also monitor monthly and special programs from the three networks, weekend news shows, and special news interview programs, such as "Meet the Press," "60 Minutes," and "Face the Nation."

Radio coverage includes ABC Information Service, CBS Radio, Copley News Service, CNN II, Mutual Life Style Reports, National Public Radio, and UPI Radio.

Tapes of television news clips are costly but often worth it. A printed copy of the audio part of a video release can also be obtained for a number of major television markets. If the client's story is used, the company receives a printed copy showing the media facts, including audience size, date and air time, plus a transcript of the story.

Advance notice should be given clip services on TV distribution or possible coverage, to get maximum use of the service. If a story is used by more than one station, order just one tape.

Because the print clipping services don't monitor all television outlets, you may need one that provides the most extensive monitoring service if you have a major broadcast campaign. I have found Radio/TV reports in New York quite cooperative in obtaining taped transcripts and written reports. What they can't get from New York, the odds are they can get from the other markets they cover.

Editorial Information

Sometimes it is necessary to have the name and address of a particular editor at a particular publication. There are a number of directories available; at least one should be a part of every publicist's library. Media directories give you not only names of editors, but also information about the publication's audiences and focus. Keep very much in mind, however, that there is a lot of turnover on editorial staffs.

Standard Rate and Data Services

Most advertising departments subscribe to this multi-volume service. It's a good place to start if you're looking for information on editorial staff, circulation, demographics, and so on. It sometimes is overlooked by publicists seeking editorial information, but I have found the large volumes full of useful data. It's quite expensive compared with other directories, but well worth it if you're handling both advertising and publicity.

Bacon's Publicity Checkers

Bacon's publishes two annual domestic media directories listing more than 5,500 business, farm, industrial, and consumer magazines in the United States and 330 in Canada, arranged in 143 market groups. Complete mailing and contact data are provided, including editor names, frequency, circulation, addresses, and telephone numbers. In addition, directories are coded to indicate what type of material the publication will consider, for instance case histories, photographs, news releases, literature releases, and personnel announcements.

Volume II is a directory of 1,700 daily newspapers and the editors of 23 news departments by name. Contact information is given on 7,500 weeklies and weekly publishers groups. Other sections show Canadian dailies, the black press, news services and syndicates, and special lists of dailies by circulation and ADI groups. Bacon's is very useful as a way to find the newspapers circulated in particular states and cities. It is less useful in identifying editors by name, because of the turnover among newspaper staffs.

The two volumes are published every October; paste-in revisions for both are sent in January, April, and July.

Bacon's also publishes the *International Publicity Checker,* with "complete and accurate media information for magazines and newspapers in Western Europe." It lists 9,979 business, trade, and technical magazines, plus 1,036 national and regional daily newspapers, with full mailing, telephone, Telex information, translation requirements, and publicity codings.

Another useful Bacon's publication is *Media Alerts,* which gives advance information on special issues and features being planned by a number of publications. While many publicists can get special-issue information from advertising reps and through media calendars in media kits, this volume is invaluable in targeting issues for possible tie-in.

Working Press of the Nation

A four-volume set, published annually: Newspaper Directory, Magazine Directory, Radio and Television Directory, and Feature Writer and Syndicate Directory. While the first three volumes contain valuable information on each medium listed, the names of editors may not be up to date, simply because it's an annual. If you compared one year with a previous one, you might be surprised by the number of personnel changes that take place.

Writing and Photography Services

No doubt you will often work with individual freelance writers and photographers in your local area. Here I will describe three services that can help get a story and/or photos virtually anywhere in the country. If you have a limited staff, can't afford an agency, or have spot work, these services can be of inestimable value. Here again, the descriptions are based on my own experiences, and should not be taken as an endorsement.

Unless you hire a service you have worked with before, they may not know much about your business. But because most are experienced journalists, they usually know how to dig in and get a story — provided you give them sufficient background and direction. That means a complete direction sheet as described in Chapter 6.

Creative Communications Services (CCS)

This firm is based in California, but it can handle a story or photo assignment anywhere in the United States. You, the client, pay a fixed cost whether CCS is doing the story in Dallas, Seattle, or Miami, because CCS has its own staff of photojournalists based all over the country. At a given time, a reporter may be doing a number of stories in a certain area of the country for a number of clients.

The clients pay only for the work, not for travel costs, which are covered in the basic fee. The only drawback is that you might not get your story immediately. It may mean waiting a week or more until the firm has other stories lined up in the same area. If a story is needed in a rush, then you pay travel expenses.

With proper planning and scheduling, such as for a case history, I have had excellent results from CCS. Photos have been good, and most ran with the stories. CCS also will, for a modest fee, place stories it writes in appropriate media.

Oesterwinter Associates

I have known Horst Oesterwinter for a number of years. He is an outstanding photographer and understands very well the needs of product publicists. His firm will do just photography for a fixed fee anywhere in the continental United States, and also photography and reportage for a fixed fee.

McCann Associates

Bob McCann, former head of UPI's commercial photo division (Compix), took it over a few years ago when the wire service dropped it. His network of working newspaper photographers and reporters can be retained on a flat-fee basis, plus travel expenses, for either story coverage, photos, or both. He also has contacts with a number of "strategically located award-winning annual report and illustration specialists," who are available for a higher fee. I have used his reporting service and also worked with his "top photographers," and have been satisfied. They got what I requested, and then some.

Strictly Photo

Here are two companies I have found that provide good nationwide photoservice.

You can call on the services of some 120 top magazine photographers through Black Star Publishing Company. It also has a large stock photo library, with photos for just about any situation from historical to heavy industry to broad consumer areas. These can add interest to a feature story or your company magazine.

Wagner International is another good photo service. If you are looking for a newswire quality photo, and if Bob Goldberg shoots it, it will stand a good chance of making either or both of the national wires. If it doesn't, you pay only expenses. There is a flat fee if the photo is used on only one wire, a higher fee if used on both.

244   *The Complete Book of Product Publicity*

I've had good success in getting wire coverage as long as the photo has been shot by Goldberg or someone else at the service.

With these two—and several other good photo services—you can be assured of getting dramatic shots, the kind wire services like to see. Figure 11-1 is a good example.

Figure 11-1. This photo by Bob Goldberg of Wagner International was used on the Associated Press wire. The wire services will use good photos that tell a story. The photo ties into spring gardening, a popular topic.

Mat and Syndication Services

Mat services (also known as syndication services) take your material, develop an angle, write copy, and distribute it to weekly and small dailies, all relatively inexpensively. The term "mat" comes from the days of letterpress printing, when a matrix (mat) or form from which printing plates were made was sent to newspapers. Because most publications today print by offset, camera-ready copy is sent. These services also prepare and release material for TV and radio. These services are best used when publicity is needed for a mature consumer product, as an extension of an ongoing publicity program, or when all else fails.

They can be useful; they do produce clippings. The audience for the newspaper services is the readers of weekly newspapers, shoppers, and small dailies. If reaching these audiences is important to your product, then these services should be part of a program. Certainly if a campaign is directed to a specific income level of newspaper readers or a demographic group, then a mat service can be a supplement to it. But no publicity program should have a major emphasis on commercial mat or syndication services. And if your agency brags about all the clippings it got from a story about a particular product, and the clips resulted from a mat or syndication service release, then you should ask the agency what else it has done for you. If it's very little, it's time for a serious review of your account. The fact is that you don't need agency help to develop mat or syndication releases. If you wish to cut costs, work directly with the service.

Three Typical Services

There are a number of these services; rather than trying to name them all, I'll just describe three I'm familiar with. Nearly all do the same thing; it's a matter of trying one or two to find the one you can work with best.

One such service is the *North American Precis Syndicate*, which reaches suburban newspapers. Readers of these papers form an impressive audience and are located within commuting distances of major markets. Camera-ready stories are sent on a wide variety of subjects — food, fashion, industrial news, religion, government information, sports, household hints, and more.

North American also produces a "Radio Roundup," which is said to generate more than 200 placements, and "TV Takes" (color slides and a brief script), which can produce about 40 placements.

One of the more sophisticated services is *Metro Associated Services Inc.* In brief, it works this way: Clients provide Metro with typewritten copy and photos. For an all-inclusive fee per column inch (it was $82 in 1985), Metro distributes the copy in camera-ready form to about 4,500 newspapers in the United States and Canada. If necessary, it will advise you on copy and photos so that they will be editorially acceptable.

Four options are offered:

1. Special editions scheduled throughout the year to coincide with newspapers' publication of special advertising supplements. For example, Christmas, spring and fall home improvement, and back-to-school.
2. A "timely features" program, not geared to a special theme, but offering tie-ins with Halloween and child safety, as examples.
3. Prime Cuts, an appropriately named service just for food; offers an opportunity for seasonal recipes.
4. Custom sections can be tailored to a client's own needs, and range from a single tabloid page to a complete 24-page section with a color cover.

Metro claims that the special section concept works best because it provides the newspapers with editorial "fillers," which the papers use to put together their own special sections. The *Los Angeles Times* and New York *Daily News* subscribe to Metro service, but Metro points out that these and other large metropolitan dailies "*do not normally make use of our material.*" Prime users are newspapers of 30,000 to 40,000 circulation and less.

Metro also offers some good advice: It will not guarantee pickup, but says to "narrow the gap" clients should keep product mention to a minimum, copy should be written in a "low-key" manner, and photos should contain people using the product and not just straight product shots.

Associated Release Service has a basic mat and offset release service with a price scale based on the number of column inches and the number released, up to a maximum of 3 column inches and 7,810 newspapers.

It also offers special feature pages, and a monthly column syndicate sent to weeklies and dailies that have agreed to run the column—for example, a sports feature on fishing. Brand names, of course, can be mentioned, if not overdone, provided something of interest and new ideas are offered each time.

The company also will produce and distribute one-minute news clips for TV news programs. Cost varies according to location and the number of stations to which the news clip is released.

TV slide releases and "filmed vignettes" are serviced to news editors, women's program directors, and sports editors. The slide releases consist of a script and slides, from one- to four-color. Vignettes are three- to five-minute videotapes produced for commercial and cable stations.

Radio releases also are prepared and distributed. These can be sent as exclusives in a given city or market or can go to a few selected stations or to all. The rationale for offering an exclusive is that the station is more likely to use it. This only works if there is a good story to tell. I suggest that the make-up of the radio audience is more important in determining whether the release is likely to be aired. Radio material can be keyed to news, sports, farm, and other program directors. Associated also has a program to reach home economists.

Determining Usage

Mat and syndication services retain the same clipping services to report usage, so the chances are you may get a number of duplicate clippings. You will not be able to cut your costs for the service by using only your own clip service, and it may not be worth the effort to try. Clipping is part of the package price.

For broadcast usage, these services find out if radio and TV stations use their material by enclosing a prepaid postcard with the material when it is sent. It should come as no surprise that many news directors and program managers neglect to return the card. This is the exception to the rule of not calling an editor to see if a release has been used. Calling may be the only way you'll find out.

If the broadcast department of your agency is handling the news clip or other type of media "news features" to TV or radio, the agency will follow up with the stations by telephone if there is no response within a given period of time. Mat services normally don't do this. On the other hand, they are inexpensive. Be aware that they probably will not get coverage for you in major markets or on major television programs.

Don't fall into the trap of confusing results from mat distribution, either in print or broadcast, as reaching your target audiences. These services should be looked upon only as peripheral to a program, and by no means the heart of it, numbers notwithstanding.

If any of your activities could benefit particularly from radio coverage, you may want to employ the services of News/Radio Network. It has been working in radio publicity for many, many years, and understands how radio works as well as any service. It can be of real help in extending the reach of such things as press events, trade shows, and new product introductions. The company offers a number of different services at different rate structures.

I have used the service to cover products of consumer interest. One example involved an exhibit at a boat show. The service sent a correspondent who did 60- and 90-second interviews with exhibitors using my company's product. The interviews were fed to preselected markets, and also to "Audioline," a phone service by which stations call in and record for their own use items of interest. We selected key markets in the Great Lakes and coastal areas because we were targeting prospects for purchase of boats longer than 20 feet.

Film and Videotape Producers

Other services include film producers and TV news clip producers and distributors.

Over the years, I have made a number of films, and have been involved with directing, writing the narration, and editing. This hands-on experience has taught me more about what goes into a successful film than I might have learned had I hired a production company. Even so, I recommend hiring a producer to do the work. You still have to stay close to the production, but you can free yourself from worrying about all the detail work.

One big question is whether to use film or tape. I prefer film if the show is going to be used with large audiences. As of this writing tape colors can be washed out and fuzzy when the image is much larger than the standard monitor size. The technology exists to transfer from tape to film and from film to tape, with good to excellent results. I prefer film for a sharper image and more sparkle in the colors, but *only* if not for publicity. For publicity purposes, you can't afford *not* to shoot tape because it is fast, easy to edit, and doesn't need processing. The best reason, though, for shooting tape is that TV stations no longer use *film* clips.

But in any case you must have more than a verbal agreement with the producer. The work should be "for hire" and the contract should state clearly that the negative, B rolls, prints, tapes, soundtracks, and all other original materials belong to the client, not the film company. You may wish to have the producer store these elements, particularly film, because it should be kept in a film vault. However, if the firm gets into financial difficulties, you will still be able to recover these elements because the contract clearly specifies ownership.

There used to be a rule-of-thumb for film costs of $1,000 a finished minute — a ten-minute film would cost $10,000. This was a myth then, and even more so today. If a producer cites a per-minute cost, get someone else. Costs are affected by a thousand variables — location, lighting, sound, talent, time, script, special effects, opticals, and on and on. There is no way to figure it on a per-minute basis.

There are a number of excellent producers who can handle video news clips from idea through production and distribution. You can be sure that few will turn you down if you approach them with a subject for a video news release, even if it doesn't meet broadcast "news" guidelines (see Chapter 9). If you can find a producer who will work with you to develop your idea, and who isn't afraid to tell you if he believes it won't work and you will be wasting your money, stick with him. He probably has been successful.

Better still, work with an agency on broadcast publicity. It's probably just as cost-effective as doing it yourself.

Resources

Associated Release Service
2 North Riverside Plaza
Chicago, Ill. 60606
312-726-8693
Offices in New York, Los Angeles, San Francisco, Washington, and Atlanta

Bacon's Clipping Bureau
332 South Michigan Avenue
Chicago, Ill. 60604
800-621-0561
In Illinois: 312-922-2400

Black Star Publishing Co. Inc.
4500 Park Avenue
New York, N.Y. 10016
212-679-3288

Burrelle's Press Clipping Service
75 East Northfield Road
Livingston, N.J.
201-992-6600, 212-227-5570, 800-631-1160

Creative Communications Services (CCS)
P.O. Box 1007
Encinitas, Calif. 92024
619-436-2279

Luce Press Clippings
42 South Center
Mesa, Ariz. 85202
602-834-4884
Offices in New York, Chicago, and Topeka, Kans.

McCann Associates
Station House, Suite 234
900 Haddon Avenue
Collingswood, N.J. 08108
609-858-3033
Office in New York

Metro Associated Services Inc.
33 West 34th Street
New York, N.Y. 10001
212-947-5100

News/Radio Network
800 Ogden Avenue
Suite #4
Downers Grove, Ill. 60515
312-963-4455
Offices in New York, Chicago, Milwaukee, Phoenix, and Los Angeles

North American Precis Syndicate
201 East 42nd Street
New York, N.Y. 10017
212-867-9000
Offices in Chicago, Washington, and Studio City, Calif.

Oesterwinter Associates
Interstate Photography and Reporting
10447 Merriman Road
Cupertino, Calif. 95014
800-FOR-PHOTO
In California: 408-257-7222
Office in New York

PR Aids Inc.
330 West 34th Street
New York, N.Y. 10001
212-947-7733
Offices in Atlanta, Chicago, Southfield, Mich., Los Angeles, Minneapolis, Pittsburgh, and Washington

PR Data Systems Inc.
15 Oakwood Avenue
Norwalk, Conn. 06850
203-847-0777

PR Newswire
150 East 58th Street
New York, N.Y. 10155
212-832-9400
Offices in Boston, Los Angeles, and Miami

Radio/TV Reports
41 East 42nd Street
New York, N.Y. 10017
212-599-5500
Offices in Skokie, Ill., Novi, Minn., Los Angeles, and Chevy Chase, Md.

Wagner International Photos
216 East 45th Street
New York, N.Y. 10017
212-661-6100

Working Press of the Nation
The National Research Bureau Inc.
310 South Michigan Avenue
Chicago, Ill. 60604

12
Measuring Publicity Effectiveness

Many of the ideas in this chapter were contributed by James D. Culley, Ph.D. A former associate dean of the College of Business and Economics at the University of Delaware, Dr. Culley is a senior marketing research specialist in Du Pont's Corporate Marketing Research Division.

A critical step in product publicity is research. Through research, the publicity manager attempts to answer questions like these:

- What should we say?
- How did we do?
- Would we have been better off if we had tried something else?

For too long, measuring the effect of publicity activities has meant nothing more than counting news clippings, broadened in recent years to include air mentions and video news clip showings. But clippings, per se, tell you little except the degree to which the media used your materials.

Measuring means more than counting. It means three-dimensional evaluation. Evaluation of product publicity efforts is essential, to improve the effectiveness of these programs and to ensure proper accountability. Without measurement, weak and useless publicity efforts may be repeated in the belief that they have been effective. Or effective efforts may be abandoned because their contributions were not appreciated. Also, most people work harder knowing that their efforts are being evaluated.

Still, many companies and agencies fail to do any real evaluation. Prudently managed companies that would never think of appropriating funds for advertising without first carefully studying the purpose, cost, and the expected yield, continue to spend relatively large sums on product publicity with only a vague idea of what such efforts have accomplished.

Why is this? Actually, there are several common obstacles to evaluation:
- Time.
- Money.
- Indifference. Product publicity is sometimes only a small part of a total marketing effort, and so management decides it does not need much research attention.
- Resistance to control. Public relations firms and advertising agencies are often openly hostile to attempts to measure the effectiveness of their work. Many publicity managers will be quick to protest that "everyone is an expert" in their field. Enlightened managers, on the other hand, recognize the difference between opinionated criticism and a detached, quantitative evaluation of publicity efforts.
- The belief that publicity (unlike advertising) does not lend itself to measurement and control. While it may be difficult to pass judgment on the artistic aspects of the discipline, the end products of such creativeness — awareness (having heard of a product), knowledge (having learned something about the product), attitudes (having formed an opinion about the product) — can be assessed in the same way as the end product of other activities of the business.
- The belief that the techniques of measurement are too costly or too inaccurate.
- The belief that the complexity of the marketing communications efforts makes it impossible to assess publicity's contribution to the whole.

Even so, the evaluation process cannot be overlooked. Publicity research can give us many useful answers:

1. Was the effort adequately planned? Was it planned with measurable objectives?
2. Did those concerned understand the job that needed to be done? Did they understand the expectations?
3. How could the results have been more effective? Were realistic goals set?
4. Did the effort reach all members of the pertinent (target) audience?
5. Could better provisions have been made for unforeseen circumstances?
6. Did the program stay within budget? If not, why?
7. What provisions were made for measuring results? Were the efforts effective?
8. What steps can be taken to improve future product publicity efforts?

Why Clear Goals Are Essential

When research on publicity efforts is suggested, the question immediately arises: "What should we measure against?" The answer, of course, is against the goals, the expected or intended results. Unfortunately, many publicity campaigns are carried on without any clearly stated goals. When pressed for a statement of the precise goals of a particular campaign, most publicity managers can furnish reasonable objectives, but in many cases these objectives were articulated after the fact. All too often, those concerned with a company's marketing communications programs are not clear on what they were designed to accomplish.

Agreed-upon goals are essential to the intelligent measurement of publicity results. To be sure, the results of one campaign can be measured against the results of another without such goals, but that won't tell you whether the results match your expectations or the money spent to attain them. One thing more: the expected results must be realistic, or any measurements of them are likely to be worthless.

Consumers buy a product at the end of a learning process in which they first become aware of the product or brand, then develop a favorable attitude toward it, and finally decide to make a trial purchase. Therefore, the best behavioral measures of product publicity performance relate to consumer awareness, knowledge, or attitudes rather than to actual sales.

Suppose a manufacturer wants to attract new customers and sees the basic publicity goal as persuading existing customers to look for the brand the next time they shop. An appropriate behavioral measure of this goal might be whether some number of store customers ask to see the brand. And an operational publicity goal might be expressed in terms of desired level of requests, not in terms of sales.

In industrial marketing, too, sales changes are not an adequate measure of publicity effectiveness. Here the goal of product publicity might be to support sales representatives by helping to create leads and communicating information about the company and its products. Product publicity often plays a less significant role in precipitating actual purchase decisions among industrial buyers, and so it is especially important not to measure product publicity performance in terms of sales. (In rare instances, a sale can be related to a specific publicity action, such as a broadcast that triggered an interest in a product. Even so, there is a salesperson involved with the customer to close the sale and write the order. Unless there is a definite statement by the prospect that he was sold on the product by the broadcast, these are difficult to track and verify.)

Where Research Fits

Perhaps one way to appreciate the role of research is to look for a minute at the overall flow of the publicity process. Then we can see at what point research fits in, and how it affects successive steps. Figure 12-1, developed with my associate Dr. Arthur Beard, shows the flow of information from the program through the audiences.

Figure 12-1. Product publicity flow.

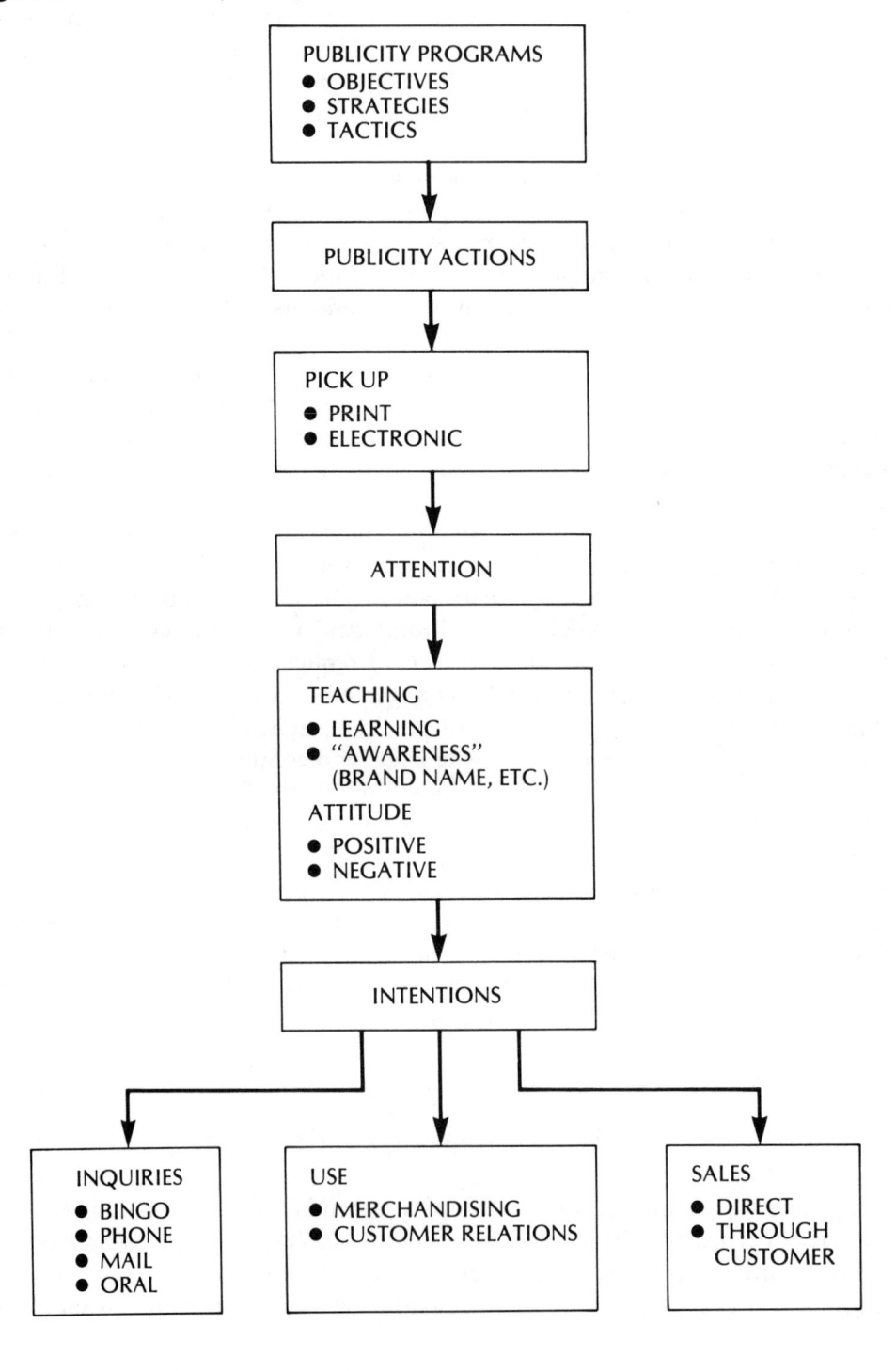

```
┌─────────────────────────┐
│  PUBLICITY PROGRAMS     │
│  • OBJECTIVES           │
│  • STRATEGIES           │
│  • TACTICS              │
└───────────┬─────────────┘
            ▼
┌─────────────────────────┐
│  PUBLICITY ACTIONS      │
└───────────┬─────────────┘
            ▼
┌─────────────────────────┐
│  PICK UP                │
│  • PRINT                │
│  • ELECTRONIC           │
└───────────┬─────────────┘
            ▼
┌─────────────────────────┐
│  ATTENTION              │
└───────────┬─────────────┘
            ▼
┌─────────────────────────┐
│  TEACHING               │
│  • LEARNING             │
│  • "AWARENESS"          │
│    (BRAND NAME, ETC.)   │
│  ATTITUDE               │
│  • POSITIVE             │
│  • NEGATIVE             │
└───────────┬─────────────┘
            ▼
┌─────────────────────────┐
│  INTENTIONS             │
└───┬───────────┬──────┬──┘
    ▼           ▼      ▼
┌─────────┐ ┌────────────┐ ┌─────────────┐
│INQUIRIES│ │USE         │ │SALES        │
│• BINGO  │ │• MERCHAN-  │ │• DIRECT     │
│• PHONE  │ │  DISING    │ │• THROUGH    │
│• MAIL   │ │• CUSTOMER  │ │  CUSTOMER   │
│• ORAL   │ │  RELATIONS │ │             │
└─────────┘ └────────────┘ └─────────────┘
```

Measuring Publicity Effectiveness

The process begins when the publicist develops a program, which spells out objectives and the strategies and tactics needed to accomplish them. Then particular actions take place involving the tactics used in the strategic program. Assuming these are successful, the media, both print and electronic, then "pick up" the message.

The next step in the process is audience attention. If the audience is seeing or hearing the message, then it is possible to do some research.

Thus, marketing research enters, to measure whether the audience reached through the media learned anything or became more "aware" of a given product or its benefits, and whether attitudes toward the product have changed, either positively or negatively. Even if it is determined that brand awareness has been generated, this does not mean that the recipient will react positively, or at all.

Having received the message, the audience will do one of two things: ignore it, or take further action. One kind of action would be to ask for more information. Inquiries can take several forms: telephone, mail, oral, or reader service or "bingo card" in many trade publications.

The results of the program may also be used in other ways, such as merchandising the clippings, the media data reports, or other information gathered to show a customer (or management) how well publicity is working for him. Often this entails writing a case history on a customer's use of a product, placing it in an appropriate journal, and "merchandising" it back to the customer, or using reprints as sales promotion material.

The audience actions may also result in sales, either direct or through a customer store. Sales increases may be measurable when they are related to a specific action such as the flu alert program or the Halloween promotion mentioned in Chapter 11. Most often, however, it is difficult to relate sales to publicity because there are other influences at work, only a few of which are marketing communications. All are carrying a message to the audiences in one way or another, and all may have an effect on sales.

Awareness can also be difficult to measure. First, it is far easier to measure what was learned from a program if you start with a measured base than to try to measure only after specific actions are taken. Also, measurement is particularly hard if a stated objective is something like, "to raise the awareness level to 20 percent from 10 percent the year before." Unless publicity is the only communications technique being used, other factors influence how much an audience becomes aware of the product. For instance, the awareness level for a new farm chemical introduced a few years ago jumped from 0 percent to 35 percent in six months in large part because of widespread mention in farm media. However, at the same time salespeople and dealers armed with sales literature were at work. Since these sales personnel could not possibly reach every member of the target audience, it was assumed that publicity played a major role in the learning and awareness jump. This was a proper assumption, although it would not be possible to determine the *exact* extent to which publicity was responsible.

How to Plan the Research Program

First, remember what you're hoping to achieve with research. It is dangerous to rely on only the number of clippings generated by a press release. What you want to know is the degree of interest, what was learned, and what actions the consumer might be expected to take. How the target audience (not the media) is *responding*, and how it sees the product in relation to its own needs. And that kind of information is not available from clippings.

When planning your research program, you must decide several things: Should you do it yourself or use an outside source; should you do pretesting or post-testing, or both; which of the many sources of available information will you call into play; and which of the various measurement tools will you incorporate into your program.

We will look at all these questions in some detail. But first, a warning must be raised. However they are obtained, and whatever form they take, the results of research must be used with discretion and tempered with good judgment. While it can be interesting and useful, for example, to find out what employees want to see in a company publication, the real job is not always to give readers what they want but to get them to read the information deemed important, accept it as valid, and take some positive action.

Outside or Inside Evaluation?

Some organizations hire outside research agencies to help in evaluating their publicity efforts. (A few large public relations firms have research divisions, but even they may go outside for special programs.) Going outside offers these significant advantages:

- An outside firm can take an independent point of view and is unaffected by the client organization's biases.
- Outside research agencies offer a wide variety of experiences and special skills that the client organization may not have.
- Outside organizations can be used only as needed, making them more flexible than a company's employees.

On the other hand, external research agencies have certain disadvantages:

- Outside research agencies may be unfamiliar with the organization's products, competitors, and environments. Educating an outside agency often takes time and money that could be invested instead on internal research.
- Outside research agencies are less accessible than internal research units,

which may impede communication and extend the time needed before a study can be completed.
- The cost of hiring an outside research agency is often greater than the cost of using internal researchers, especially for small projects.

Pretesting or Post-testing?

Evaluation takes one of two forms: pretesting or post-testing.

Pretesting will tell you whether the planned materials actually convey your message in an understandable way, and whether there are any possible backlash effects. If pretesting reveals confusion, your materials can be edited at this early stage, before the full program is put into action.

Pretesting is valuable not only in determining the after-effects of a specific program but in advancing your knowledge of a particular situation. There are a number of maxims that are heard in the business, but pretesting tends to cast some doubt on their validity. For instance, "What people know about a subject depends roughly on the amount said or published about it." On the contrary, increased flow does not necessarily spread information effectively. Another example is, "If people know you better, they will like you more." Some studies of big business have indicated the opposite. Familiarity, however, can lead to favorability.

If a planned activity is pretested, then it stands to reason that post-testing and a method of ongoing tracking are also needed, particularly if the campaign is to be a long one.

Post-testing tells you whether you reached the goals you set for your program. It is based on what was learned during pretesting. You go back to the audience queried in the pretesting program and measure change: in awareness, learning, actions taken, positive and negative attitudes.

Post-testing can also offer knowledge that can help a marketer respond better to the needs of the audiences in the future. The result may be a different copy emphasis, for example.

PR Data Reports show results of publicity based on clippings and raw data. This information can be valuable in measuring results in one year against those in a previous one. But marketing research such as pre- and post-testing goes further to give the publicist, marketing, and management a look at how the target audience (not the media) is *responding* to an action, and how that audience sees the product in relation to its own needs.

Which Information Resources?

The diversity of information available about companies and markets is staggering. Consider the following questions, which you as a product publicist should ask yourself:

What is the potential for a new product or service?
How much is being allocated to advertising, personal selling, and merchandising?
Is the company adding or deleting products to improve the profitability of its line?
Are prices being changed and, if so, by how much?
What distribution channels are being used?
What are the major competitors for the product?

All that data, from both inside and outside the organization, can and ought to be turned to your use when designing the research. Don't reinvent the wheel; first see if the data already exist. Look for:

Trade association data
Customer lists
Company annual reports
Sales call reports
Financial information:
    credit
    discount analysis (by customer, region, etc.)
    budgets
Special marketing research studies
Syndicated research services (Nielsen, Arbitron, Standard Rate and Data Service)
Multiclient studies
Competitor annual reports
Inventory reports
Sales:
    by product
    by product line
    by customer class
    by region
    by salesperson
    by competitors
Census data
Marketing research reports
Life cycle analysis
Departmental budgets
Manufacturing cost reports
Secondary literature
Supplier annual reports

Research Tools

Publicity managers have at hand a number of research tools, measuring devices, if you will, that can be used to provide all sorts of data at several points through the publicity process. One word of caution, however: They measure only the bits and pieces, not the overall program. The total efforts must be kept in view: advertising, sales promotion, and activities by the sales staff. Periodically the total program must be looked at, as well as its parts, and its results measured against the objectives.

An important measurement is what happened when the leads you developed were qualified by telemarketing and followed up by the sales staff. Do you know how these turned out? Were they converted to sales, and how much (in dollars) was earned? For consumer products, it may be a little more difficult. But it is possible to track movement through distributors, jobbers, and retailers. Can you derive, from an analysis of your results, a return on investment?

Media Research

Many of the best-known and most commonly used research tools have to do with measuring media and their audiences. One popular model defines the product publicity process in six distinct stages, three so-called exposure stages (characteristics of the media putting forth the message) and three response stages (characteristics of the audience receiving the message). Measurements can be made at each stage (see Figure 12-2) to estimate the effects of product publicity.

Vehicle Distribution

This is data about magazine or newspaper circulation or the number of television or radio sets available to carry a message. There are a number of techniques available to gather this data, and the accuracy of the information is relatively free of controversy.

The Audit Bureau of Circulation (ABC), the Business Publications Audit of Circulation (BAPC), and Verified Audit Circulation (VAC) audit the circulation of paid subscriber magazines, free subscription magazines, and paid and nonpaid newspapers and magazines, respectively. For the broadcast media, the measure of vehicle distribution is much less important because more than 98 percent of all U.S. households have at least one television and radio set. For television and radio, the most important research question relates to vehicle audience.

Vehicle Audience

This is the number of people exposed to the media vehicle — the number of readers of a given issue of a magazine, or the number of viewers of a specific

Figure 12-2. Measurement techniques for six publicity stages.

Stage	Example of Technique
Exposure Stages	
Vehicle distribution	Circulation data
	Television and radio ratings
Vehicle audience	Audimeters
	Diaries
Message exposure	Readership or recognition tests
	Psychological measurement devices
	Recall measures
Response Stages	
Message perception	Learning measures
	Opinion measures
	Attitude measures
Message communication	Learning measures
	Opinion measures
	Attitude measures
Message response	Sales measures

television show. The vehicle audience is typically larger than the vehicle distribution, because more than one person reads the same magazine or watches the same television set. The magazine and newspaper audience is usually measured by so-called pass-along studies.

Two organizations are active in this area. Simmons Market Research Bureau uses a cluster sampling procedure to measure readership. Some 19,000 respondents a year are shown logos of magazine titles and asked to pick "those that you might have read or looked into during the last six months, either at home or someplace else." This is verified again in an interview, after the respondent goes through a stripped-down version of each magazine.

Mediamark Research Inc. draws a cluster sample of about 30,000 individuals (15,000 in the fall and 15,000 in the spring) and measures readership with a modified recent reading method. Respondents are given a list of more than 150 magazines and asked to sort a deck of cards containing the magazine logos and indicate those they read in the last six months, and then in the last publication interval.

The Audit Bureau of Circulation's Newspaper Audience Research Bank provides survey data on what kind of people read what parts of a newspaper on a given day. It combines data provided by cooperating newspapers in the top 100 markets. The Simmons Scarborough Company, a part of the Simmons Marketing Research Bureau, periodically conducts surveys on most major newspapers to measure the audience size and demographic profile.

Two companies dominate the television ratings business: A. C. Nielsen for national data and Arbitron for local. Television audience data are collected by four methods: diary, meters, coincidental telephone recall, and personal interview recall. In the diary method, viewers record the name of the shows they watch and mail the diary back to the research firm. Because it is inexpensive, this is the main way of measuring local television audiences. The major disadvantages are that respondents may fail to record shows they watched, or forget that they watched, or even untruthfully record what shows they watched.

Problems with diaries led to the use of meters to record what channel a set is turned to and when it is on. Because meters are expensive, they are used mostly for national ratings, although Arbitron uses meters for its local ratings in Chicago, New York, and Los Angeles. Nielsen uses both diaries and meters to determine national audiences. Meters do not record whether anyone is watching the set while it is on, a problem that some researchers estimate produces an error factor of up to 25 percent.

In coincidental telephone recall, a sample of households are called and asked what show is being watched at that time, if any, and asked to identify the sponsor or product being advertised. This method is quick and relatively inexpensive but it works only during certain hours (8:00 A.M. to 10:00 P.M.); it excludes nontelephone homes; and rural homes are underrepresented because of the cost of sampling them. The personal interview is sometimes used for special audience studies. The disadvantage is that respondents often have a poor memory, and personal interviews are time-consuming and thus expensive. Questions must be skillfully drawn so that the answers are not biased.

Measurement of radio audiences presents some unusual problems because radios are used almost everywhere. The only major supplier of radio audience data is Arbitron, using a mail diary method. During the selected seven-day period in which ratings are taken, the sample respondents are called twice to make sure they understand the required task and are reminded to complete and return the diary. Demographic data are also collected.

For the product publicist, the problem with all this is that it is expensive, and few syndicated sources are available. Publicists must usually rely on information supplied by the media themselves, which of course suggests the possibility of a bias.

Message Exposure

This is the actual number of people who have read a particular article or seen or heard a particular broadcast message. It is typically much less than the vehicle audience; people may be exposed to a certain media vehicle but not notice a particular story.

Readership or recognition tests are used to gather information about message exposure. Typically, respondents are shown the cover of a magazine or newspaper and, if they indicate they have read it, the interviewer asks questions about the stories inside. Readers and nonreaders are counted, and readers are tabulated as having "noted" (those who remember seeing the story), "associated" (those who read enough to recall the major part of the story), and "read most" (those who could recall more than half the points made in the story).

Recall and awareness tests are used to measure respondents' attention to print and broadcast stories. For example, a folio test groups together several stories from a recent issue of a magazine. Respondents are asked to leaf through the stories and indicate whether they recall seeing each story. Besides providing a measure of message exposure, such tests yield data about viewers' comprehension and motivation, which may be useful in developing future publicity actions.

Inquiry tests also are used to measure the relative effectiveness of various types of publicity, particularly for industrial products. The number of requests for more information indicates the effectiveness of the story in arousing interest among the readers. Requests for information is a measurable objective. Most of my associates have found that a new product announcement story will generate as many inquiries as an ad (sometimes more) and that telemarketing followup will identify as many qualified inquiries as comparable advertising.

A variety of psychological measurement devices also can be used to evaluate message exposure and attention. Two new ones are the psychogalvanometer or "lie detector"—a camera that measures dilation of the pupils of the eye—and voice pitch analysis to indicate the viewer's emotional involvement and learning pattern.

Message Perception and Communication

Opinion and attitude measurements are aimed at the receiver's perception of the message. Opinion tests usually treat consumers' reactions as being one-dimensional; they simply indicate a liking or disliking of some object. Attitude measures are more sophisticated; they attempt to measure not only the different dimensions of people's feelings, but also the intensity of those feelings. Typically, fewer people actively perceive a story than those exposed to it; fewer still actually take some action in response. There are also ways to measure what the respondent has learned from the message.

Message Response

The desired long-range effects of a product publicity effort are increased awareness and knowledge of a product and a better understanding of its benefits, leading to increased sales and profits. In their simplest form, sales measures relate sales volume or market share for a preceding period to results obtained by the current publicity effort. If sales or marketing share improve enough, the communications effort is judged effective. Usually it is not possible to link sales directly to publicity efforts unless publicity is the major communications tool.

Message Research

Another category of research tools are those used to gain information about the content of a message. Many of the methods that are used for pretesting ads can also be used for evaluating a product publicity piece before it is released.

Portfolio tests involve exposing respondents to a package of stories or broadcast messages with both test and control pieces in the group. The effectiveness of the test copy is measured by the respondents' ability to recall the story and then recall specifics of the story. The major limitation with these tests is that recall may be affected by a respondent's level of interest in the story.

Mock-ups of magazines are sometimes used to test potential publicity releases under natural readership conditions. Test stories are inserted into a magazine that is then distributed to a random sample. The respondents are told that the publisher is interested in their evaluation of the editorial content and they are instructed to read the magazine in a normal way. A followup interview covers both editorial and advertising content. Measures taken might include awareness, recall, copy readership, and product interest induced by the story.

Laboratory procedures can be used to test such things as copy readability and broadcast story interest. One procedure uses an eye camera to track the movement of the eye as it examines a story. The story copy is then examined to determine which sections receive and hold attention, which parts are interesting, which parts had to be read more than once, and so on. Unfortunately, interpreting eye movement is difficult. Does lingering at a given location indicate interest in the idea or poorly worded copy?

The tachistoscope is another physiologically related testing device. It allows for presentation of story copy under different levels of speed. Researchers can measure the rate at which a story conveys information.

I know of no firm that has conducted laboratory research on editorial copy, but it might be a worthwhile university research project, of interest to communicators.

Readability Tests

A number of useful yardsticks for evaluating the reading ease for printed materials have been developed. Four of the better known measures are:

1. The Flesch Formula, which quantitatively measures both reading ease and human interest. Reading ease is measured by the number of syllables in words and by sentence length. Human interest is measured by the number of personal words per 100 words and by the number of personal sentences per 100 sentences.

2. The Gunning Formula, which measures reading ease in such areas as the average sentence length, number of simple sentences used, portion of familiar words, portion of abstract words, percentage of personal references, and percentage of long words.

3. The Dale-Chall Formula, which measures reading ease by analyzing the length and the proportion of words outside the Dale list of 3,000 most commonly used words.

4. The Cloze Procedure, which measures the help provided the reader by the context of the total message. Reading samples have every nth word omitted. Success of subjects in filling in missing words on the basis of other parts of the message measures the item's readability.

Measuring Media Pickup

One simple measure of success is whether publicity was effective in reaching media audiences; tools to measure this aspect can be among the most important of all for publicity managers. The significant question here is whether the media pickup actually included the copy points that you consider important.

You can be reasonably sure that a program was successful if the targeted media used the stories, the features, the news clips, or the releases, and if the main copy points came across. The program is less successful if the media used only a couple of lines and no photo, or broadcast the video clip at 2:00 A.M.

In short, success cannot be measured in terms of clip tonnage, but rather on the basis of whether it reached the targeted audience through the right media, and whether the media did or did not bury it and cut it so much that the prime messages were lost.

This will not, of course, measure whether the audience learned from it, but it will indicate that media objectives were met—and that is half the battle.

Measuring "Media Buy"

PR Data Systems, Inc., a commercial firm, can be a valuable aid in measuring the "media buy" and can help an organization advance beyond counting, once the product publicity objectives are spelled out. Here is how it works. Client firms of PR Data feed their copy point objectives into a computer to provide a yardstick against which results can be measured. PR Data then analyzes each of the organization's releases (and features). The resulting data base indicates numbers of uses, the messages carried, and the percent of media in the prime target area. The reports also show other "raw" data such as total clippings in inches or broadcast minutes, total circulation, story treatment, and ad value on an "if purchased" basis. (Ad value is better translated into either a cost per thousand or return on investment.)

Although PR Data does not measure the effect of a story or program on the reader or viewer, it has its advantages. The data can be compared with data from previous time periods, to see how well a program is doing or what must be changed or reemphasized to reach the predetermined objectives.

In addition to reporting results to management, the data can be used to show management the results of your efforts periodically — to make it clear to management that you are carefully and continually tracking and analyzing your program in their interest. This helps ensure their continued support.

Then, as a diagnostic tool, the reports enable you to detect weak areas, such as media not reached for some time (and whether a visit to the editor to determine why the releases have been rejected is in order). You can also see if predetermined copy points are being delivered, whether a shift in strategies is called for, or even if a release performed well in its targeted media area.

Last but not least, PR Data does substitute electronic muscle for human labor in analyzing clippings by calculating volume, circulation, geographic coverage, and working out an array of percentages that help a corporation quantitatively plan and evaluate its efforts.

A company's reports can be set up to measure many other aspects as well. The reports can be structured to track performance in a plant community, or a broad range of public issues including governmental affairs, environment, security analysts attitudes, stockholders. To demonstrate the variety and scope of information available, a series of typical reports for Snow Skis, a hypothetical company, is included in Appendix D.

Collecting the data, however, is the beginning, not the end. Considerable time is involved in analysis, planning, and reporting to make the data meaningful to the company. Time is needed to set up the reporting system so that the data received meet the needs of the company. Additional time must be dedicated to analyzing the results. But the time is well worth it. My own experience has shown that marketing management appreciates this kind of information and becomes more supportive of the publicity program and is likely to approve publicity budgets with fewer questions and reservations when it can be shown that publicity is making an important contribution.

These reports place publicity on the same level as advertising. Advertising and marketing professionals have accepted the discipline inherent in buying and applying research, which, in turn, has generated management support.

Data similar to what's been discussed here are currently being used by GTE Electrical Products, according to Vincent D'Alessandro, vice president, public affairs. He's using these types of reporting systems to develop and, when necessary, revise his product publicity plans. Data gathered in 1985 were utilized in 1986 planning. Now, for the first time, he is sending quantified reports to senior management. Reports will also be made to the heads of two GTE businesses—precision materials and lighting products—and, eventually, to marketing.

D'Alessandro's assessment? "Absolutely superb." But he cautions that you have to make certain assumptions and take the time so that the system works properly.

Other Information Sources

There are other data bases that can search for and provide a wealth of information about a company from a wide variety of sources. This information is not used very often for product publicity; it is more valuable when a company needs to know what is being said about it for corporate concerns and programs.

1. *Nexis.* Very briefly, an on-line data base that can search for media reports (including product publicity) about a company. It includes what was once the New York Times Information Bank. Abstracts of stories as well as complete articles from some trade publications, professional journals, major dailies, and financial publications; wire services, PR and Business Newswires, BBC, Reuters, and Asian wires, as well as access to brokerage reports, government documents, and others. Agnes Galbán, senior vice president for research at Hill and Knowlton, calls it a "joy to use." Many agencies and corporations use its services.

2. *Dow Jones News.* This service, which Galbán calls "structured and inflexible," provides *Wall Street Journal, Barron's,* and Dow Jones wire copy in a matter of minutes after printing. It has complete text of the *Wall Street Journal* back to 1979 (as of early 1986). Information can be obtained about a company through its stock symbol but for only 90 days previous to request. It can be accessed by subscribers to MCI Mail for a per-minute fee.

3. *Dialog.* A subsidiary of Lockheed Aircraft Corporation, it has about 200 separate data bases on a wealth of subjects, from the arts through the sciences and business. Some of the data are in abstract form, some in complete text.

Other Uses of Research

There are some other areas of research that relate to public relations and at times will have a relationship to product publicity. Areas that lend themselves to research include literature searches, community attitude studies, focus group interviews on products and value perceptions, competitive research (what is being said about the competition and what the competition is saying about us), overviews of an industry, preacquisition studies, executive profiles and backgrounds, and even some advance work relating to the appearance of an executive on a panel show (what kind of folks are the *other* guests or panelists?).

13
Reporting and Merchandising

After all your programs have been written and all your campaigns have been carried out, you have one more responsibility: It is time to report your successes (or failures) to top management. If the programs were set up in such a way that they can be measured, reporting is much easier.

It would also be easier if you were reporting on an advertising campaign. Advertising people are much more diligent about presenting the results of their efforts, and they do it in such a manner that there is little mystery about it. They also seem to have more data to present: ad tear sheets, tapes of television commercials, examples of direct mail campaigns, cost per thousand figures, Arbitron and Nielsen numbers, readership reports, reach, pass-along data, inquiry tallies, and more. They present their results in an attractive package, with color slides and professionally done charts. And one thing more: They have an audience that understands advertising better than publicity.

Public relations people in the past have been too casual about reporting results. They focus more on getting the release printed, the photo used, the story placed, than on trying to determine if all the effort was worth it. Sometimes they just pass around clippings (maybe in a scrapbook, maybe not), and assume that everyone knows about and appreciates all that has been done. Success is judged solely by clippings; usually no one asks whether the clips are from the target media, or whether the stories actually convey the company's message.

But this may be changing. Marketing executives have begun asking for proof that publicity is productive and cost-efficient. This has spurred publicity people to look at ways they can demonstrate that indeed publicity is worth the investment, that management need not rely just on faith.

Granted it is not easy to determine if attitudes have been changed because of a public relations program. (It's much simpler to measure an increase in sales because of an ad campaign.) But there are ways to find out how to do the job better, which actions are most effective, and what can realistically be expected. Also, remember that some tools are available for reporting.

First, Gather Your Data

The first thing you need to do is to find out if you have anything to report. T. M. (Sam) Egbert, head of GE's news bureau, suggests an approach. "Measurement is relatively simple. At the end of the year, we compare what we actually produced with what we said in the plan that we would. Almost always, we meet or exceed our promises, in part because we propose realistic plans. We do not overpromise because our PR professionals know the limits as well as the possibilities of PR and usually succeed in tempering the sometimes inflated hopes and expectations of marketing and general management personnel."

Look at your original publicity plan, and ask yourself five questions:

1. Did you get the editorial coverage you set out to get? Did you reach your audience through the media that spoke most directly to them?
2. Did you deliver to that audience the copy points you set out to deliver? If so, then you were at least partly successful.
3. Did you get good treatment in the media? Were your stories used without significant cuts? Did you get good positioning in the publication? Were your spots broadcast when people were listening, and not at 3:00 A.M.?
4. Were your photos used?
5. Did you get brand identification? That is, did the reader or viewer, when asked, know what product was being discussed?

The media tallies you generated during the research phase, or the reports from PR Data Systems (see Chapter 12), can be very useful at this stage, since most of the data you need for your report is already here.

If your answers to the five questions were affirmative, then your program can be considered successful—the communications objectives set for publicity were reached. You are now ready to take the results of the publicity part of your marketing communications program to your management and marketing group. Or are you?

Only if marketing and management understand product publicity to begin with. They have seen the print ads and the television commercials from the advertising staff. They have seen the clippings or tapes from the publicity program. But the big question is, do they understand the significance of what publicity has accomplished? Most will not. They may need a refresher course on publicity before you present your results. It doesn't have to be long.

Then, Set the Stage

Publicity has to be first positioned in the communications matrix. You might wish to begin with a review of how a market gets information about your products: salespeople, literature, trade shows, direct mail, letters, phone calls, competition, magazines, newspapers, television, radio, word of mouth.

It will be well worthwhile to spend 10 or 15 minutes reviewing the value of publicity, and emphasizing its contribution to the marketing communications program. Here's an idea to build upon: Nothing sells like success, and nothing sells success like publicity. It's your job to convince marketing that you have the skills and the talents to take their story to the marketplace.

Review the overall objectives of publicity:

1. Establish product knowledge among key purchasing influences.
2. Reinforce the reputation of your product and your company among its customers. (Show the various tactics you used to accomplish these goals.)
3. Extend the reach of marketing.
4. Promote unadvertised products. (Review the differences between advertising and publicity.)
5. Position your company in its markets.
6. Create a strong presence in the media vis-à-vis competition.

As an example, take them through the steps involved with introducing a new product:

Research
Introduction to media
Case histories
Product improvement publicity
Exclusives
Roundups, trends
Photography
Editorial contacts

It's particularly important to use a simplified life-cycle curve (see Chapter 2) to relate your activities to the marketplace. Thus, if there is little activity in a particular area, it may be because the product or service is in a declining market and editorial interest has waned. Conversely, you can show where you are placing more emphasis, such as in maturing markets, and justify a shift in focus or a budget change.

You can show that publicity will help generate sales leads. Reprints of an article can be used as a sales aid to trigger new business. You can also point out that the editor has in effect endorsed the product, because it was passed along to the readers — your customers or potential customers. This is highly credible evidence of the value of your product.

Example of a Promotional Package

Here is an excerpt from a presentation developed by one of my colleagues. It's one of the best I have seen to sell the concept of publicity to marketing. This particular program was business-to-business and did not involve many consumer products. But the idea and approach can be adapted for just about any program.

A Strong Case for Publicity . . . It's Valuable

That's right. Publicity is a valuable marketing tool which may have more impact on readers than any other. Because, in order to warrant publicity, a company must do something significant to earn the attention of media. Money simply can't buy this kind of attention — or its dramatic effect on readers.
Through publicity, a company can gain:
- Credibility. People are often skeptical of promises that businesses make. But when the message is delivered by objective sources such as journalists, the audience is more likely to believe it.
- Recognition. Publicity makes a company a "newsmaker," strengthening its image as a supplier worthy of attention.
- Wider audience reach. Publicity can reach key people within a company who influence buying decisions, but whom the salesman may never meet. And news gets people talking at all business levels. Such word-of-mouth communication is a strong marketing medium.
- Competitive edge. Reading good things about a product helps customers to differentiate a company from the competition. It gives them a reason to choose one product above the others.

And everyone benefits!
The salesperson: Case history reprints and article clippings offer salespeople an extra merchandising tool which demonstrates to customers that we are committed to helping them market their products. This adds value to a sale. Also, the salesperson is personally credited for each story he or she submits.
The customer: When used as the subject of a case history, the customer receives exposure in the press and gets extra marketing tools in the form of article clippings and personalized case history reprints.
End users: They get the qualitative information they need to make educated buying decisions. When chosen as the subject of a story, end users also reap the benefits of publicity and get personalized case histories as well.
For our company: It's a great opportunity to demonstrate our unsurpassed experience and our commitment to helping customers market the product.

Another part of the presentation encouraged marketing and sales personnel to submit ideas, made it easy for them to do so, and provided four-color reprints of published articles.

The Reports

Reports can be made monthly or bimonthly. They can be joint presentations by agency and staff, or by the agency alone. They can be either written or oral, although written reports will usually suffice.

In addition, it is highly worthwhile to present to management, either alone or with the agency, an annual "stewardship" report. It can be either written or oral, and it's a good idea to present it at the same time as the advertising report, to show an organized marketing communications approach.

The publicity part should include:

1. A review of objectives reached.
2. A summary of accomplishments: increased awareness, more inquiries, inquiries converted to actual business.
3. A candid assessment of objectives not reached, and why.
4. Brief comments on the coming year, to hitchhike past accomplishments, correct course, or suggest new approaches.
5. Bar and pie charts based on PR Data System information are quite helpful. If any research project has been undertaken, such as measuring learning or awareness from a market research program, a summary is appropriate here.

The stewardship report is not meant to be used as a program presentation; the program for the coming year should be more detailed and given separately.

Merchandise Your Publicity

Publicity needs constant sell to show how it can contribute to marketing, how it works, its advantages and limitations, and how it fits in, with advertising and promotion, to a total communications program. Because of the fluid nature of many marketing organizations, the need for publicity must *constantly* be asserted. It is far easier to justify advertising because the costs are set and the message is delivered according to a planned structure and specified media.

One excellent way to sell your program on a steady basis is to merchandise its accomplishments. One technique for this that I have admired is called "The

Communigram," a simple one-page flier with an attractive letterhead. It is sent periodically to marketing, the sales force, distributors, retailers, whatever the audience you want to reach informally. It's a good way to remind the marketing and marketing support organizations that you are working for them.

You might open with a heading like this:

> Hot Runners in the Press Recently Have Been:

> The compact aircraft radar system release: Mailed 10/22/86 to 45 commercial and military aircraft publications. Twenty used the release; 87 inquiries generated.

Select two or three good items for each mailing. Include photos wherever possible.

When you pull off a major event, be sure to let your people know about it. Do a mailing in two parts. First send a report of the event itself, mentioning editors who attended and their television or daily press pickup. Include a copy of the press kit. Follow three months later with a report on the number of stories, key media use, inquiries, and so on.

In a somewhat more elaborate vein, Hill and Knowlton produced a four-color multi-page brochure highlighting the agency's success in promoting National Photo Week. This was the culmination of an extensive program developed to solve a problem. The trade association for the photographic industry, Photo Marketing Association, recognized that action was necessary to motivate more consumer interest in photography. Surveys showed that with high-tech competition for discretionary spending, the enjoyment of photography was being eclipsed. Cameras were sitting unused on closet shelves.

The results of a detailed program were impressive, and the report to photo retailers called it: "A picture of success . . . May 7th through 13th marked the first National Photo Week and thanks to the efforts of hundreds of retailers, finishers, suppliers and equipment manufacturers, it was a huge success." The report left no doubt that the promotion was indeed a success and recognized the contribution of the members of the association.

In another example of this type of effort, the former Carl Byoir & Associates agency conducted a menswear media tour for the Wool Bureau to explore ways to extend the impact of the existing advertising program through selected public relations techniques. Here, as reported by the Byoir agency, is a description of the tour:

> The tour was undertaken in five primary Wool Bureau markets which were selected by [Wool Bureau executives]. These markets were: Denver, Detroit, Minneapolis, Phoenix and Philadelphia. The tour took place during the months of September and October. Preparations were initiated in early July.

They were handled by the Byoir agency in conjunction with the Bureau staff.

As a result of the tour, the Wool Bureau received extensive, in-depth media coverage in each of the five targeted cities. This included 19 newspaper articles, two magazine articles, one hour and 45 minutes of radio air time and two hours of cable television coverage. This coverage achieved an estimated 5.1 million audience impressions.

Transcripts were provided for each of the appearances on broadcast media to show how the messages were delivered, and the questions answered.

In each of the five targeted cities, a Bureau spokesman conducted university seminars on "value dressing" for business and marketing students. In this manner he was able to speak virtually one-on-one with a total of 370 students about the advantages of wool as well as tips on building a quality wardrobe.

This report is far more than a scrapbook of clippings. It explains the rationale for the tour, the elements needed, and the activities involved in packaging the tour and developing an appropriate theme for the media interviews and seminars. It analyzes the results for each city, including transcripts of broadcast coverage and copies of print-media stories.

Turn Publicity into Sales

Product publicity does not exist in a vacuum. Your goal is more than filling a scrapbook with clippings, more even than producing a professional presentation of your achievements. Your goal, let's not forget, is to contribute to and enhance the marketing efforts of your company. You're part of the marketing team, and the value of your achievements in product publicity is the part they play in the team's overall success.

Your publicity campaign may result in a record number of customer inquiries, but that means little until those inquiries have been converted into sales. Your job now is to track and qualify those inquiries for sales to follow up on. Follow up again on the sales call to see if you can document any sales. This information will be a very powerful addition to your publicity report.

Many of the leads generated by publicity will come through reader service numbers, sometimes known as "bingo cards." Many trade publications offer their readers this simple way of requesting more information. A code number appears at the end of an article or an item in the new product column. A postage-paid bingo card, on heavier paper, is bound into the publication. All a reader has to do to get additional information is remove the card, circle the appropriate number, and mail it to the magazine. The publication then sends the person's name, job title, and address to the appropriate companies.

Bingo cards can be a good source of bulk inquiries, but only if they are sent to the right person in the company. You can help. At the bottom of a news release or story, write: Note to editor—Please send inquiries to Room X0987, then your company's name and address. The "room number" is a tracking number set up for inquiries on this product release (or ad) only. These are simple to set up with your company mailroom.

Consumer magazines have shopper's services and similar devices, but usually only in conjunction with ads. They are rarely available for editorial mentions, unless it is strictly a new product that is being cited.

With customer inquiries in hand, telemarketing begins. It should be done by someone who understands how inquiries work and can set up a series of questions to determine the degree of interest, how the product might be used by the person who made the inquiry, whether that person can influence buying decisions, make recommendations to purchase, or approve purchase, whether the person only wants more product data or prices, and whether that person buys any other products from the company. If there does seem to be a high degree of interest, then at the close of the call, it must be determined whether a sales or technical representative should be contacted, or whether the person at the other end is ready to place an order.

The questions must relate to the potential purchaser and must be structured properly. The goal is to elicit information without appearing to be pushy. If there is immediate interest, a salesperson *must* make a call.

"Hot" leads should be turned over to the marketing manager or a district sales office. To make sure they were pursued, part of the qualification process in telemarketing should be a call—two to three weeks later—to these hot prospects to find out if they were contacted by sales.

Often publicity will generate more leads than advertising. But unfortunately, advertising leads are often regarded as better ones than those from publicity. We must work to change this attitude. You may be sure that your colleague in advertising knows the exact number of inquiries, has qualified them, and has a good idea of the number that were converted to sales. There is no excuse for publicity people not doing the same thing. Then, when it's time to report, they too have some hard data to present and valuable information to help them plan for the future.

An objective of publicity people should be to bring merchandising and self-promotion to the same level as their advertising counterparts. If this happens, there will be more support for their efforts and a clearer understanding of what they do.

Appendix A: Trivial Pursuit® — A Case Study of a Publicity Campaign at Its Best

"Trivial Pursuit" may very well rival Monopoly as one of the most popular board games around. Getting it to that position took a very creative and aggressive marketing communications campaign.

Pezzano+Company, a New York public relations and marketing communications firm, was given the account, and a budget of $40,000, just a few weeks before the 1983 Toy Fair. The company required "a unique program . . . to introduce the game and create the demand which would make it sell."

A four-part campaign was developed to reach successive audiences. The overall goal was to create awareness and consumer demand.

Part 1: Buyers

Selchow & Righter had the U.S. rights for the game. The company had a well-deserved reputation among buyers as a producer of "quality classics" — which meant that buyers felt they didn't need to pay too much attention to the company at the Toy Fair, since they basically already knew what products they would be buying from the company over the year. The agency wanted to surprise them, to make them sit up and pay attention.

To do this, the agency produced a series of four teaser mailings timed to reach buyers during the weeks before the fair. Each one was hand addressed and mailed in the smallest envelope the post office would deliver, on the theory that buyers get hundreds of big envelopes and perhaps a small one would get their attention.

Inside each was a foldover card, in the "Trivial Pursuit" colors, which opened to include a sample of an actual "Trivial Pursuit" card. By the time of the fair, each of the 2,000 game buyers had received three mailings. A fourth note was sent as a "thank you" after the fair to reinforce the message.

The response was overwhelming. Buyers called the Selchow & Righter offices if they had not received a mailing or if another buyer got two cards and they received only one. (Doubles were sent to some intentionally, but cards were not duplicated.) Not only did they ask for additional cards, they came to the company's showroom at the Toy Fair and ordered games.

Part 2: Opinion Molders

The next objective was to create public awareness before the game was in the stores. The targeted audience was opinion molders, and finding them was easy: many celebrities were mentioned in the game. The agency hired a celebrity service to find the addresses of all living actors, producers, directors who had been "immortalized" in the questions. Each then was sent a copy of the game with a personal note from Richard Selchow, chairman of the company.

The agency says, "Even we were surprised by the results." Letters began pouring into the company's headquarters, thanking them for the game and talking about how much they enjoyed it. Included were letters from celebrities such as Charlton Heston and Larry Hagman. Such letters were very important in the agency's early efforts to get publicity—everyone wants to write about celebrities.

Part 3: Trivia Buffs

The agency also began getting the word out to trivia buffs, a natural audience for the game, for example a New York disc jockey who is considered the trivia expert of his station and the city. There were more like him around the country.

To interest them, the agency offered a promotion. It would supply the games if the disc jockeys would ask a question over the air and have their listeners call in with answers. The first correct ones would receive the game. Result: More than 150 radio promotions took place in 1983, in markets ranging from New York and Los Angeles to smaller cities and rural communities.

Part 4: The General Public

At this point, word of the game was spreading. Copies were available in stores and sales were brisk. The agency was set for the final phase.

While it would seem that "Trivial Pursuit" generated its own publicity, this was not the case in the beginning. A carefully orchestrated media campaign to acquaint reporters with the story of the game was put into action. Celebrity comments were important, but everyone wanted sales figures. The agency scheduled a media tour for the inventors to talk about the game and the future editions, which were already planned. Samples of the game were sent to media people, and the agency spent a lot of time contacting the editors and answering questions over the phone.

The publicity job became easier as it appeared the game was an industry phenomenon. But agency management of information became more complex and critical. The strategy focused on three needs: being responsive to media inquiries, maintaining interest among media for the game and new editions, and creating new story lines and ideas to keep the publicity level high. And these principles guide the agency even today.

Results

The initial plan called for six months of activity. The agency stayed within the budget. There were no expensive press conferences or special events. Outlays were mainly for production, telephone and office expenses, and staff time.

The real measure of the success was in sales of the game. There was no advertising budget, yet from a forecast of 300,000 units for 1983, sales actually reached 1.5 million units — and would have been higher if the company had been able to make more games. Through 1984, about 22 million games had been sold in the United States. This represents about $650 million at retail. In 1983, retail sales of board games industrywide were *only $360 million.* Today, 15 percent of all U.S. households have at least one copy of "Trivial Pursuit." The game will be sold in nearly every language, each one adapted to the market with local and international trivia. Countries include France, Germany, Holland, Australia, Great Britain, Japan, and South American and Asian countries. There are currently about 120 imitations on the market.

As you can see from this case study, even with what might be identified as a "hit" before it is even promoted, achieving success took careful and creative planning. Few publicists are likely to have such a winner, but all can learn to plan carefully, with one eye on the budget and another on the target audiences.

Appendix B: Tip Sheet

What follows is an example of a tip sheet sent to describe the elements of a video news clip and B roll. This clip was about a promotion for simulated diamonds that used "Spic and Span" cleanser. In this promotion, boxes of the cleanser contained either a real diamond or a manmade zircon crystal known as Cubic Zirconia, or CZ. Consumers had a one in 4,500 chance of finding a real ⅓-carat diamond.

Description

The attached newsclip (:90) and B roll footage (6:15) can be used to create three stories.

1. CZ Story

The newsclip can be used in its entirety and tells the CZ story. It also includes mention of the multi-million dollar CZ promotion which is currently under way. Audio track 1 (containing narration) could be replaced with your reporter's narration. (The newsclip script is attached.)

2. Spic and Span Diamond Promotion Story

Newsclip and B roll footage can be used in conjunction with location footage of shoppers buying specially marked boxes of Spic and Span at a local grocery store. B roll footage documents the promotion beginning with armored security truck arrival of CZs; workers at D. L. Blair in Blair, Nebraska counting out CZs into plastic packages of 4,500 stones each; production line footage from plant in Cincinnati of individual CZs being placed in boxes of Spic and Span; and assembly line shots of specially marked Spic and Span boxes.

3. Valentine's Day Feature Story

With Valentine's Day just around the corner, a new twist on an age-old tradition may be in the offing: Instead of buying her a box of candy, give her a box of soap—it may have a diamond in it.

Appendix B

Newsclip Script

Suggested live lead-in: Diamonds are a personal gift. Very personal. Now a low-cost version is making its debut—in a soap box. ——— has the story.

Video	*Audio*
Close-up of a diamond ring on woman's hand with husband looking on. Close-ups of expressions of love and affection. Dissolve to exterior shot of diamond district taken from New York City's 47th Street. Shot of window shopper is also included.	Diamonds have come to symbolize a sweetheart's expression of love and affection—the only limitation being one's imagination or, more often, one's pocketbook.
Cut to various shots of CZ jewelry. Shots of uncut CZ crystals and unmounted cut CZ stones illustrate how CZs are "grown." Close-ups of CZ jewelry show the variety of types of jewelry made with CZs.	Now the first truly convincing simulated diamond is fast becoming a nationwide trend. Cubic Zirconia, or CZ, is a man-made, crystal-forming mineral. First "identified" in 1969 in France, CZs are the finest quality man-made diamonds available and now account for a multimillion dollar industry.
Cut to comparison shot of CZ and diamond jewelry. Three rings of the same style are shown side by side.	In fact, CZs look so much like natural-mined diamonds, they pose a definite identification problem for the jewelry industry.
CZ expert is shown talking about characteristics of CZs. Interspersed with close-up shots of the expert are shots showing how a CZ is strong enough to cut glass.	*Sound bite:* Marvin Bankoff, President of MSB Industries, one of the largest producers of CZ jewelry in the world, discusses the special qualities of CZs.
CZ and diamond jewelry shown with "price tags" illustrating difference in price.	But the best thing about CZs is their price—a quality, one-carat CZ may be less than one percent of the cost of a one-carat diamond.
The sequence shows production line workers dropping the diamonds and CZs into boxes of Spic and Span from three different angles. A line shot with Spic and Span boxes moving (already packaged) is shown to illustrate the "specially marked" boxes. The 1-to-4,500 ratio is shown using one diamond to a pile of 4,500 CZs.	CZs have become so popular that even the makers of Spic and Span are getting into the act, making the single largest CZ purchase in history for use in a promotional giveaway. During February—but only for as long as supplies last—consumers will find either a ⅓-carat genuine diamond or CZ in every specially marked box or bottle. Each shopper has a one in 4,500 chance of finding a natural-mined diamond.

Video	*Audio*
More shots of CZ set jewelry are shown and a shot of a pile of CZs follows. Hands come in and pick up the CZs. Freeze frame on sparkling CZs.	Because CZs look deceptively like diamonds and cost considerably less, diamonds may be forever, but fellas, CZs may be *your* best friend.

Editor's Note

The following newsclip contains a :90 story on the growing interest in simulated diamonds, especially the high-quality cubic zirconia (CZ). Right now, 2,250,000 CZs and 500 diamonds can be found in specially marked boxes and bottles of Spic and Span as part of a nationwide promotion.

The newsclip (with split audio track) is followed by 6:15 minutes of B roll footage. Channel 1 has narration. Channel 2 has sound bite and music.

CZs are discussed by Marvin Bankoff, President of MSB Industries.

For further information contact: Colleen Growe, Hill and Knowlton, Inc., 420 Lexington Avenue, New York, NY 10017, (212) 697-5600 Ext. 3676.

B Roll Footage Shot Sheet

The total running time for this segment is 6:15.

1. Spic and Span with Cubic Zirconia shots. (Total Shots: 3)
2. Security truck brings CZs to D. L. Blair where workers pack CZs into plastic bags. (Total Shots: 5)
3. Spic and Span production line shots. (Total shots: 7)
4. Sound bite of Marvin S. Bankoff, President, MSB Industries, who demonstrates a device which can be used to authenticate genuine diamonds from CZs.
5. Sound bite of Marvin Bankoff, who gives a technical description of how CZs are manufactured.
6. Sound bite of Carolyn Garrido, jeweler, discussing why people buy CZs.
7. Exterior shots of NYC 47th Street diamond district. (Total shots: 5) Also includes a running shot of entire street.

Appendix C: Media Briefing Manual

Summary of Media Training for Media Briefing Workshop

I. The Role of the Media
   A. Importance of communicating to the media
      1. The news media's assignment
      2. Your public image
      3. Today's business communicates
   B. Importance of knowing needs of media and how to meet them
      1. Complexity of your issues
      2. Consequences of mishandled interview
      3. Differing needs of the media (broadcast and print)

II. The Message
   A. Your publics
      1. Who are they?
      2. What are their attitudes?
   B. Your message
      1. Primary points
      2. Secondary points
   C. Response to the other side

III. Getting their attention: How the media works
   A. What they are looking for
      1. Print
      2. TV
      3. Radio
   B. How they work
      1. Print
      2. TV
      3. Radio

* The material in this appendix is used by permission of Joanna Hanes, Hanes & Associates.

Agenda

TIME

(9:00 a.m. Coffee)

9:30–10:30 a.m.	Introduction Role of the Media Your Message How the Media Works
10:30–10:45 a.m.	Coffee Break
10:45–11:30 a.m.	Print Interviews Broadcast Interviews Radio Interviews The News Conference
12:00–1:30 p.m.	Lunch
2:00–3:30 p.m.	Television Training Studio Situation Critique
3:30–3:45 p.m.	Coffee Break
3:45–5:00 p.m.	Studio Situation Critique

Basic Briefing Points

- Buildings may meet fire safety codes, but the materials inside are the biggest killers in residential fires. Mattresses, bedding and upholstered furniture were involved in 45 percent of the fatal fires reviewed by the National Bureau of Standards.
- 930 fatalities were attributed to bedding fires in the U.S. in 1981. Fires in upholstered furniture took 1,400 lives. The Consumer Product Safety Commission calls these materials "the biggest killer of all the products under the jurisdiction of the agency."
- The number of school, college and university fires increased from seven in 1971 to 42 in 1980, with a loss of 21 lives and $16 million. Educational facilities lost $184 million to fire in 1981, an increase of 82.2% in only 12 months (over 1980).
- The fire problem in this country is out of control and growing. Multiple death fires increased 70% in the past decade. Estimated property losses from building fires in the U.S. in 1981 increased almost 7% over 1980 to $6 billion.
- National building codes do not regulate the flammability of upholstered seatings or mattressess.
- Fire hazards can be substantially reduced by the use of upholstery materials with good open flame resistance and low smoke generation properties.
- Neoprene foam is the safest upholstery material, producing less smoke, heat and

flame than polyurethane or flame-retardant cotton constructions. It is available now.

Briefing Outline for Neoprene Cushioning Material

Introduction

Here are the main points, in order of priority:

1. The peril
2. The remedy
3. The misconception that led to the peril
4. Credentials of the spokesperson: his personal involvement
5. Testing information
6. What you can do: next step for the concerned

Short Statement

The following statement should last approximately 30 seconds:
Students in our nation's residence halls face a deadly and pervasive peril, resulting from mattresses that can go from ignition to pools of flammable liquid and noxious gases in a matter of minutes.
They and their parents need to let the proper authorities know of the danger and specify mattresses that resist flame propagation, such as low smoke neoprene foam.

Interview Points

For this short version, lasting four minutes, state the following and also briefly explain how you became involved.

> Students in our nation's residence halls face a deadly and pervasive peril. They are being supplied with mattresses that are extremely flammable and can create enough smoke and heat in a matter of several minutes to virtually eliminate the chance for escape.
> The principal culprit is polyurethane, which burns easily, melting into pools of flammable liquid and producing noxious gases that can, in minutes, cause a "flashover" situation, or rolling wave of fire throughout the room. It has been called "liquid gasoline."
> Because of this problem, I now specify mattresses with low smoke neoprene foam, which resists flame propagation. I came to this conclusion after three years of testing following a fire in a student's room that left me with no explanation as to why it had burned so rapidly in a supposedly "fireproof" construction building.

Media Briefing Manual

Interview Points

For a longer version, lasting eight minutes, add the following to the short statements:

Most of us are under the misconception that "fireproof" structures and meeting structual fire codes are enough. But these codes do not apply to the contents of the building, only the structure. A parallel may be drawn between a contents fire in a fire resistant building and a fire in a furnace. The contents are the fuel and the building is the furnace.

The number of fires in schools, colleges and universities in the United States increases every year, in part because of the increasing use of materials that have been called "solid gasoline."

Think of fire control as a three-part effort. The first is prevention, the second is regulation over the construction of the building, and the third is regulation over the contents of the building. Up to now, the emphasis has been on the first two, to the point where public buildings can be certified for occupancy before there is a piece of furniture or upholstery in place.

Also explain these items:

- What the difference is in flammability standards that relate only to ignition
- Why there is a need for different standards in residence halls
- How the different products tested out in this regard

Appendix D: PR Data Reports for Snow Skis, Inc.

The information provided for Snow Skis, a fictitious ski manufacturer, illustrates some of the broad range of information that is available. Keep in mind when reviewing these samples that each company's program is developed to meet specific needs.

The PR Data Analysis of press clippings provides a report on four basic elements for the current report period and as compared with the prior year.

1. Raw data; a count of:
   number of clips
   photographs
   column inches
   circulation figures
   comparable ad $ value
2. Media analysis; a breakout of clips by type of media:
   daily newspapers
   weekly newspapers
   trade magazines
   consumer magazines
   business finance publications
3. Content analysis; an in-depth analysis of message content of clips based on a predetermined list of story messages that support the communications objectives of Snow Skis, Inc.
4. News release usage; a report on all news releases distributed by the number of clips generated and circulation.

Figure 1 (all figures can be found at the end of this appendix) is a chart reporting on raw data comparing the year 1985 with the previous year. In every category of activity, with the exception of photos, the company has increased its publicity coverage. More important, 86.1 percent of the clips analyzed showed they were within the target media range — a very high score. Slightly more than 10 percent were the result of a news release or press conference. Because photo use dropped off considerably, this tells the publicist to examine the quality of photos that were sent, and determine if they are suitable or acceptable to the media to which they are directed.

Ad value is shown here measured by column inch or minute of air time. While this is high, it might better be expressed in terms of return on investment or cost per thousand, rather than just what the time and space would have cost had it been purchased. A return on investment is calculated by dividing the dollar amount of the comparative ad value of the space or time into the amount of money earmarked for publicity in a given time period, or for one activity such as a press event. The cost per thousand is obtained by dividing the total circulation by 1,000, then dividing that into the total equivalent advertising value. Showing the equivalent ad value as "here is what this would have cost us had we paid for the space" does not account for a higher validity of publicity compared with advertising, and possible higher readership compared with advertising, pass-along readership, and other factors. Comparative ad value equivalent totals based on gross circulation also do not account for publications that normally might not be used for advertising because they are not cost efficient reaching target media.

Figure 2 shows percent of use by various media for each medium. Note that most of the use was on television (clips), and the largest "circulation" also was television. Daily newspapers reach a large share of the target audiences as well. These results may suggest that the company devote more effort to reach consumer and ski magazines and support dealers through trade publications in the next year.

Figure 3 shows the number of clips and corresponding circulation for each media category.

Figure 4 takes the same information and relates it to inches of print/minutes of time and shows the corresponding ad value. Figure 5 is the same information on pie charts to show percentage results for each medium.

The Added Value

If a company has planned well and identified the key copy points it wishes to emphasize in its communications program, the delivery by publicity of these points can be tracked by clipping analysis. Snow Skis Company has five different types of skis in its product line. Figure 6 shows very quickly how well each fares in terms of clipping and circulation. Pro Model KX2 did quite well, with 85 clips and a 6,633,000 circulation, but the intermediate model did even better, with 127 clips and a circulation of 8,604,000.

Figure 7 shows how well the publicity for the company's skis fared in reaching its designated markets. The clips chart on the left shows that 18.8 percent of the clips were in the top 150 markets. The right pie chart shows that 20.8 percent of the circulation was in these markets. For the top 50 markets, 27.1 percent of the clips were from media reaching these markets, with 20.9 percent of the circulation. "All other" markets garnered the largest number of clips and the most circulation. Is this bad? Perhaps it is because the company is not reaching what it has defined as its top markets. However, there appears to be interest in the company's products by media in the "all other" category, so it would be worthwhile to explore the reason for this interest.

Figure 8 shows totals for raw data for 1986 (four quarters plus annual total) with comparisons for each quarter of the previous year and the total year, plus percent of change. This chart shows positive news for news clippings (negative news can also be measured). Other similar charts can be produced to show print inches/broadcast (television and radio) minutes; clip circulation reach, including TV and radio audiences; clip advertising values; and photographs. I recommend that management and marketing not be presented with publicity results using this format; rather, you can plot the data on bar charts. We use a Hewlitt/Packard plotter for many of ours, and PR Data also has excellent plotter capabilities.

Copy Points

The value of the data in this category is not only to see how well you are doing, but help evaluate an ongoing program and plan future ones.

Figure 9 lists some general activities undertaken in 1986. Under the heading Marketing Support are eight categories. The first, New Product Introduction, shows (from left to right) that the publicity appeared in 89.2 percent of the targeted media, a change of 752.9 percent higher than the previous year. Current messages (CUR MSG) for the quarter reported was 40, with a cumulative (CUM MSG) of 145. The total circulation for this was 21,091,651. The number under Reach—In Millions is the quarter in which the messages appeared. The chart shown is for the total year, because it shows a "4" signifying fourth quarter.

Figure 10, Products, provides even more worthwhile data. By looking at each copy point, the publicist is able to see how well the messages were delivered. Note that of the messages for the Intermediate Skis, "space age materials" totaled only 21. This may not be important, but "hold an edge," and "little maintenance, waxing" may be. Compared with "tough, abrasion resistant," they are not appearing nearly as much. If it is important to the company to get these messages across, the publicist must develop material that emphasizes these points. One would assume that the points are listed (as they should be) in the order of importance.

The data for the Pro Model should be evaluated in the same way.

The summary of the raw data for this company showed that photo use was down. But there was good news too, as shown in Figure 11. A small-circulation publication (probably a newspaper) ran a six-column photo. And the final items show that there were eleven cover photos, compared with five the previous year—a jump of 120 percent. If the cover photos related to a story inside, this is an indication that the company is placing strong feature material.

Finally, as shown in Figure 12, data can also be reported on use by syndicates and wire services, if publicity ran in these media.

PR Data Reports for Snow Skis, Inc.

Figure 1. Raw data.

Objective Program Growth: In four out of five raw data areas the clip totals show growth over the same period in 1984.

	1984	1985	% Change
Clips	1,675	6,025	+259.7
Inches/Mins.*	15,343	15,516	+ 1.1
Circulation	192,584,875	561,704,588	+ 19.7
Ad $ Value	$690,772	$1,284,071	+ 85.9
Photos	566	303	− 46.5

Of the 1,675 clips analyzed, 86.1% were within the defined target markets and 10.1% were determined to be the result of a news release or press conference.

Major stories/announcements of the year:

1. Snow Skis receives Award—199 clips; 45,847,513 circulation
2. New line introduced—113 clips; 6,203,375 circulation
3. Winter Olympics sponsorship—3,316 clips; 379,912,537 circulation
4. Skis of Champions—61 clips; 7,506,780 circulation

---

* For measurement purposes, one minute of broadcast time is the equivalent of one inch of print in the reports.

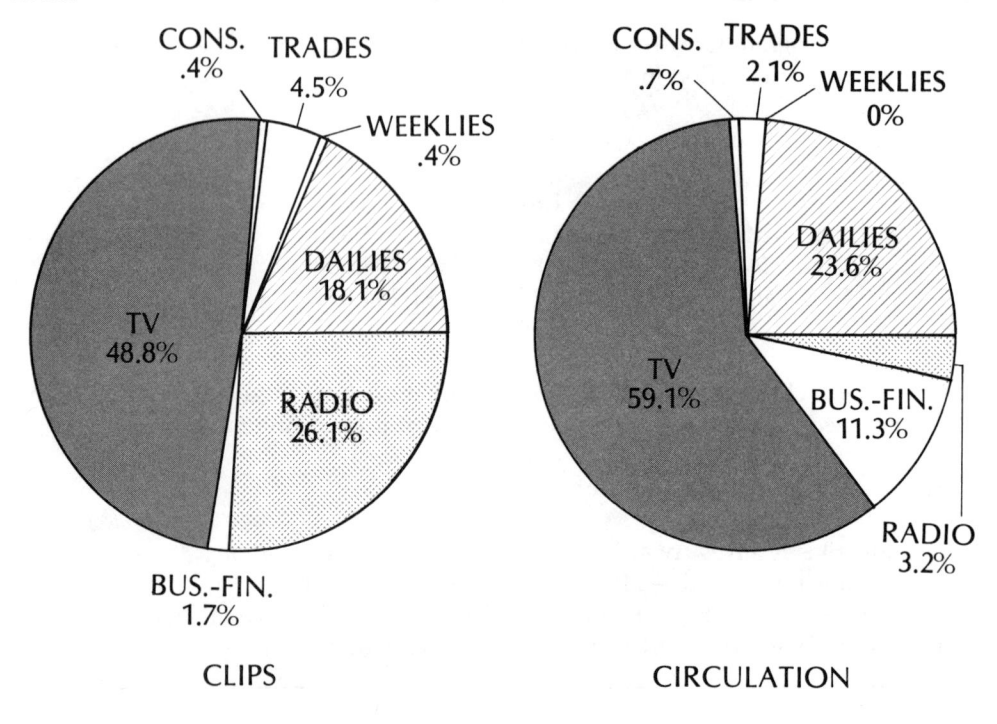

Figure 2. Snow Skis, Inc.: Percentage totals by media category, January–December 1986.

CLIPS

- CONS. .4%
- TRADES 4.5%
- WEEKLIES .4%
- DAILIES 18.1%
- RADIO 26.1%
- BUS.-FIN. 1.7%
- TV 48.8%

CIRCULATION

- CONS. .7%
- TRADES 2.1%
- WEEKLIES 0%
- DAILIES 23.6%
- BUS.-FIN. 11.3%
- RADIO 3.2%
- TV 59.1%

PR Data Reports for Snow Skis, Inc.

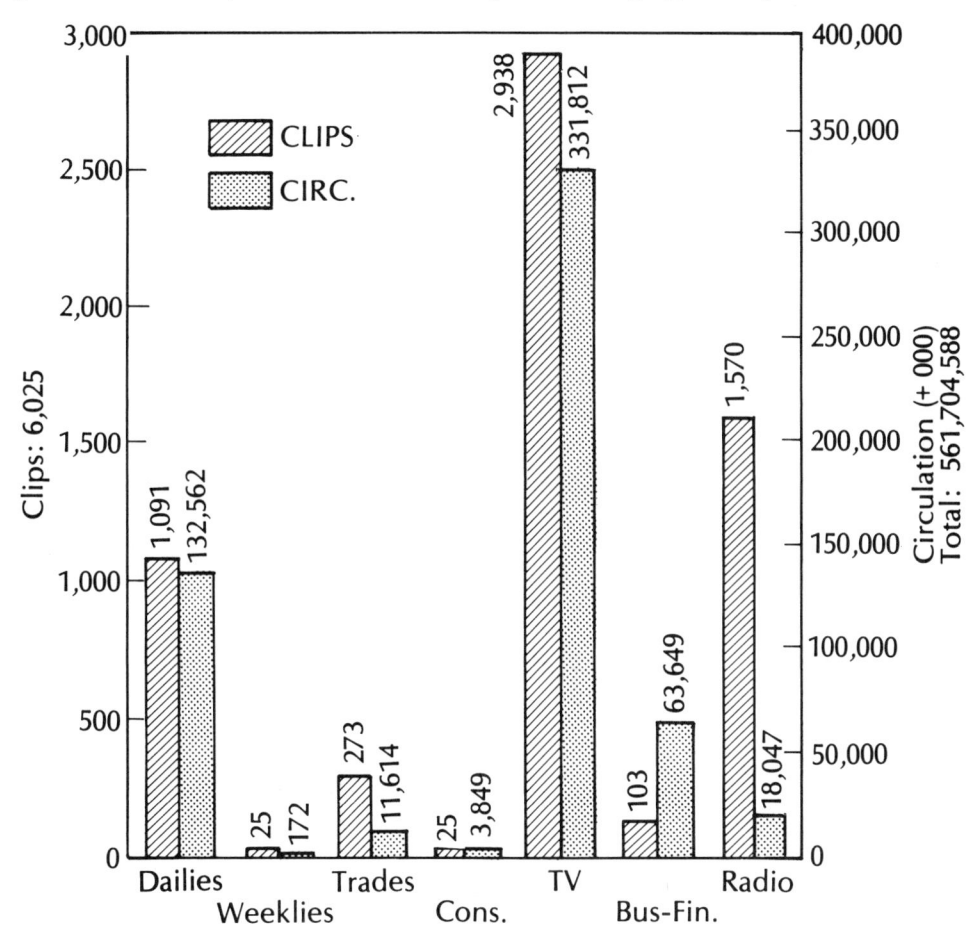

Figure 3. Snow Skis, Inc.: Numerical totals by media category, January – December 1986.

Figure 4. Snow Skis, Inc.: Inch/minute totals by media category, January–December 1986.

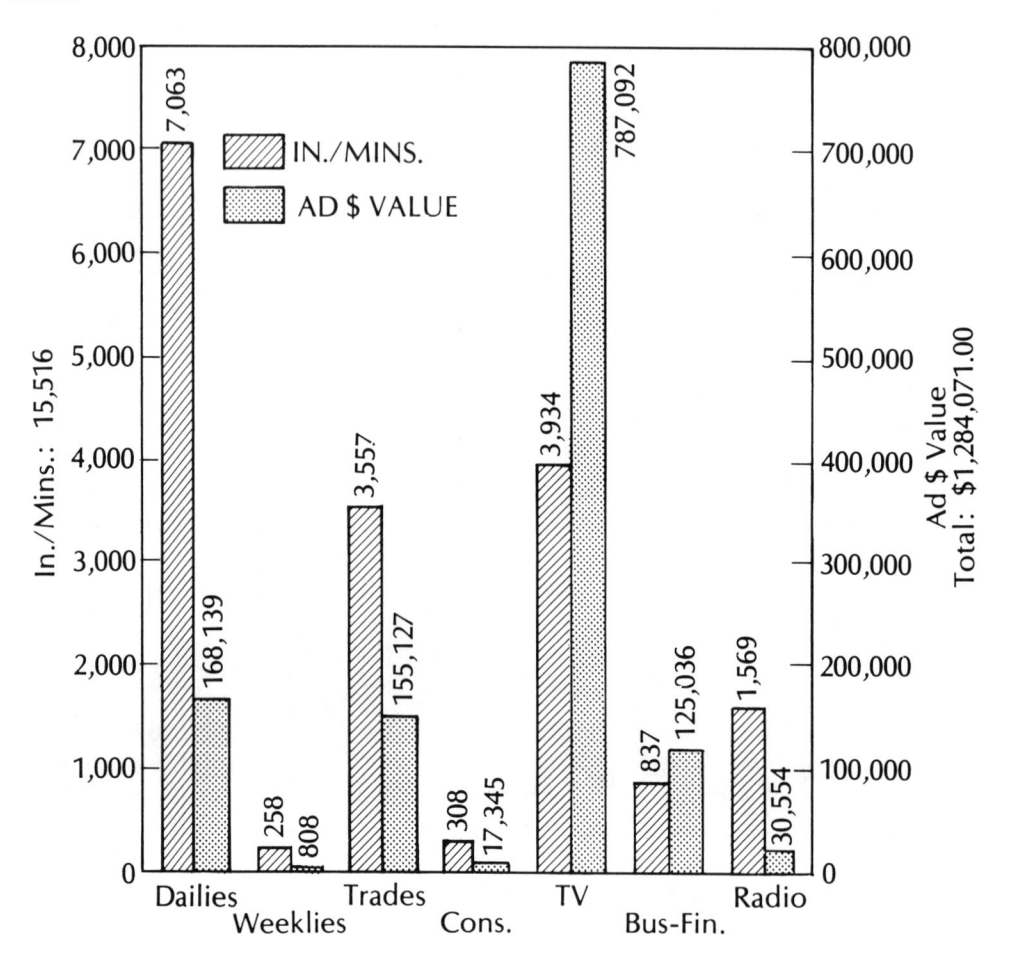

Figure 5. Snow Skis, Inc.: Percentage inch/minute totals by media category, January–December 1986.

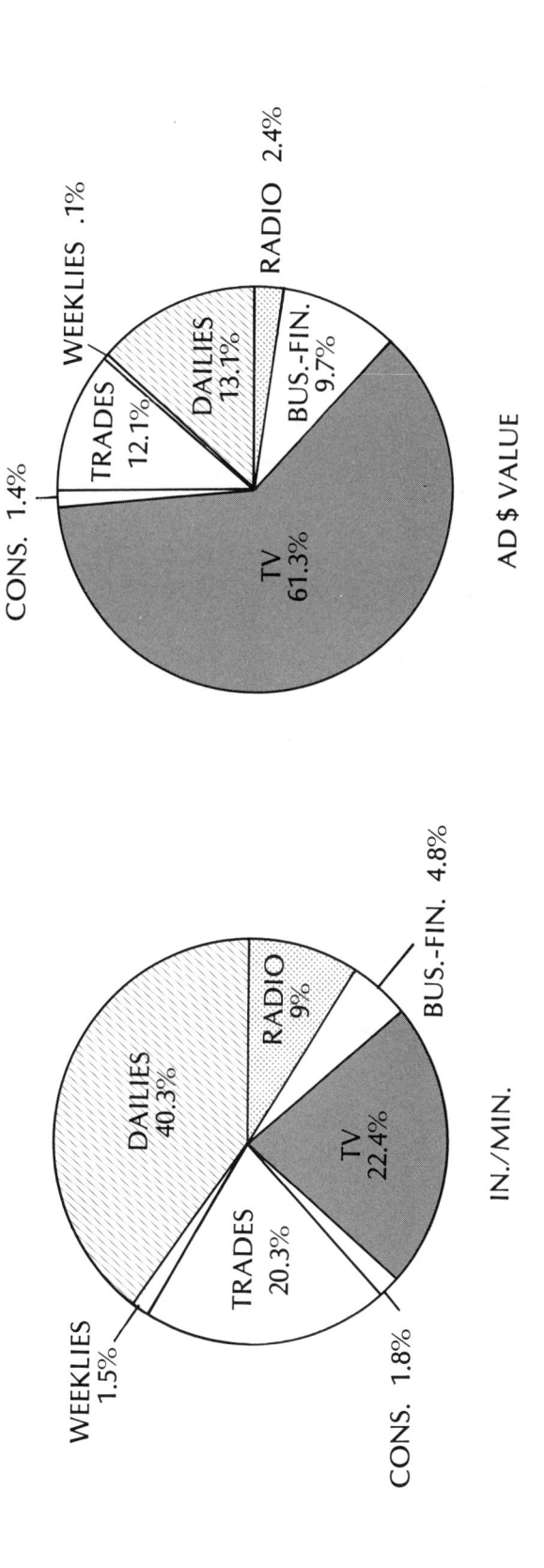

294 *Appendix D*

Figure 6. Snow Skis, Inc.: Product exposure.

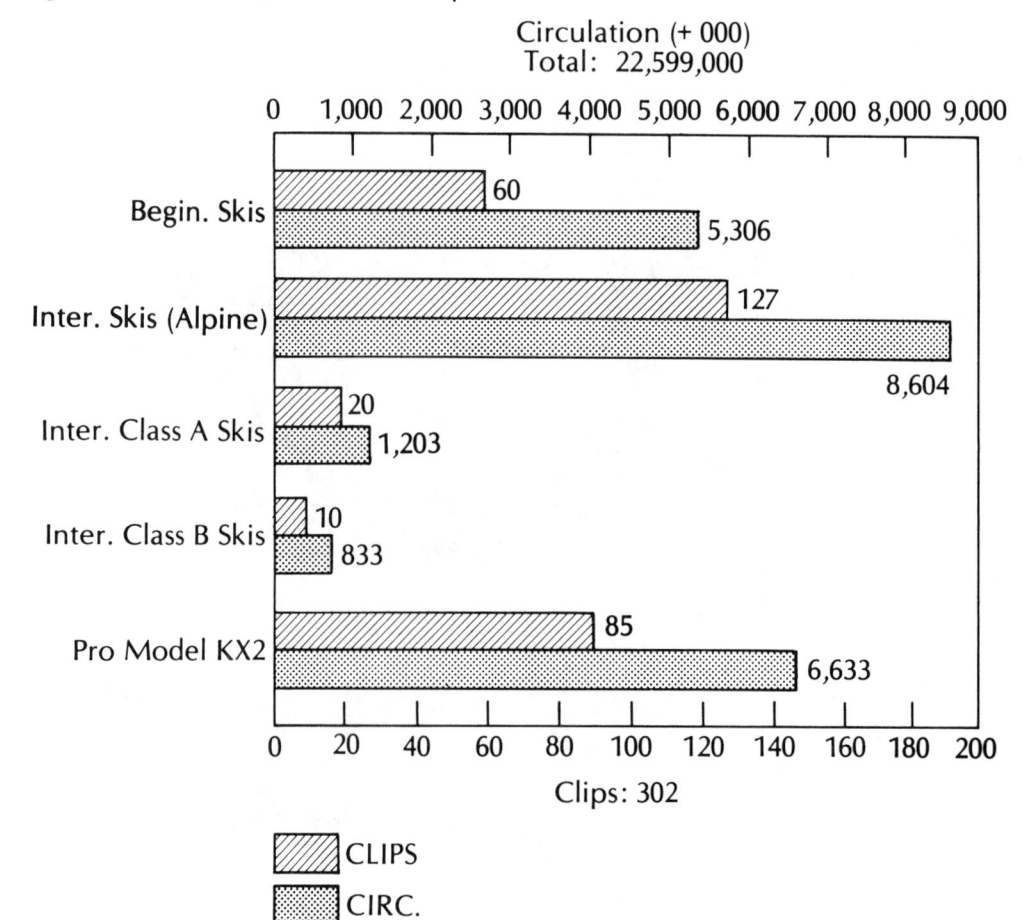

Circulation (+ 000)
Total: 22,599,000

Product	Clips	Circ.
Begin. Skis	60	5,306
Inter. Skis (Alpine)	127	8,604
Inter. Class A Skis	20	1,203
Inter. Class B Skis	10	833
Pro Model KX2	85	6,633

Clips: 302

CLIPS
CIRC.

PR Data Reports for Snow Skis, Inc. 295

Figure 7. Snow Skis, Inc.: Percent target.

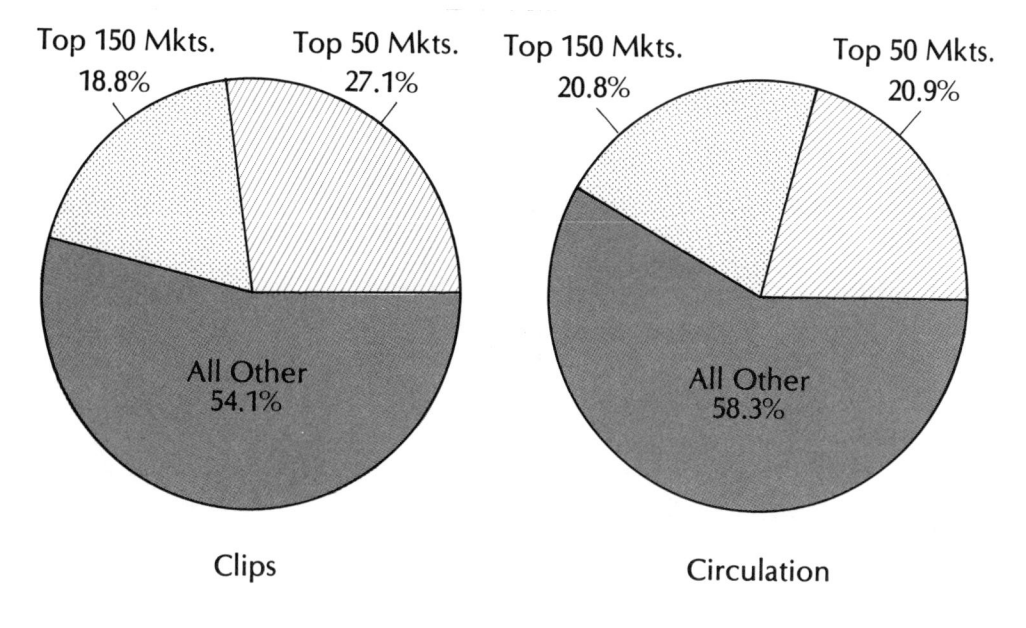

Clips:
- Top 150 Mkts. 18.8%
- Top 50 Mkts. 27.1%
- All Other 54.1%

Circulation:
- Top 150 Mkts. 20.8%
- Top 50 Mkts. 20.9%
- All Other 58.3%

Figure 8. News clippings: Overall totals for positive news.

This chart is based on raw clips.

	Dailies	Weeklies	Trades	Consumer	Bus.–Fin.	Television	Radio	All media
First Quarter 1986								
1986 Totals	102	7	61	5	20	218	1,568	1,981
1985 Totals	521	24	75	8	37	296	—	961
Percent change	−80.4%	−70.8%	−18.7%	−37.5%	−45.9%	−26.4%	—	+106.1%
Percent target	100.0%	100.0%	100.0%	100.0%	100.0%	100.0%	100.0%	100.0%
% News releases	75.5%	42.9%	42.6%	40.0%	70.0%	0.0%	0.0%	6.2%
Percent all media	5.1%	0.4%	3.1%	0.3%	1.0%	11.0%	79.2%	100.0%
Second Quarter 1986								
1986 Totals	463	10	49	—	29	762	—	1,313
1985 Totals	63	6	125	18	27	—	—	239
Percent change	+634.9%	+66.7%	−60.8%	−100.0%	+7.4%	100.0%	—	+449.4%
Percent target	100.0%	100.0%	100.0%	—	100.0%	100.0%	—	100.0%
% News releases	28.9%	20.0%	24.5%	—	31.0%	0.0%	—	12.0%
Percent all media	35.3%	0.8%	3.7%	0.0%	2.2%	58.0%	0.0%	100.0%
Third Quarter 1986								
1986 Totals	472	5	111	7	40	1,956	2	2,593
1985 Totals	126	5	82	10	21	—	—	244
Percent change	+274.6%	+0.0%	+35.4%	−30.0%	+90.5%	100.0%	100.0%	+962.7%
Percent target	100.0%	100.0%	100.0%	100.0%	100.0%	100.0%	100.0%	100.0%
% News releases	14.0%	20.0%	22.5%	14.3%	10.0%	9.6%	0.0%	11.0%
Percent all media	18.2%	0.2%	4.3%	0.3%	1.5%	75.4%	0.1%	100.0%
Fourth Quarter 1986								
1986 Totals	54	3	52	13	14	2	—	138
1985 Totals	46	4	103	9	54	28	—	244
Percent change	+17.4%	−25.0%	−49.5%	+44.4%	−74.1%	−92.9%	—	−43.4%
Percent target	100.0%	100.0%	100.0%	100.0%	100.0%	100.0%	—	100.0%
% News releases	16.7%	33.3%	44.2%	53.8%	21.4%	0.0%	—	31.2%
Percent all media	39.1%	2.2%	37.7%	9.4%	10.1%	1.4%	0.0%	100.0%
Total Year 1986								
1986 Totals	1,091	25	273	25	103	2,938	1,570	6,025
1985 Totals	756	39	385	45	139	324	—	1,688
Percent change	+44.3%	−35.9%	−29.1%	−44.4%	−25.9%	+806.8%	—	+256.9%
Percent target	100.0%	100.0%	100.0%	100.0%	100.0%	100.0%	100.0%	100.0%
% News releases	26.2%	28.0%	31.5%	40.0%	29.1%	6.4%	0.0%	10.1%
Percent all media	18.1%	0.4%	4.5%	0.4%	1.7%	48.8%	26.1%	100.0%

Figure 9. Marketing support.

% Tgt.	% Change.	Cur. Msg.	Cum. Msg.	Description	Circulation Cumulative	Reach — In Millions 0 → 15 → 30 → 45 → 60 → 75
				Marketing Support:		
89.2	752.9+	40	145	New product introduction	21,091,651	12334444
87.6	103.8+		53	Advertising & Sales Promotion	5,143,935	11
79.4	64.9−	13	67	Shows/Exhibits	8,464,806	223
91.2	200.0+	8	39	Product endorsements	1,780,946	2
90.3	145.8+	4	59	Consumer Education	3,580,881	2
91.4	24.4+	14	240	Special Promotions	53,336,952	2223333333333333333
94.3	38.1+	5	29	Market Growth	6,806,410	334
86.0	75.0+	4	21	Marketing Support, General	1,371,661	3
88.4	31.4+	88	653	Subtotal	101,577,242	

Figure 10. Products.

% Tgt.	% Change.	Cur. Msg.	Cum. Msg.	Description	Circulation Cumulative	Reach—In Millions 0 → 4 → 8 → 12 → 16 → 20
				Products:		
				Intermediate Skis (Alpine)		
69.4	145.0+	8	49	Lightweight	2,196,258	122
70.3	72.7+	10	57	Turn easily	3,796,366	112334
55.6	56.0+	5	39	Hold an edge	2,572,408	1133
62.3	145.8+	4	59	Little maintenance or waxing	3,580,881	12233
65.4	91.1+	11	107	Tough, abrasion-resistant	14,834,521	1111111112233333333344
66.7	75.0+	4	21	Space age materials	1,371,661	13
60.2	120.6+	14	75	Many different lengths	4,205,651	112233
59.4	99.5+	56	407	*Subtotal*	32,557,746	
				PRO Model		
80.1	119.2+	9	57	No chatter	2,981,693	1223
78.9	38.5+	1	18	Superior performance	1,200,747	13
80.3	90.9+	6	63	The "racers' edge"	5,559,247	11111111
81.2	63.2+	4	31	Rigid underfoot	1,786,973	133
81.9	38.5+	1	18	Flexible at tip and tail	1,200,747	13
86.4	80.0+	11	54	Excellent turn response	9,690,586	1112333333333444
86.3	140.0+	12	60	Holds edge on hard snow/ice	3,152,607	12234
84.2	89.3+	38	301	*Subtotal*	25,572,600	
88.6	58.3+	182	1361	JAN–DEC 1985 TOTAL	159,707,588	
75.5		261	860	JAN–DEC 1984 TOTAL	99,236,705	

PR Data Reports for Snow Skis, Inc.

Figure 11. Photographs.

% Change: '85–'86	Photos 1985	Photos 1986	Description	Circulation 1986
−7.8%	51	47	½ Column picture	2,803,666
−20.7	82	65	1 Column picture	7,436,740
−60.0	280	112	2 Column picture	12,242,408
−55.0	120	54	3 Column picture	5,974,598
−47.8	23	12	4 Column picture	808,359
−83.3	6	1	5 Column picture	17,206
+100.0	0	1	6 Column picture	6,000
+120.0	5	11	Cover picture	147,581
−46.5%	567	303	Photographs TOTAL	29,436,558

Figure 12. Syndicates.

% Change: '85–'86	Clips 1985	Clips 1986	Description	Circulation 1986
+56.5%	352	551	Associated Press (AP)	44,397,534
−72.1	212	59	United Press (UP)	3,508,194
+66.6	3	5	Dow Jones (DJ)	933,007
+100.0	0	2	Editorials	87,808
+100.0	0	2	Agence France Presse (AFP)	12,000
+100.0	0	2	Wall Street Journal	83,050
+150.0	2	5	Reuters	1,266,255
+100.0	0	5	Christian Science Monitor	257,114
+100.0	0	1	Chicago Trib/NY News	15,815
−100.0	1	0	Chicago Daily News/Sun Times	0
+100.0	0	19	LA Times/Wash Post	2,238,802
+88.8	18	34	New York Times (NYT)	2,612,602
−91.6	12	1	MAT Mailings	1,800
+100.0	0	4	Other Syndicates	156,490
+100.0	0	2	Gannett	73,149
+15.3%	600	692	Syndicates TOTAL	55,643,620

Index

abbreviations, 137–138
A.C. Nielsen, 261
actualities, 183–184
ad agencies, 55
advertising
   and editorial contacts, 45–46, 93–94
   as press conference alternative, 230
   vs. publicity, 4
agency briefing paper, 60–61
Alexander, Roy, 219
   on agency selection, 51–52
Alexander Company, press conference of, 219–220
American Management Association, 42
application features, 10, 111
Arbitron, 261
Armstrong Company, 162
Associated Press Stylebook, 136
   for photo release captions, 162–163
Associated Release Service, 246, 249
Association of National Advertisers, 42
attitudes, measurement of, 262
audience
   in information flow, 255
   share of, for broadcast media, 171
   see also target audience
audiences of publications, 108
   and feature acceptance, 116
   and targeting of news releases, 97
Audit Bureau of Circulation, 259
   and Newspaper Audience Research Bank, 261
awards, news releases for, 99–100
awareness
   measurement of, 255
   testing of, 262

backgrounders, 79, 112–113, 114–115
Bacon's Clipping Bureau, 238, 239, 249
   for release distribution, 234
Bacon's Media Alerts, 110
Bacon's Publicity Checkers, 200, 241–242
Bacon's Publicity Directories, 72
Bacon's Radio/TV Directory, 177
Ballentine, Andrew, on product publicity, 12
Beard, Arthur, on information flow, 253
Bernstein, Theodore *(Careful Writer)*, 137
bingo cards, 274
Black Star Publishing Company, 243, 249
Branciaroli, Cathleen, 228–229
brand names, in editorial copy, 5
Broadcasting Magazine, 177
broadcast media, 171–191
   clippings from, 240
   contacts for, 173
   nature of, 171–174
   vs. print media, 172–173
   uses of, 173–174
   see also radio; television
broadcast news release, 8–9
   see also video news releases
Broadcast Publications Inc., 177
broadcast publicity, agencies for, 49
budgeting, 27–31
   departmental, 29–31
   fact gathering in, 28–29
   for media tours, 184
   overruns in, 29
   for press conferences, 201–203
   for public relations agencies, 58, 61
   for special events, 31
Burrelle's Press Clipping Service, 238, 249
Burson-Marsteller, 187

Business Marketing, 87, 88
business objectives, creativity and, 40
business publications, 72
Business Publications Audit of Circulation, 259

cable systems, 172
Cannon, Don
  on editor/publicist relations, 76, 78, 88, 89
  on news releases, 96, 98
  on press conference format, 214
  on reading trade publications, 75
capitalization, 136
captions, for photographs, 162–163
Careful Writer (Bernstein), 137
Carl Byoir agency, 174, 273–274
case histories, 10, 109
celebrities
  for media tour spokesman, 187–188
  permission from, for photographs, 158
Chemical Engineering ("How to Write for Chemical Engineering"), 111–112
Chemical Week, 78
clipping analysis, by PR Data Systems, 236
clippings, and publicity success, 268
clipping services, 42, 238–240
  budgeting for, 28, 29
  charges of, 240
  competitors' stories from, 21
Cloze Procedure, 264
color photographs, 155
communications, role of, in publicity plan, 22–23
communications analysis, 20–21
communications counseling, 42
communications paths, to customers, 14–16
communications plan, drafting of, 60
communications strategy, planning for, 1
company, referring to, 139
comparison, writing style for, 137
competition
  communication by, 21
  in market summary, 19–20
  mention of, in feature stories, 109
confidentiality clause, in agency contract, 57
consumer publications, 72
consumers, and publicity evaluation, 253
contingency funds, in budgeting for agencies, 51
contracts
  with photographers, 165, 168

  with public relations agencies, 59
copyright laws, photographs and, 165
Creative Communications Services, 67, 242–243, 249
creativity, and business objectives, 40
customer attitudes, in market summary, 20
customer benefits, in market summary, 19
customers, communications paths to, 14–16

D'Alessandro, Vincent, on publicity evaluation reports, 266
Dale-Chall Formula, 264
datelines, 131
deadlines, 118, 145
departmental budgets, 29–31
Design News, 108
Dialog, 266
direct mail press conference, 229
distribution, in market summary, 20
distribution services, 233–238
  budgeting for, 30
Donath, Bob, on public relations and editors, 88
Dow Jones News, 266
Dreger, Don
  on news releases, 96
  on press conference expenses, 201–202
  on technical story development, 107–108
Du Pont, 32, 49

editing, by publicity manager, 38, 44
editorial contacts, 11, 81, 233
  and advertising, 45–46, 93–94
  budgeting for, 31
editorial deadlines, 118
editorial material, 1, 78
  payment for, 104–105
editors, 72–73
  calls from, 84–88
  cold contact with, 78–80
  expenses of, for press conferences, 201
  gifts to, 80
  information on, 241–242
  learning about target audience from, 22
  meeting with, 93
  publicists' knowledge of, 76–84
  relations of, with publicists, 45, 70
Egbert, T.M. (Sam), on understanding publicity evaluation, 269
Elements of Style (Strunk and White), 136
entertainment, budgeting for, 31

Index

errors in news stories
  correction of own, 144
  dealing with, 142–144
ethics and television publicity, 179–180
evaluation, *see* publicity evaluation
Evans, Harold *(Newsman's English)*, 140
evergreen stories, 9, 179
exclusives, 9, 117
  photographs for, 151

fact gathering, in budgeting, 28–29
Fairchild publications, 103
feature stories, 9–10, 105–127
  bull's eye targeting for, 107
  chances of placement of, 118–119
  checking and review of, 124
  headlines for, 130
  ideas for, 119–120
  interviews for, 120–122
  lead paragraph for, 131–132
  placement of, 113, 116–119
  recycling of, 125
  sending fundamentals of, 106–107
  types of, 109–113
  writing process for, 119–127
Felcyn, Keith, on editor/publicist relations, 77
film, 28, 247–248
financial information, in market summary, 20
financial publications, 72
Flesch Formula, 264
followup, commitment to, 27
foreign countries, style for, 139–140
freelancers, 42, 66–67
free publications, 75
Friedman, Marvin
  on broadcast publicity, 172, 176
  on satellite transmissions, 180
  on teleconferences, 212

Galbán, Agnes, 266
General Electric, 49
generics, trademarks used as, 141
gifts, to editors, 80
Goldberg, Bob, 243
  on photographers, 164
  on photographs, 152
"Good Morning America," media tours and, 186
Gordon, Jerry, 173
  on radio broadcasts, 184

on television news releases, 180
Gunning Formula, 264

Hancock, Nick, on photographs, 151
Hanes, Joanna, 218
  on broadcast media, 174
  on press conference invitations, 206
  on radio broadcasts, 184
  on television contacts, 176
Hanes and Associates, press conference of, 218, 220–221
headlines, 128–130
Hill, Gary
  on radio broadcasts, 184
  on television publicity, 177–178
Hill and Knowlton, 273
  press conference of, 221–223
host, use of, 139
"How to Get Your News in a Business Publication" (Maclean Hunter Publishers), 6, 87
"How to Write for Chemical Engineering" *(Chemical Engineering)*, 111–112

impact, use of, 139
International Publicity Checker, 241
interviews
  for feature stories, 120–122
  focused, 229–231
  one-on-one, 228
  publicist role in, 189–190
inverted pyramid style, for releases, 101
italics, 136

Jeff Blumenfeld and Associates, 48, 150
Jennings, Carol
  on agency selection, 52–54
  on relationship with agencies, 57–58
Johnson, Gale, on agency budgeting, 59

key media, identifying, 71–75
kitchen setting photography, 162
Kodak, 32

Larimi Communications, 177
lead paragraphs, 131–132
leads, from publicity, 275
legal approval, of news stories, 146
Liddell, Jerry, on network shows, 186
local television, media tours and, 186

log, of calls from editors, 84
long-range planning, 4
Luce Press Clippings, 238, 249

Machine Design, 107–108
Maclean Hunter Publishers ("How to Get Your News in a Business Publication"), 6, 87
Madison Avenue, 55
magazines, *see* publications
management
    and editorial relations, 89–91
    and editor/publicist relations, 70
    understanding of publicity by, 268–270
market share, in market summary, 19
market summary, in publicity plan, 17–20
marketing communications, 2–3
marketing communications plan, 13
marketing objectives, vs. communications objectives, 23
marketing research, 20
    budgeting for, 31
markets
    in market summary, 19
    and targeting of news releases, 97
mat services, *see* syndication services
Maycumber, Gray
    on contacts with editors, 77
    on entertainment expenses, 59
    on publicists, 86
McCann Associates, 243, 249
media
    key, 71–75
    publicist's understanding of, 39
    target, 14
media alerts, 177
Media Alerts (Bacon's), 110, 242
MediaBase, 234
media briefing manual, 282–285
media buy, measurement of, 264–266
Media Comparability Council, 75
media directories, 42
media list development, by PR Data Systems, 235
Mediamark Research Inc., 260
media objectives, in publicity plan, 25–26
media pickup, measurement of, 264
media plan, 62
media profile, 73–74
media relations, mature products and, 36

media tours, 184–191
    budgeting for, 184
    merchandising of, 191
    planning for, 184
    selecting targets for, 186–187
    spokesman for, 187–188
    training for, 188–189
message exposure, 262
message perception, 262
message research, 263–264
message response, 263
Metro Associated Services Inc., 245–246, 249
models, working with, for photographs, 170
movies, budgeting for, 31

new products
    agency involvement in, 58
    broadcast media for introducing, 173
    budgeting for publicity of, 31
    news releases for, 99
    stories on, 10
news, sources of, 171
news events, 174
news judgment, of publicity manager, 38
News/Radio Network, 247, 249
news releases, 7–8, 95–105
    agency time required for, 63
    budgeting for, 28
    checklist for, 148
    cost of, 30
    DOs and DON'Ts of, 143
    follow-ups on, 87–88, 94
    headlines for, 129
    lead paragraph of, 131–132
    radio, 9, 246
    time for using, 99–100
    timing of, 103–104
    video, *see* video news releases
    writing process for, 100–103
    see also photo releases
news stories
    editor's role in, 133–135
    errors in, 142–144
    format basics for, 128–132
    speeding up approval for, 144–146
    style for, 132
    time requirements for, 145
Newsman's English (Evans), 140
newspapers
    clippings from, 240

Index

editors of, 73
   mailing photographs to, 164
   media tours and, 187
Nexis, 266
North American Precis Syndicate, 245, 249

Oesterwinter Associates, 67, 243, 249
office expenses, 29
one-on-one interviews, 228
opinion tests, 262
out-of-pocket costs, for agencies, 59
Oxford Book for Writers and Editors, 140

parameter, use of, 139
pass-along studies, 260
peripheral services, *see* support services
Pezzano, Linda
   on communications, 38
   on marketing public relations, 12
   on public relations agencies, 48
Pezzano+Company, 276-278
photographers, 42, 164-170
   contract for, 165, 168
   freelance, 67
photographs, 11, 150-170
   budgeting for, 28, 30
   captions for, 162-163
   color, 155
   costs of, 168, 170
   distribution of, 163-164
   files of, 43
   good quality, characteristics of, 152
   kitchen settings for, 162
   mature products and, 35
   models for, 170
   of products, 159
   releases for, 155, 157-158
   services providing, 242-244
   shooting in studio for, 161-162
   shooting on location for, 159-161
   technical tips on, 153-155
photo releases, 152
   caption for, 162
post-testing, in publicity evaluation, 257
PR Aids Inc., 234, 250
PR Data Reports, 286-299
   and publicity evaluation, 257
PR Data Systems, Inc., 234-236, 250, 264-266
press briefing tour, 228-229

press conferences, 192-231
   alternatives to, 194, 228-230
   budgeting for, 201-203
   direct mail, 229
   editor's viewpoint on, 194
   environment for, 197, 199
   examples of, 218-222
   invitations to, 206-207
   media selected for, 200-201
   objectives of, 193
   planning for, 197-212
   presentation at, 213-214
   press kits for, 209-210
   project preview for, 195-197
   registration at, 212-213
   rehearsals for, 207, 209
   security for, 209
   site selection for, 203-206
   slides for, 209
   as teleconferences, 210-212
   timing of, 203
press events, 10-11
press kits
   distribution of, at press conferences, 212
   for press conferences, 195, 209-210
   for trade show press room, 226
   for video news releases, 180
press updates, 226-227
pretesting, in publicity evaluation, 257
prime media, and success of publicity, 25
print media
   broadcast media vs., 172-173
   see also newspapers; publications
PR Newswire, 237-238, 250
product descriptions, in market summary, 18
product life cycle, 2
   in market summary, 18-19
   publicity plan and, 32-36
product publicity, *see* publicity
product reinforcement, broadcast media for, 174
products
   backgrounders on, 113
   newsworthiness of, 32
   photographs of, 159
Professional Guide to Public Relations Services (Weiner), 177, 232
professional standards, 40
program development, 41
promotion, internal, 43

proprietary information, 86
PRSA (Public Relations Society of America), 40, 42
psychogalvanometer, 262
publications
   audiences of, and release targeting, 97
   free, 76
   style of, 78
   see also newspapers
public figures, permission from, for photographs, 158
publicity, 2, 3
   asserting need for, 272–274
   in communications program, 33–34
   definition of, 1
   elements of, 7–11
   limitations of, 6–7
   objectives of, in reporting, 270
   promotion of values of, 43
   readership of, 6
   results of, 5–6
   success of, 25
Publicity Club of New York, 40, 42
publicity evaluation, 251–267
   consumers and, 253
   information resources for, 257–258
   inside or outside, 256
   measurement of media buy for, 264–266
   measurement of media pickup for, 264
   obstacles to, 252
   planning, 256–258
   pretesting or post-testing for, 257
   publicity goals and, 252
publicity evaluation research tools, 259–267
   message exposure, 262
   message perception, 262
   message research, 263–264
   message response, 263
   vehicle audience, 259–261
   vehicle distribution, 259
publicity manager, 37–46
   agency coordination by, 44–46
   authority of, 44
   qualifications of, 38–40
   responsibilities of, 40–43
publicity plan
   elements of, 17–26
   and evaluation, 269
   objectives of, 11
   organization of, 14–17

   preparation of, 13–36
   timing in, 32–36
publicity professionals
   advertising professionals and, 4
   tasks of, 8
publicity reports, 268–275
   form for, 272
   publicity objectives in, 270
public relations, vs. product publicity, 2
public relations agencies, 47–68
   beginning relationship with, 56–64
   benefits of, 48–49
   budgeting for, 28, 55, 61
   complaints about, 64
   complaints from, 65–66
   contracts with, 59
   cost of, 29, 50–51, 63
   drawbacks of, 49–50
   and editorial contacts, 71, 88–89
   editorial review of work by, 44
   vs. in-house publicity, 50
   news releases from, 102–103
   and press conferences, 227
   publicity manager and, 44–46
   reports from, 62
   role of, in publicity plan, 26
   schedules for, 61
   selection of, 51–56
   turnover in, 57
Public Relations Journal, 179
Public Relations Publishing Company, 177
Public Relations Society of America (PRSA), 40, 42

quality control, 40–41
questionnaires, to editors, 22
Quirk, Eileen, on newsworthiness, 32
quotes, 138

radio, 183–184
   coverage by clipping services, 240
   measuring audiences of, 261
   media tours and, 187
   releases to, 9, 246
   statistics on, 171
Radio/TV Reports, 250
readability tests, 264
reader service numbers, 274
recall tests, 262

Index

recognition tests, 262
reference books, on writing, 137
research, *see* publicity evaluation
resource management, 42
retainer arrangement, for agencies, 59
roundtables, 10, 112, 229
roundups, 10, 109–110
Rumrill-Hoyt, 110

said, use of, 139
sales
    and publicity evaluation, 253
    relating publicity to, 255, 263, 274–275
sales representatives, learning about target audience from, 22
satellite transmission, of video news releases, 180–181
schedules, for agencies, 61
security, for press conferences, 209
Seidel, Eric
    on filming for television, 182
    on making broadcast contacts, 176
Shultz, Ernie, on ethics in television publicity, 179
Simmons Market Research Bureau, 260
    and Simmons Scarborough Company, 261
slides, for press conferences, 209
special events
    budgeting for, 28, 31
    news releases for, 100
special interest, news releases for, 100
special issues, 110
speeches, news releases for, 100
Standard Rate and Data Services, 72, 200, 241
standards, professional, 40
strategic programming, 11
strategies, in publicity plan, 23–24
Strunk, William (*Elements of Style*), 136
subheads, 130
superlatives, 5, 136
support services:
    clipping, 238–240
    distribution, 233–238
    editorial information, 241–242
    film and videotape producers, 247–248
    syndication, 245–247
    writing and photography, 242–244
support services, directory for, 232
syndication services, 245–247
    budgeting for, 31

tachistoscope, 263
tactics, 24
    budgeting for, 30
    in publicity plan, 25
talk shows, 172
taped actuality, 183–184
tape recorders, at interviews, 122, 228
tapes, budgeting for, 31
target audience
    action by, and publicity success, 16
    in publicity plan, 21–22
target media, 14
technical articles, 10, 111–112
technical support group, learning about target audience from, 22
teleconferences, 210–212, 221
television, 174–182
    directories of, 176–177
    ethics and, 179–180
    making contacts in, 176–178
    media tours and, 184, 186
    placing prepared story on, 179–180
    planning for, 182
    ratings bureaus for, 261
    statistics on, 171
    story characteristics for, 175–176
Television Digest, Inc., 177
third-party endorsement, 5, 10
timing, of publicity, 24
tip sheets, for video releases, 279–281
titles, of individuals, 138
"Today" show, media tours and, 186
Tortolano, Bill
    on press conferences, 213, 214
    on relevance of news releases, 97
trade publications, 72
trade shows
    budgeting for, 31
    contacts during, 80–82
    press events at, 224–226
    press room at, 226
trademarks, 140–142
training, publicity manager responsible for, 41–42
travel, budgeting for, 31
travel time, for freelance writers, 67
trend features, 10, 110–111
Trivial Pursuit, publicity campaign for, 276–278
trust, in editorial relations, 89–91

turnover, in public relations agencies, 57
TV Publicity Outlets, 177
Tylenol, 33

unfavorable stories, publicists and, 92–93

"value in use," 20
vehicle audience, 259–261
vehicle distribution, 259
verbal communications skills, 38
Verified Audit Circulation, 259
video news releases, 8, 173, 179
   cost of, 181
   filming of, 181–182
   media tours and, 190
   tip sheets for, 279–281
videotapes, 247–248
   budgeting for, 28
visit reports, 82–84
voice pitch analysis, 262

Voros, Gerald, on advertising and public relations, 55–56

Wagner International Photos, 243, 250
Wall Street Journal, press conferences and, 200
Warrilow, James, on publication content, 108
Weiner, Richard *(Professional Guide to Public Relations Services),* 232
White, E. B. *(Elements of Style),* 136
women, as publicity professionals, 55
Women's Wear Daily, 103
work for hire guidelines, for photographers, 165
Working Press of the Nation, 72, 200, 242, 250
writers
   fees of, 67
   freelance, lists of, 42
writing
   agency time required for, 63
   guidelines for, 135–140
   standards of, 41
writing services, 67, 242–244